Globalization, Democracy and Gender Justice

Globalization, Democracy and Gender Justice

Edited by

M.R. Biju

Associate Professor,
Post-graduate and Research Department of Political Science,
Sree Narayana College, Kollam, Kerala.

New Century Publications
New Delhi, India

NEW CENTURY PUBLICATIONS
4800/24, Bharat Ram Road,
Ansari Road, Daryaganj,
New Delhi – 110 002 (India)

Tel.: 011-2324 7798, 4358 7398, 6539 6605
Fax: 011-4101 7798
E-mail: indiatax@vsnl.com • info@newcenturypublications.com
www.newcenturypublications.com

Editorial office:
LG–7, Aakarshan Bhawan,
4754-57/23, Ansari Road, Daryaganj,
New Delhi – 110 002

Tel.: 011-4356 0919

First Published: **2012**

ISBN: **978-81-7708-305-7**

Published by New Century Publications and printed at Salasar Imaging Systems, New Delhi.

Designs: Patch Creative Unit, New Delhi.

PRINTED IN INDIA

About the Book

Globalisation implies widening and deepening integration with the globe, i.e. with people and processes abroad. Globalisation is widely seen as the most important factor that could influence economies of nations the world over in the new millennium. Globalisation has also resulted in the creation of a new business framework. More changes can be expected in the business scenario specifically in terms of openness, adaptiveness and responsiveness.

With the growing globalization and liberalization of the economy—as well as increased privatization of services—women as a whole have been left behind. Mainstreaming of women into the new and emerging areas of growth is necessary. This will require their training and skill upgradation in emerging trades, encouraging them to take up vocational training and employment in the boom sectors. This will also require women to migrate to cities and metros for work. Hence, provision of safe housing, and other gender-friendly facilities at work will need to be provided.

Against this backdrop, this collection of 9 research papers —contributed by renowned academicians—embodies critical analysis of various aspects of the core issues under investigation.

About the Editor

Dr. M.R. Biju is Associate Professor, Post-graduate and Research Department of Political Science, Sree Narayana College, Kollam, Kerala. He headed two major research projects on Panchayati Raj Institutions funded by the Ministry of Panchayati Raj, Government of India, and University Grants Commission (UGC), New Delhi. He has to his credit several books and research papers on social, political and development issues.

Dr. Biju was the recipient of the UGC Post-doctoral Research Award for 2004-07. He is the editor of *South Asian Journal of Socio-Political Studies (SAJOSPS)*.

Contents

Contributors

M.M. Verma	Associate Professor, Faculty of Social Work, Mahatma Gandhi Kashi Vidyapeeth, Varanasi.
Arvind Singh	Head, Department of Political Science, KGK Post-graduate College, Moradabad.
Swami Prakash Srivastava	Associate Professor, Department of Economics, Dayalbagh Educational Institute, Agra.
Ramakrishnan Ramaiah	Secretary, Department of Home Affairs, Government of Nagaland, Kohima.
M.R. Biju	Associate Professor, Post-graduate and Research Department of Political Science, Sree Narayana College, Kollam, Kerala.
Sudha Menon	Programme Director, Skill Building and Training at SEWA, Ahmedabad.
Dolly Phukon	Assistant Professor, Department of Political Science, Dibrugarh University, Assam.

Introductory Note by the Editor

The 1990s witnessed a paradigm shift towards market oriented economic policies and a careful dismantling of obstacles in its wake. This has helped the smaller, emerging economies gain access to world markets, emergent technologies and collaborations. This has also given them a window to the developed world and helped them understand the significant role of globalisation as an instrument, which could be utilised not just to achieve economic efficiency, but also eradicate poverty.

The issue that concerns developing countries is how one can ensure greater participation of the weaker economies in the global process and what needs to be done to ensure that the course of globalisation benefits more people in more countries. The uneven and unequal nature of the present globalisation is manifested in the fast growing gap between the rich and poor people of the world and between developed and developing countries; and by the large differences among nations in the distribution of gains and losses.

With the growing globalization and liberalization of the economy as well as increased privatization of services, women as a whole have been left behind and not been able to partake of the fruits of success. Mainstreaming of women into the new and emerging areas of growth is imperative. This will require training and skill upgradation in emerging trades, encouraging more women to take up vocational training and employment in the boom sectors. This will also require women to migrate to cities and metros for work. Provision of safe housing, and other gender friendly facilities at work will need to be provided.

The issues arising out of globalization in a democratic set up and its impact on women are discussed in this volume.

In the inaugural chapter M.M. Verma, highlights the issues related to globalization process in India and the third world. According to him, the emerging world economy is swayed by capitalistic ideology which pleads for an enhanced and freer play of market forces and removal of all barriers to free global trade 'Stabilization' and the 'SAP' are the key phrases associated with the consequent process of economic restructuring. He further states that the central agenda of the globalization process seems to facilitate abolition of all sorts of barriers to global trade and commerce as well as minimization of the state intervention not only as a producer and promoter but also as a regulator. Thus, it postulates the dilution of the goals of the welfare state. Such concepts as equity, full employment and distributive Justice, etc, naturally, do not fit in with this neo-capitalistic ethos. Therefore, the poor, the down trodden, the women and children as also all the weaker sections of society are supposed to bear the brunt of new world order. The paper brings out the legitimate concerns of all these sections in the light of the new LPG regime.

In chapter 2 Arvind Singh focusses on the myths and realities of globalization. To him globalization has been one of the most frequently used expression in economic and political Discourse over the last two decades. Its merit and demerits, advantages and disadvantages and as to who would be its beneficiaries and loosers has been debated ad infinitum. Thousands of papers and articles in newspapers and academic journals; and scores if not hundreds of books and monographs have been written on the subject. International Financial Institutions, multinational corporations, governments of most of the developed countries and many influential intellectuals, economists and politicians have never got tired of admiring it as a natural and necessary process with immense potential for the betterment of mankind. On the other hand, a number of independent intellectuals, economists, social scientists, NGOS, trade unions, and civil society groups have exercised serious reservations, if not opposition, to globalisation project. They have particularly cited the iniquitous consequences on poorer countries, disadvantaged group, labour and the environment.

According to Arvind Singh, the period after 1950 was marked by the integration of national economics to a magnitude never witnessed earlier in the mankind's history. The current phase of integration is also strongly influenced by the developments in information technology[1] and the concomitant increase in the literacy levels worldwide. Technology has given impetus to innovation in telematics, computers, fiber optics, satellite and other communications; their convergence with television, electronic bourses for trading stocks, bonds, currency, commodities, future options and other derivatives; and the global explosion of e-commerce and the internet. The increasing access to education has ensured that literacy levels are increasingly on the rise, thereby affording opportunity to state and non-state actors to sell their ideas and perspectives with greater ease and speed.

The Present globalization seems to be creating new horizons, and spaces of contestations for the nouvea rich elites, corporations and the Transnational Corporations. With the settling nuances of Financial Discipline being imposed globally by multilateral institutions such as WTO, IMF and World Bank the entrepreneurial juggernauts, and venture capitalists, having at their disposal Transnational Finances, have never had so easy to fulfill their goal of maximizing profits.

In chapter 3, Swami Prakash Srivastava made a study on India-ASEAN Trade Agreement and its impact on Indian Economy. According to him, the agreement comes at a appropriate time taking into account the current world economic crisis. ASEAN includes Brunei, Cambodia, Indonesia, Laos, Malaysia, Myamar, the Philippines. Singapore, Thailand and Vietnam. The Southeast Asian bloc of about 550 million people is forging free trade pacts with key regional economies including China and India to ensure it does not become economically sidelined. ASEAN itself aims to achieve a single market and manufacturing base by 2015. The agreement is a partial one, covering only "normal" trade items, primarily industrial goods, and excluding many agricultural and handicraft items deemed sensitive. The ASEAN-India deal also excludes agreements on investment and services.

Swami Prakash further states that, the agreement has been hailed as a milestone following years of tough negotiations between ASEAN and India, its seventh largest trading partner. It covers billions of dollars in trade and a market of 1.7 billion people. The signing came ahead of a meeting in Bangkok of finance ministers from ASEAN and its regional partners China, Japan, South Korea, India, Australia and New Zealand. The free trade agreement between India and ASEAN took six years to finalize. It was originally scheduled to be signed last year but was delayed by India, where the government was gearing up for elections. The pact will eliminate duties on 4,000 items or 80 per cent of the tariff lines by 2016 accounting for 75 per cent of trade. India has excluded 489 items from the list of tariff concessions and 590 items from the list of tariff elimination to address sensitivities in agriculture, textile, auto, chemicals, crude and refined palm oil, coffee, tea, pepper etc. The agreement also provides for bilateral safeguard mechanisms to address a sudden surge in imports after it comes into effect. In such an eventuality, if it hurts a domestic industry, safeguards measures including imposition of safeguard duties may be put in place for a period up to four years.

India and ASEAN, according to Swami Prakash are currently negotiating Agreements on trade in Services and Investment, which were to be concluded by December 2009. The current Agreement in goods will provide an impetus to the negotiations in service pact. India's total trade in services was US$ 137.5 billion in 2006 compared to US$ 280.9 billion for ASEAN. Similarly, FDI attracted by India in 2007-08 was US$ 24.6 billion whereas ASEAN countries attracted FDI US$ 60.5 billion in 2007.

The author in his conclusion observes that the Indian economy is of similar size to China, Japan and South Korea, countries with which ASEAN has already signed FTAs. Under the agreement, ASEAN members and India will reduce import tariffs to zero for more than 80 percent of their total imported goods between 2013-2016, while import tariffs for sensitive goods will be reduced to 5 percent by 2016. Signing the free trade in Goods Agreement with the Association of South East Asian Nations has evoked mixed reactions in India. The plantation sector, the marine products industry and some light manufacturing industries are feeling threatened by this agreement. This is not completely unexpected as some of the ASEAN countries have a much higher level of efficiency in these sectors as compared to India. The signing of the agreement signals India's firm commitment to its "look east policy" of building upon its historical links with the countries of the South East Asia region and further deepening and widening this partnership. Domestic manufacturers, for their part, distrust these bilateral agreement due to the handicap of inverted duty structures where the duty on the finished product is lower than on raw materials. This acts as a disincentive as finished products can be imported at lower duties.

Swami Prakash Srivastava in his second paper (chapter 4) on Global Climate Change and its Impact on Indian Economy states that the industrialized nations are primarily responsible for the high volume of carbon emissions. Hence, they should share a certain percentage of their GDP with developing nations to enable access to green technology. But as usual, industrialized nations have been shrinking any commitment regarding reduction in carbon emission. Instead, they have been demanding action from developing countries like India. If carbon emissions continue to increase at the current rate of 3 percent per year, then we would overshoot the threshold limit for climate change catastrophe in the next 20 years, in half the time that was projected earlier. Such a disaster scenario would play out, say researchers, only if there is no abatement of emission worldwide and if we assume that no scientific method would be employed to remove excess carbon from the atmosphere.

The World Bank, in a presentation based on preliminary results of a modeling study, has pointed out that power consumption and, therefore, the GHG emissions in India are bound to increase 3.5 times the 2007-08 levels by 2031-32 due to increasing urbanization, electrification and household incomes. This could be brought down to 2.7 times the 2007-08 levels with stringent energy efficiency measures, the study results show. The World Bank modeled what are technically called marginal abatement cost curves-statistical projections of how much it would take to reduce GHG emissions from different sectors of the economy. The figures from the bank come as scientific evidence in favour of the Indian government's International position. India has long contended that taking severe emission reduction targets can only come at the cost of its poor and that India which already has an extremely low per capita emission needs the carbon space to pull its people out of poverty and provide basic amenities like power, sanitation and water to all. The industrialized nations as well as some international NGOs continue to argue against the position claiming that India is hiding its inaction behind its poor. But the bank has concluded after its study that this increased demand for power is not to support a life style or consumption patterns displayed in developed countries but to provide basic energy services and support a growing economy The bank in its draft report has admitted that the 11th Plan of the Indian government was the best low carbon plan the country could adopt with the current set of technologies and continue to grow economically.

India's energy demand, according to Srivastava, is likely to increase threefold by 2030, a substantial portion of which will be met through fossil fuel, which will cause emission of greenhouse gasses to go up sharply, says a report by management firm McKinsey & Co. Suggesting initiatives such as expanding programmes to increase energy efficiency, developing clean sources of power generation and creating energy efficient infrastructure, the report-Environmental and Energy Sustainability: An Approach for India-argues that India could reduce emissions by 45 percent and lower energy consumption by 22 percent by 2030. In terms of energy alone by 2030, India is likely to need between 760 GW and 790 GW of installed power capacity. Overall coal demand is likely to cross 2.4 billion per annum. India may have to import 10 times its own production of oil and up to 40 percent of its coal needs by 2030.

According to the author, India has demonstrated that it takes the climate change issue seriously: the National Action Plan on climate change has spelt out the details of implementation of eight missions and is to soon establish a climate change mitigation authority that will set targets to reduce emissions by 2020. India has a ministry dedicated to promotion of alternative energy and several projects are underway to promote adaptation measures. Far more could be achieved if developed countries deliver the promised financial and technological assistance. The Ministry for Environment and Forests might appear to be grandstanding by declaring that India is willing to specify the amount of emissions it could cut to demonstrate its green credentials.

Yet, the political rhetoric does indeed reveal a milestone achievement in the way India has evolved from a diffident bystander at international climate change meets to a more vocal and confident frontline participant. This is a good sign, since India badly needed a makeover of its negotiating profile in order to be heard at international climate change meetings, particularly since there is mounting pressures from developed countries to include emerging economies like India and China in an emission reduction protocol that would be time bound and mandatory. All along, the focus in India has been more on adaptation to the effects of climate change-for instance on how to face the challenges of environmental degradation, changing crop patterns and vanishing habits. The official approach to climate change is now beginning to seriously consider effective mitigation measures that would result not only in reducing dependencies on conventional fossil fuel and oil imports but also expanding and intensifying investment in alternative clean energy solutions.

In chapter 5, Ramakrishnan Ramaiah, examines the power sector reforms in India. It is a detailed comparative study of four states in India–Karnataka, Maharastra, Punjab and Tamil Nadu.

Electricity according to the author, is the most necessary and critical infrastructural input in the development and growth of economy of any country. Consumption of energy, and more particularly of electricity, is recognized world over, as the most important index of the extent of industrial and economic advancement of the country and living standards of people (Shahi, 2005). The development of other sectors of economy depends on the development of power sector. Though power sector in India achieved significant growth in the past fifty years, the sector has been suffering from inadequate generation capacity to meet the demands of all consumers, operational and functional inefficiencies with high transmission and distribution losses, theft of energy, poor metering etc. The main purpose of the research is to find out the performance of the selected state utilities in realising the objectives of the reform initiatives after the enactment of Electricity Act, 2003 such as reducing transmission and distribution losses, bringing in competition, more investments, improving system efficiency, meeting the demand gap and rationalization of tariff structure in order to provide quality and reliable power at affordable prices to all.

After a systematic and detailed enquiry on the various aspects of the topic, the author concludes his investigations by stating that, the enactment of Electricity Act, 2003 provided the needed momentum for the power sector to grow. Maharashtra and Karnataka followed the Orissa model and unbundled the electricity board, created separate companies for generation, transmission and distribution and constituted regulatory commission. Among the left over states, Tamil Nadu has already taken initiative to unbundle the SEB. Punjab is yet to unbundle the board.

In chapter 6, M.R. Biju, discusses in the significance of Right to Information in India as a tool for democratizing politics and administration. According to him, transparency seems to be the only means for sustaining democratic governance. That is why the right to information has been legislated in about 70 countries of the world, and another 30 countries are in the process of legislation.

It was in this context that the RTI was enacted in India in 2005. The experience of five years shows that the response to this Act has been very positive and optimistic. It has also been widely welcomed by the people at all levels. They have been seeking various types of Information from different authorities. The RTI Act confers on all citizens the right to seek information and makes it the duty of the public authorities to disseminate the same for better governance and accountability. It covers the central, state and local governments and recipients of Government grants but does not apply to the intelligence and security organisations except if the information released to the allegations of corruption.

The author also focuses on the major impediments in its implementation and also few suggestions for its effective functioning in the days to come. Knowledge and information according to M.R. Biju, is the prerequisite for the enjoyment of this right because the lack of authentic information on matters of public interest leads to the wild rumors. Freedom of speech and expression includes the right to receive and collect information. Since the democracy is the government of the people who are the sovereign masters. There can be no government by the people if they are ignorant of the issues to be resolved, the argument for and against different solutions and the facts underlying those arguments. The taxes collected by the government belong to the people. They have the right to know in what manner they are being governed and how their money is being spent. The business of the government should be a participatory process. The fact should be made public. Only a fully informed citizenry can be better equipped for the performance of these duties.

The author further observes that, the Right to Information Act enables the citizens to get the required information for the redressal of the grievances within a specified time from the date of filing application. Any citizen can ask for information under this law by applying in writing or through electronic means to the Public Information Officer (PIO). Specifying the particulars of the information sought for. The right to information has been judicially recognized as a part of the fundamental right to speech and expression. Information is sine qua non for the efficient functioning of democracy. It keeps the people informed about the socio-political and economic affairs and issues. In a developing country like India, the availability of the information is required to be assured to the people in a simple and speedy manner because the development process depends on it.

M.R. Biju concludes his study by stating that, over the past few years, RTI has gained increasing importance in the human rights discourse as well as the larger democratic discourse. Since a democratic government must be sensitive to the public opinion for which information must be made available by it to the people. Effective accountability rests on the peoples' acquaintance with the information. A system that operates in secrecy tends to loose the faith of the people as much as its own legitimacy and credibility. Openness and full access to the information are the two pillars of the democratic state. It will equip the citizens to participate meaningfully in the democratic and political process.

Sudha Menon in chapter 7 has made a study on Social Entrepreneurship in India. According to her social entrepreneurship is a relatively new concept in development and social science literature. It implies applying business skill in social issues. In other words, social enterprise is an initiative which identifies a social problem and finding out a solution using the entrepreneurial skills and principles. It is self-sustaining on one side and maximizes social return on the other. Social entrepreneurs try to solve a social problem through inventing new approaches, harnessing managerial skill and applying business models which are replicable, scalable and sustainable. This paper has been divided into three parts. The first part of the paper briefly introduces the concept and examines various approaches towards social entrepreneurship. In the second part, the author attempts to analyze the social entrepreneurship initiatives of SEWA and its content and spirit. The concluding part critically examines lessons learnt and future challenges ahead.

According to Sudha Menon, the success of social enterprises in SEWA contributes an important ingredient to social enterprise theory- Community participation, community ownership and collective demands are more important in social enterprise than financial and other assets. Re-integration of business and social goals requires a perfect blending of social value generating structure with revenue generating business models. The unique Model–ownership model in which stakeholders own the enterprise and they take the responsibility of maintenance of the system-is the greatest asset of SEWA. Success of SEWA mainly depends on the two important assets- social capital and human capital. Through the effective leveraging of managerial techniques and skills; SEWA can certainly make any social enterprise sustainable.

Dolly Phukon in chapter 8 dwell upon the linkage between democracy, media, and gender. According to Dolly, women are still dramatically underrepresented in formal political institutions and decision-making bodies worldwide. In many countries women are not at all adequately represented in political parties, legislatures or the courts of law. Thus, it can be said that politics continues to be a masculine dominated activity. Even if women are admitted into the higher levels of government, they are entrusted with responsibilities which may be characterized as feminine.

Although women were incorporated in large numbers into the workforce and although quotas ensured their presence in political institutions, little effort was made to change cultural attitudes or to challenge the domestic division of labour. Ultimately, economic and political mechanisms to sustain the public role of women collapsed with the regimes that introduced them and that role in itself was discredited. Further, attention is drawn to the revival of local patriarchalism in the form of conservative, religious and nationalist forces. Politics has been constituted as a man's business to which women are not suited and male participants have been mandated to intervene in the domestic sphere in the form of legislation and constitutional clauses explicitly oriented towards 'enabling' women to stay at home, limiting their capacity for reproductive self-determination and thus their access to the public sphere.

Thus democracy has defined itself in fairly restrictive terms; it allows for formal equality but obviously this is not enough. A very little attention or no attention is given to factors that prevent or inhibit women from participation in the democratic process or public sphere on an equal basis, factors such as institutional structures and relationships in the workplace, the family, the community etc. The mere granting of rights doesn't help to alter people's attitudes and perception regarding those they consider inferior, whether these are women or dalits.

Dolly further states that, gender discrimination has been a universal phenomenon in human history from time immemorial. On account of her biological constitution, social taboos and scriptural sanction, the social position of the woman has always been considered as inferior and subordinate to man in society. In every society people as male and as female are expected to make some exclusive role performance. This role internalization is done through the process of gender socialization. The expected role performance of the female places them in a secondary position in the social structure and in the minds of men and women alike. Women are never viewed as persons on their own rights.

Moreover women don't view themselves as autonomous being due to their cultural socialization. Because of their marginalization in society, women hardly exist as a public phenomenon. Psychological orientations develop in the given social environment. Interest in Politics or Public sphere is created through the socialization process. The socialization process conforming to cultural norms continue to create interest in politics. But female roles are traditionally defined to be home oriented along which the learning develops. Interest is therefore created in the private sphere activities. The political and democratic rights conferred by the democratic system serve as opportunities for the citizens to participate, but if there are significant differences in motivation and societal inputs, the new participatory opportunities under the democratic polity would mean more inequality in participation.

Globalization according to the author, has brought new challenges to the democratic role assigned to the media. The advertisers become the primary customer of the print and visual media through which they reach the customers who happens the readers or viewers of the media. With the economic liberalization in the third world countries including India, the fashion industry has developed. The fashion industry in collaboration with the media creates role models in order to urge women to look this way and that, promote products which, they claim will enhance or even enable one to be beautiful. Thus with the growth of fashion industry women's beauty became one of the most important definition of femininity.

The precondition for successful democracy according to Dolly is gender equality so that both men and women could equally participate in governance and developmental process in a country. Even though women in a democratic society is assumed to be enjoying their rights to the fullest extent, in reality women's democratic freedom are curtailed by the rigidity of the prevalent social customs of the society. The position of women in the society is determined on the basis of the social values, and the trends or tendencies prevailing in the society. Thus, the relation between women and media in the Indian democratic setup could be determined after analyzing the position of women in the Indian society and culture. The Indian society is highly stratified one and thus the position of women depends upon the class they belonged to.

In chapter 9, M.R. Biju presents a study on the political significance of the Fifteenth Lok Sabha Polls (2009) in India. According to M.R. Biju, the election to the fifteenth Lok Sabha was a land mark in the politics of India in more than one sense. The personality of Dr. Manmohan Singh, policies of the UPA Government, Rahul Gandhi's contribution to the Congress party particularly in UP, weaknesses of the NDA especially the BJP and confusion in the third and fourth fronts were responsible for the spectacular victory of the Congress and its allies. Belying expectations of a fragmented verdict, the mandate was decisive in favour of the Congress led United Progressive Alliance.

According to Biju, the triumph of the Congress was actually an aggregation of specific success across different States. The party retained its base in Andhra Pradesh, cut its losses in Madhya Pradesh; recovered lost ground in West Bengal, Kerala, and Rajasthan; and combined well with its allies in Maharashtra and Tamil Nadu. There was no one big surprise anywhere, but the party pulled out one small surprise after another across the regions of India. When it seems to take the long view in Uttar Pradesh and Bihar and spurned alliance offers by regional players, few predicted any immediate gains for the party. But now, one of the significant features of this election is surely the re-emergence of the Congress as a key player in Uttar Pradesh, India's most populous state. The same strategy did not work of course in Bihar, where the alliance of the Janata Dal (United) and the Baharatiya Janata Party rode on the good track record of Chief Minister Nitish Kumar. At the same, the Congress seems to have sown the seeds of its own resurgence by adopting a long-sighted strategy in the two key Hindi speaking States.

Moreover, in 2009 Polls, the voters appeared to have delivered a decisive mandate, came that heralded a new era in Indian politics. The verdict provided greater stability to the national government and reduced the bargaining and black mailing capacity of coalition allies vastly. Moreover, the verdict eliminated the need for a Congress Left coalition and was widely seen as paving the way for greater economic liberalization. The verdict, especially the success of the Congress in U.P catapulted Rahul Gandhi to the centre state of National Politics. The verdict was no doubt a vote for stability, ongoing economic reforms and certainly a vote against, the regional and caste based parties like RJD and BSP. The new and vibrant strength of the Congress will give rise to the impression that national parties were back at the centre-stage of Indian politics. Further, the 2009 Poll also proved as to how state-level alliances failed and the entire poll process was centered around national political issues. The credibility of the stable government by the third front was doubted by electorate' thus they noted for an alliance which they thought would offer a stable government.

M.R. Biju concludes his detailed study by stating that, the electorate indisputably noted for a stable government at the Centre. The vote was for a dispensation which was wedded to help the poor and the middle class. The progressive forces of all lives must comprehend the essence of these results and extend constructive support to the ruling dispensation, which has secured the clear mandate to rule for five years beyond all expectations embodied in poll surveys.

Over and above, in 2004 onwards the UPA Government at the centre initiated a politically conscious approach shifted away from mere technocratic strategies of governance. Both the language of politics and direction of policies were pinpointing for the middle class and downtrodden. It has helped the Congress Party in 2009 to launch a platform aimed at the above such groups. The net result was nothing but the resurgence of the Congress party–party of the middle class and the poor. However, both the party and its leadership have to work over time to retain its mass base in the days to come. There lies the destiny of the UPA.

I wish to express my deep sense of gratitude to the esteemed contributors to this anthology of articles. The views and opinions expressed by the contributors are of immense value for researchers, policy makers and planners for rejuvenating policies and programmes on the core areas of the volume. Thanks are also due to Sri Jinesh Vellimon for providing excellent secretarial assistance.

I take this opportunity to record my thanks and affection for my wife Jaya, daughter Aishwarya and son Anantha Padmanabha for sparing me the time to complete this volume.

Finally, I thank Mr. Sandeep Sury, Chief Executive, New Century Publications, New Delhi, for his co-operation and understanding to bring out this volume in time.

Kollam M.R. Biju

1

Globalization, India and the Third World

M.M. Verma

Introduction

The current global economy is passing through an era of Liberalization, Privatization and Globalization (LPG). This emerging world economy is swayed by capitalistic ideology which pleads for an enhanced and freer play of market forces and removal of all barriers to free global trade 'Stabilization' and the 'SAP' are the key phrases associated with the consequent process of economic restructuring. The first stands for a sharp reduction, preferably elimination of a government's deficit, and the second strongly advocates wholesale privatization and rapid marketisation of economy" (Jha, 2003; 593). At the beginning of the current era in 1991 with the collapse of the USSR, it was publicized that by liberalizing and privatizing their economies, the erstwhile socialist and welfare states would immensely benefit in terms of free global trade, expansion of industry, food security and elimination of poverty, etc. However, during the last almost two decades of the new world economic order the indigenous industrial base of many developing countries has been fast disappearing. People, en masse, have been losing their jobs due to the trend of right sizing and the repetant global recession. The number of unemployed youth is on an unprecedented increase even in the developed economies of the world.

The central agenda of the globalization process seems to facilitate abolition of all sorts of barriers to global trade and commerce as well as minimization of the state intervention not only as a producer and promoter but also as a regulator. Thus, it postulates the dilution of the goals of the welfare state. Such concepts as equity, full employment and distributive Justice, etc, naturally, do not fit in with this neo-capitalistic ethos. Therefore, the poor, the down trodden, the women and children as also all the weaker sections of society are supposed to bear the brunt of new world order. The paper brings out the legitimate concerns of all these sections in the light of the new LPG regime.

Concept of Globalization

'Globalization refers to the process of integration of the world into one huge market' (Ashwathappa, 1997; 39). This process 'involves growing economic interdependence of countries worldwide' (Singh, 1998). The European Commission recognizes it as a 'process by which market and production in different countries are being increasingly interdependent due to dynamics of trade in goods and services and flow of capital and technology" (Sengupta, 2001; 3118). It is often seen as a series of efforts in order to develop free markets, privatize state enterprises, deregulating trade and business and expanding Foreign Direct Investments (FDIs) in different countries. Thus, the process of globalization aims at integrating the economies of the world in terms of trade and commerce sans barriers, free flow of financial and human capital and the uninterrupted transfer of technology, etc. To achieve this goal of integration, gigantic transformation of the economic, social and cultural structures which are full of numerous heterogeneities, is essential. Also, since all the countries and regions of the globe are at varied levels of socio-economic development, the modes, extent, process and the impact of globalization are bound to vary. It has far reaching implications for all segments of the society.

The globalization process has brought sweeping qualitative changes in the world economic system which "can be attributed to factors such as the advent of new global markets in services, increase in mergers and takeovers, weakening of anti-monopoly laws and the rise of global consumer markets and consumer brands (Hyman, 1999). One important prerogative of the agenda of globalization is to create such conditions in various countries as facilitate the adoption of a policy of non-discrimination between domestic and external industrial and business firms. By implication, it means that these states, which till recently protected domestic firms from external shocks, are now obliged to offer 'home treatment' to foreign firms.

Thus, the domestic enterprises are now open to global competition and are also subject to facing fluctuations of the global markets. It implies that the domestic firms have to rationalize themselves by adopting such measures as technological upgradations, downsizing of workforce, renegotiating conditions of work with the employees, removal of all hurdles to free in-flow of foreign capital, etc. Thus, globalization may be as the process of liberating the economies from the communist, socialist and welfare state politico-economic structures and paving the way for establishment of a global capitalistic economic system which entertains no restrictions on free global trade in commodities and services and has firm faith in allowing and facilitating a free play of market forces.

Economic Reforms in India: A Review of Achievements

The Government of India declared its New Economic Policy in 1991 as a part of Structural Adjustment Programme (SAP) as advocated by the Brettenwood Institutions. The new policy proposed to "unshackle the industrial economy from the cobwebs of unnecessary bureaucratic control" (GOI, 1991; 6). The Washington Consensus package intended to make India fiscally more prudent. It also aimed at a sharp reduction in the monetized deficit of this country. It included the following (Venkat Ratnam, 2001; 132) initiatives:

Cutting Down of Government Expenditure

- Drastic reduction in subsidies.
- Lowering of tariff and non-tariff barriers on foreign trade.

- Removal of policy preferences in the form of reservation for the public sector, Small Scale Industries (SSI) etc.
- Reform/removal of industrial licensing.
- Withdrawal of restrictions on foreign exchange.
- Dismantling of anti-monopoly legislation etc.

This package had been quite opposite to the "horrendous over activity in controlling industries, restraining gains from trade and blighting competitiveness" (Dreze and Sen, 1995) in the erstwhile policies. In the post-reform period, as Bhattacharya (1998) mentioned: "financial repression in India has decreased; reserve requirements have come down; interest rates have been deregulated, and real interest rates have risen to very high levels; and that direct credit to the government too has decreased". Even though "the performance of the economy during the period has been below potential" (Venkat Ratnam, 2001; 134), the World Bank predicts that by the year 2025 AD, Indian economy would be the third largest in the world after China and the United States (Amar Ujala, 2006; 14).

After the onset of new economic policies in India in 1991, certain laudable achievements (Verma, 2009; 2-5) have been made as summarized below:

- Forex reserves swelled to over USD 300 bn. from a meagre USD 1 bn. in 1991.
- The inflation rate based on wholesale price index has come down to negative figures from a high of around 17 percent in 1991.
- Poverty, as per the URP estimates, declined to 27.5 percent in 2004-05 as against 36 percent in 1993-94. As per MRP estimates, it declined from 26.1 percent in 1999-2000 to 21.8 percent in 2004-05 (Yojana, 2007; 17).
- During the last four years (2004-08) around, India could attract around USD 50 bn. as foreign direct investment which earlier had been a distant dream to be realized. In 2008-09, a target of USD 35 billion had been fixed. For the next 10 years, the target is USD 150 bn.
- Not only FDIs have been increasing, but Indian investment

abroad has also shown encouraging trends in terms of acquisitions, mergers and takeovers by the Indian corporate in the entire world.

- Even during the current recession, India has been one of the few countries to have achieved 6.7 percent GDP in 2008-09, which had been 7-10 percent during the last one decade.
- Gross domestic savings have been constantly increasing since 2001-02.
- Public sector savings which had been negative until 2002-03 have now become positive since 2003-04.
- Despite all the hic-ups during the recession, the BSE sensex continues to maintain the five digit mark since 2006.
- Though during the current recession our exports have declined, in the FY 2007-08 Indian exports stood at US$ 155.4 bn. (The Economic Times, 2008; 7). As compared to the pre-reform era, the balance of payments situation has now eased to a great extent. And with the setting up of SEZ and AEZ, India's trade imbalance may become a thing of past.
- Positive signals in terms of growing domestic investment opportunities have been received during the tenth five year plan period and thereafter, though, of course, the trends have been upset to a certain extent during 2008-09 due to the impact of recession.
- The reform era has witnessed a welcome resurgence of public sector leading to a constant growth of dividends from the PSUs to the government exchequer. It reflects that Indian economy has gained strength in the post reform era in both the public and private sectors.
- Even though the global recession has given a great setback to Indian job seeker abroad, Indian talents have continued to get opportunities to a great extent.

Thus, despite global recession, the current shape of Indian economy promises a better future. The ongoing LPG process has opened up numerous opportunities to face competition and achieve expansion of Indian economy. Bloomberg News recently reported that now India is fast emerging as a leading centre of mergers and acquisitions in the world. Now, she is fast emerging as a trading nation with achieving free market access to such markets as OECD, ASEAN, EU, etc.

Emerging Opportunities and Challenges

Globalization has created a number of opportunities for those who are competent, ambitious and real businessmen. According to the UNDP Report (2000), "Globalization expands the opportunities for unprecedented human advances". Globalization policy in India has accelerated the growth of Foreign Capital Investments by the MNCs who are supposed to bring with them advanced technologies, efficient management, work culture, and access to the global markets. Indian companies may get greater opportunities in a globalizing world by establishing joint ventures with foreign Companies; product based technology transfer agreements; R & D agreements; and components supply agreements, etc. There are immense opportunities for Indian Companies to build up strategic collaboration with Japanese, American, Korean Companies, etc. in order to enlarge their size and image in the global market.

Such sectors as agriculture and allied activities; construction materials; chemicals, fertilizers and medicines; management consultants; chartered accountants; software/hardware technology; diamond processing; jewellery exports, etc. have emerged as new areas having innumerable opportunities in such neighbouring countries as China, Pakistan, Nepal, Sri Lanka, ASEAN countries, etc. India has an immense opportunity of dominating in the export of coffee, sugar, tea, flowers, fruits, vegetable, agro seeds, dairy products, fish, meat, ayurvedic and herbal medicines, textiles, etc. However, the challenge ahead is how to adopt international standards of quality control and the associated sanitary standards.

Global Employment Opportunities

The greatest challenge India faces today is large-scale unemployment of educated youth. India, along with China, is rich in HR, while many developed countries are facing shortage of manpower. These countries are looking for Software professionals; Hardware professionals (technologists); Management professionals, Specialists and skilled persons in different areas. NASSCOM estimates that USA, Germany and other developed countries would annually require 50000 software professionals from India. The European Union has accorded India the status of a strategic partner. They will encourage unrestricted entry of Indian talents into their markets. In the US, Australia, New Zealand, Canada and Britain, etc., not only IT professionals but also our Doctors, Nurses, teachers, lawyers, cooks, etc. are in great demand. Australia has started a 'Skilled Independent Regional Visa Category' in order to meet out lack of professionals in the far-flung regions of the country.

In 1997, such OECD countries as, USA, Germany, Austria, Luxemburg, Switzerland, Australia, etc. had 10 percent or more of their total labour force which comprised of foreign born people. In such countries, India has better opportunities for investment of her human capital as there is an increasing trend of global business leaders deciding for more outsourcing from India (Panda,2007;45). Indians have been occupying top –notch MNC jobs because their abilities and competencies leave no doubt on the employers. However, it has become essential for the potential workers to acquire multi-dimensional skills in addition to up-gradation of their current skills in order to better harness global employment opportunities.

Opportunity to Accelerate Foreign Trade

The Foreign Trade Policy 2004-09 intended to double

Indian contribution to world trade in next 5 years. It also indented to achieve a global trade of US$ 300 bn. and 1.5 percent of the total global trade, which happened to be merely 0.7 percent at the time of the launching of the policy. It proposed a number of programmes including establishment of Services Export Promotion Council, Special Economic Zones and Biotechnology Parks etc. The policy accords top priority to agriculture. In special economic zones (SEZ) and Agriculture Export Zones (AEZ) 100 percent FDI has been permitted. China has been able to generate huge employment opportunities by enhancing FDIs and foreign exports. India too has an opportunity to achieve this.

Areas of Concern for India and the Third World

Despite all the opportunities made available to the third world by a globalizing world economy, there are many areas of serious concern for these countries. Globalization generates job insecurity, income insecurity, health insecurity, cultural insecurity, personal insecurity, environmental and community insecurity as well as a severe challenge to the national sovereignty (Thasian, 2001; 51). A discussion about the various issues/areas of concern follows:

Growing Unemployment and the Plight of Local Enterprises and Industry: Globalization has posed serious threats to employment and livelihood of the people. Automation, Computerization and Capital-intensive technologies of production have taken the toll of employment opportunities. It was argued that the lifting of industrial control and trade restrictions would result in higher output growth leading to creation of new employment opportunities and a visible fall in poverty and inequality. The trends of falling employment in the 1990s impelled the Planning Commission of India to constitute a Task Force in 2001 to report on this matter.

The Task Force (GOI, 2001) endorsed the trend of decline in employment and a consequent rise in unemployment.

Harnessing the criteria of Usual Principal and Subsidiary Status (UPSS), it reported that the annual rate of aggregate employment growth had been 0.98 percent during 1993-94 to 1999-2000 as against 2.04 percent during the period 1983 to 1993-94. The estimated aggregate employment elasticity also fell drastically from 0.41 during the period 1983 to 1993-94 to 0.15 during 1993-94 to 1999-2000 which might have been caused by the negative growth in agriculture, mining and quarrying, electricity, gas and water supply during the 1990s. As per NSS estimates, the unemployment rate in India had gone up from 6 percent to 7.3 percent during the corresponding period.

The Special Group constituted by the Planning Commission later in 2002, using the criteria of Current Daily Status (CDS) also observed a decline in the workforce growth from 2.7 percent during 1983-1993/94 to 1.07 percent per annum during 1993/94 to 1999/2000 periods despite a rising GDP from 5.2 percent to 6.7 percent respectively. The sharp decline is not only visible in the primary and secondary sectors, but also in the tertiary sector "at a time when the share of value-added in services as a proportion to GDP is increasing quite dramatically across states and India as a whole" (Bhattacharya and Sakthivel, 2003; 852).

Though the employment growth rates have shown positive trends during 2000-05, the rate of growth of employment has been lower than the rate of growth of labour force indicating an increase in the overall unemployment rate (Prasad and Anand, 2007; 48). These figures reflect dismal scenario on the employment front in the post-reform era. It is more alarming to note that the increase in the incidence of unemployment has been sharper for the relatively more vulnerable sections of India. In the post reform period, more than 700 thousand small scale industrial units and 900 companies have closed down rendering millions of workers jobless and as a result, capital worth billions of rupees has been blocked.

As per BIFR webpage(August 2006), there were 5147

enterprises in India registered as sick with a net worth of ₹ 655.56 billion against which they had accrued accumulated losses of ₹ 1291.44 billion. Out of these, only 436 units (8.47 percent) have revived. Employment of 21,87,175 workers in the rest of the units was in danger (Prasad & Anand, 2007;46). Thus, suffering in sick units is intensifying, while solutions, let alone labour friendly ones, are eluding. The Second National Commission on Labour has made certain recommendations to solve the crisis of high incidence of industrial sickness across regions and sectors. However, the major stakeholders have already disapproved the balancing exercise of the Commission. The challenge remains before the country as to how to revive our sick units.

As the domestic enterprises are facing quite intense competition from the foreign firms, the capital intensity in almost all sectors, including even in the small and unorganized sectors and services, is increasing (GOI; 2002; 24). As a result, now retrenchment, CRS, VRS, etc. have become quite common in order to achieve right sizing of the work force which creates a new category of job seekers in the market. A globalized economy is characterized by easy movements of skilled workforce across the countries. But, in the localized economies of most of the Under Development Countries, the family as a whole provides income security (Fearn, 1981; 236), which restrains people from moving out of a limited territory. Majumdar (2003; 530) also found very limited movement of people even outside the boundary of their own district for any economic purposes.

Therefore, strengthening of the local economy, characterized by prevalence of household and tiny enterprises, may be more beneficial for the rural workforce in developing countries. The development of agriculture related activities on an industrial basis, the development of local resource-based rural industries, etc. are the only routes though which the population of these countries can be productively settled. The catalyst for these has to be the State. Contrary to this requirement, the state is now gradually withdrawing from most of the sectors which had been dearer to the welfare state regimes.

Restrictions on Inflow of Human Capital: Many developed countries have shown their tendency to tighten their immigration rules in the name of national security against the fact that there were more than one billion job seekers in the world, as per the ILO Report (1997-98). These countries plead for free flow of goods and capital across borders in order to exploit the natural resources and maximize their profits from global trade, but they restrict free in-flow of job seekers from the over-populated regions of the globe. Such restrictions are against the basic philosophy of globalization. The process of Globalization will be completed only when borders of all the WTO signatories are opened up for the job seekers from anywhere in the world. Along with free in-flow of capital, technology, free trade, open competition, free entry of human capital across the borders must be allowed.

Problems of Inclusive Growth and Distributive Justice: The problem of inclusive economic growth is very basic to the survival and growth of the weaker sections of society. Development efforts must touch all sections of the society. However, fruits of globalization are being shared exclusively by the privileged classes across the globe. The World Bank Report, 2004 accepts that unequal distribution of wealth between the rich and the poor is increasing. According to the report, out of the 6 billion people on earth only one billion are rich. They consume 80 percent of the world's GDP, while the rest five billion have to live only on the remaining 20 percent. Around 2 billion people do not have access to potable drinking water, schools and basic health amenities.

A recent survey indicates that one-fifth of the world's people living in highest income countries dominate world's 82 percent of the export market; the share of the bottom fifth is just one percent. Similarly, they have 86 percent of the world's GDP whereas the bottom fifth have only one percent. Each year about 18 million people, mostly children die of starvation, malnutrition and related causes around the world. Unless we are able to sort out this problem of distributive justice, the poor of the world would question the legitimacy of the LPG process.

In 1998, out of the total poor population of the world, 43.5 percent belonged to South Asia. In India, as per NSS estimates (2004-05), 21.8 percent of the population was living below the poverty line. Any development strategy, which fails to include these poor masses, may not be acceptable. The Supreme Court of India (1993) explained the meaning of development in the case of Thomas Kocherry. As quoted by Thasian (2001), it said, "Development is not for the sake of development, but for the people; development does not mean increase of production alone but production has to be coupled with distributive justice". However, the market-led growth strategy has pushed the Indian economy in an era of 'profit over people', which goes against the democratic ethos of the country. Hence, 'the economy needs to be "re-embedded" with some form of "redistribution" his favour of the weak and the deprived, exposed to economic and social exclusion (Thakur, 2003; 646).

Even though we have accepted the path of globalization, we must always be inclined to expand our horizons as well as to protect the best interests of the country and the economically weaker sections. We have to strike a balance between LPG based economic development and the democratic need of public welfare. We have to develop some measures to achieve distributive justice. A weak, inefficient and allegedly corrupt regulatory framework cannot be expected to moderate the excesses of the market. Only effective rules and references can deliver full positive gains of the market economy.

Problem of Hunger in a Globalizing World: Globally, 37 percent of the children in the age of under five, are malnourished. The International Food Policy Research

Institute predicted that two out of every five children in South Asia will not have enough to eat by the year 2020 (Thasian, 2001; 58). Around two-third countries of the world are developing ones inhabited by the poor. If the developed world keeps on looking at these economies only as markets and continues to exploit them, the situation may worsen further.

We must remember that our infrastructure is still weak for sustainable development. Disparity across formal and informal sectors has further intensified. The fate of the working poor, the aged, the less educated and the unskilled have worsened substantially after the onset of reforms. According to UNFAO report, India has the largest number (around 2.33 million) of people affected by hunger in the world. Likewise, two-third of the mal-nourished people hail from India. Overall, 36 percent of Indian children (and 52 percent of children under 5) are mal-nourished. In India, 33 percent children are born with low birth weight, against 17 percent of those in the world. India has more persons suffering of endemic or chronic hunger than any other country, whether measured by calorie intake or anthropometrical indicators of malnutrition (Swaminathan 2007;15).

NSS Data (1999-2000) show a clear trend of decline in calorie intake. During that year, it was found that almost 77 percent of the rural population consumed less than 2400K calories which is the minimum poverty line requirement of calorie intake. The decline in per capita net availability of cereals and pulses over the last 15 years (from 510 gms. per capita per day in 1991 to 463 gms. in 2004) has been unprecedented (Swaminathan, 2007; 16). The sluggish agricultural growth rate of around three percent does not make for the any promise in near future. The sky rocketing prices of food items are making the situation even worse. Thus, the growing food gap and the diminishing purchasing power of the common masses in India and the entire world are indicating towards a horrible situation in the near future for the mankind.

Growing Rich-Poor Gap: Though the number of

billionaires is increasing and Indians are more and more joining the list of world's richest persons and the salary packages for the few are getting heavy to heavier, the plight of lower middle classes and the poverty ridden and disadvantaged sections has been assuming alarming proportions. The rich are getting richer, whilst the poor are getting poorer. The gap between the rich and the poor is ever widening. In the current period of recession when more and more people around the globe have been losing their jobs, this problem has attained a greater intensity. This is the greatest challenge to the stability of the world economic order.

During the 1990s, the GDP grew and new job opportunities were also created. But, net additions in jobs fell far short of increases in labour force (Chandrashekhar and Gosh, 2002; 643). Consequently, some gained jobs; others even improved upon the existing ones. But since the losers were not the gainers in this change, gains and pains of change got inequitably shared. This way the current growth strategy has further widened the rich-poor gap. While the "higher and average wages moved up, bottom wages fell further down. This has further intensified inequality" (Thakur, 2003; 642).

The then UN Secretary General Mr. Kofi Annan, addressing U.N. Special Conference on Globalization and Poverty in September 2004 expressing his concern over the widening rich-poor gap, called for adoption of a liberal process of globalization which could take care of the interests of the poor. He rightly warned that the people in developing countries were frightened by the process of liberalization and felt secluded and marginalized. Brazilian President De Silva expressed his anguish by saying, "After all, how many more times we shall have to repeat that the most lethal weapon of mass destruction in the world is poverty". Hence, a sincere and well-planned global effort to wipe out the menace of poverty and hunger from the world is immediately called for.

Extensive Use of Non-tariff Barriers by the Developed Countries: Certain non-trade barriers are permissible under

WTO, which the USA, the EU and Japan are using extensively to protect their industry. For example:

- Indian tea was prohibited entry into Germany on the pretext of pesticide residue. The European Union blocked groundnut exports from India due to content of aflatoxin (Banik, 2000; 4226).
- Recently, Japan rejected Indian mango because, according to them, it was not as per international standard.
- The US has initiated most of anti-dumping cases on Indian exports.
- The viability of agricultural exports of developing countries has suffered a setback due to high domestic support, high export subsidies and imposition of various trade and non-trade barriers by the developed countries. EEC, Japan and the U.S. provide subsidies to the extent of 50, 58, and 30 percent respectively of the aggregate cost of their products, while India provides only 9 percent domestic support (Chand, 2000; 3015). The developed countries keep on pressurizing the LDCs to withdraw all subsidies and support from farm and other sectors, while they themselves are still maintaining high level of support systems for their agriculture, industry and trade.

The developed countries are imposing different sanitary measures for restricting the imports of milk and dairy products, vegetables, fruits, meat and fish from India. Eco-labelling may be a new barrier to the exports from the developing countries as these countries are not in a position to maintain the norms required for the eco-labelling of their products. Thus, a situation of unequal competition has been created in the global markets against India and other third world economies.

Clout of Transnational Corporations: Dependency of the erstwhile colonies on the western economies for capital, technology and market has resulted in huge transfer of surplus from these countries on account of repatriation of profits. Also the unfavourable trade and unequal exchange has been a phenomena of the post-World War II, which gave rise to the

Trans-national Corporations (Mathew, 2001; 13). Described by the UN as 'the productive core of the globalizing world economy', the TNCs and their affiliates account for bulk of world's industrial capacity, technological know-how, and international financial dealings. However, there TNCs have been found to have been frequently involved in various sorts of malpractices, which many a times have caused national and international tensions. As expressed by Kannamma (2001; 175) the following, among other factors, have augmented the clout of TNCs:

- The increasing protection in international law of their property and other interests.
- An influential role in international bodies which regulate trade and other global issues.
- Acquiring (through mergers, etc.) an increasingly monopolistic position.

Though mostly based in Europe, North America and Japan, TNCs operate around the globe. While the world economy is growing by a mere 2 to 3 percent annually, the bigger TNCs are, as a group, growing at a rate of 8 to 10 percent (Karliner 1997). The MNCs and the WTO seek to outlaw the national laws, which restrict free trade and the super profits. They do not wish to bear even a bit of risk for their investments. They do not wish to transfer their technology to companies of the developing world. Hence, domestic units have to face unequal competition from the TNCs. For them, it is a question of survival. On the other hand, TNCs follow business just like a war. They ruthlessly attack the very existence of domestic enterprises in the host country. Initially, they sell their products on cheaper prices making the domestic industry lose their markets and eventually close down. MNCs once monopolies the market, determine the prices at their will. This process kills the entrepreneurial capability of the country and converts the society merely into supplier of cheap labour. A recently published UNCTAD report confirms such possibilities.

These MNCs enter markets in order to sell their products. They rarely aim to export the locally produced commodities. Hence, a heavy capital transfer outside the country takes place as the MNCs transfer dividends to the country of their origin, pay interests on the foreign loans and import machines from foreign markets. An over dependency on foreign direct investment is, thus, dangerous for the domestic economies of the developing world. The industrial relations situation may worsen in the countries like India as the Brettenwood Institutions, the WTO and the multinational corporations have been pressurizing the governments for effecting labour law reforms. And, the global competition has further put new pressures on national IR regimes (Hyman, 1999). The intended labour reforms (supposed to be carried out in India during the eleventh plan period) will have serious repercussions on the powers of the trade unions and would result into informalization of labour force and a decline in the real wages (Majumdar, 2003; 523).

Violation of Human Rights: The regime of human rights emphasizes the importance of human dignity; the right to work in just conditions and in return for fair wages; the right to welfare; the care for children; the equality for women; the respect for the cultural and economic rights of indigenous people; the protection of environment; the exercise of popular sovereignty through democratic constitutional orders, and the accountability of holders of power while aiming to distribute on a more equitable principle (Ghai, 1999; 250). The TNCs have over the years been found to have been involved in gross violation of all these human rights. The TNCs have often been found to be meddling in the internal affairs of the host countries or supporting such governments as had been dictatorial and human rights violators, if it was in the best interest of the company. Their involvement in the internal strifes in Chile in 1970 (Winston, 1999; 827); in Congo in 1997 (Sarangi, 1998; 3); and in Nigeria (Human Rights Watch Reports, Larrianga, 2000; 145 and 169) may be quoted as examples.

It has been generally seen that in their home countries, TNCs. "depend on democratic systems of governance, the rule of law and open societies to protect their interests and enable them to thrive. At the same time, they make enormous gains in countries where authoritarian and non-democratic regimes deliver on the promise of disciplined labour, low wages and lax controls on environmental protection and human rights. Thus, they seek to protect the gains of their exploitation in developing countries under the umbrella of their home country's democratic institutions" (Sethi, 2000). In this connection, a code of conduct for the TNCs was negotiated in the UN Conference on Trade and Development, but it was never formally approved.

The former UN Secretary General Kofi Annan's Compact (1999) calls on TNCs to assume leadership in the commitment to basic human rights principles. The global compact is based on values contained in three international agreements; the Universal Declaration of Human Rights; the ILO Declaration on Fundamental Principles and Right to Work; and the Rio Declaration of the UN Conference on Environment and Development. The principles are worthy but vague. Additionally, the UN promises that neither it will undertake any monitoring nor will the companies be under any enforcement procedure or any formal process of scrutiny. There is a dire need for not only evolving and accepting a code of ethics for these TNCs but also to develop some international mechanism in order to monitor its implementation by the TNCs in order to safeguard the human rights of the common citizens.

Globalization and the National Sovereignty: It is a matter of great concern that the World Bank, the IMF and the WTO together with the NATO and the UN have emerged as the global State. This super State is least concerned about the concerns of national sovereignty of the independent States of the world. The Supra-National monopoly capital concentrated in the MNCs is the biggest oppressive and exploitative force in the world today (Mathew, 2001; 21), as they hardly bother about the genuine national concerns of their host country.

Labour Concerns in LPG Era: The lifting of state labour protection, technological upgradation, restructuring of enterprises, contracting out of work and jobs, coercive VRS, etc. give rise to exploitative practices. In the name of reduction in labour costs, "offering lower wages, and reduced rights to sick pay, holiday entitlements, contribution to pension schemes and medical insurance (Brown and Lauder, 2001), etc. are now quite common which lead to insecurity of workmen. In the same way, casual employment, fluctuating wages and variable hours of work are also quite common. Thus, 'the lifting of state labour protection and the advent of free markets give rise to exploitative practices at work. Wages are driven to minimum' (Portes, 2000 as quoted by Noronha, 2003; 611).

Another general tendency of the companies and firms now-a-days is that they try to maintain a 'core' of indispensable key functionaries and a substitutable force of peripheral workers. This substitutability results in the erosion of workmen's bargaining power. Thus, "the days of welfare as an ideology are slowly drawing to a close. The conditions of work that existed during the pre-Independence period, gradually seem to have resurfaced" (Noronha, 2003; 612). The protagonists of the neo-liberal philosophy are pressing the Government of India hard to gradually do away with all the protective labour legislation and let the market forces have a free hand in dealing with their workforce.

Even though cheap labour may be well available in the market and the availability of the capital may be limited and costlier, the tendency is generally to resort to capital-intensive production (Mehta, 2004; 8). This tendency of the employers is bound to lead to further erosion in the wage rates and a constant increase in the prices of the commodities. Both ways the consequences go against the interests of the common citizens.

Agriculture and Women in a Globalizing Economy: In this era of Globalization, the issues of women and development as well as those related with women in agriculture are directly affected by not only the policy transformations of the national governments, but also the international agreements such as GATT and Convention on Bio-diversity and such agencies as the IBRD, the IMF and the WTO, etc. 'From the introduction of the Green Revolution technologies to the present Globalization of agriculture, there appears a rapid erosion of women's rights and control over productive resources (Reddy and Reddy, 2001; 378). The increasing mechanization of agriculture with export orientation in the new globalization and free trade regime is making the national 'agricultural policies devoid of a broader rural development and equity agenda' (Nanda, 1995).

Now, these policies are guided more 'by the transactional business and capital'. Such projects of development displace women from productive activity by appropriating or distorting their natural resource base (Shiva, 1998). The production process adopted by the MNCs generates a process of dependency of the farmers on these corporations. This process is bound to accelerate contract farms and capitalist agriculture, which will further marginalize the small and marginal cultivators and women. Economic reforms have intensified women's subordination as 'women when compared to men failed to take advantage of new work opportunities to enhance their position, and access to, and control over productive resources' (Tamara, 1997).

Globalization has, thus, failed to address gender concerns. Promotion of Bio-technologies in agriculture would lead to increasing commercialization of agriculture, decrease in Bio-diversity, degradation of environment, over exploitation of soil and ground water, and the growing power of TNCs (Kloppenberg, 1988; Shiva, 1988; Agarwal, 1988 and 1992; Reddy and Reddy, 2001). Thus, there is an urgent need for material empowerment of women through strengthening their rights in land as well as other resources to ensure that women have greater access to productive resources in the globalization era.

Concluding Observations

In the given scenario, global planning of resources is a peculiar aspect of the present techno-centric competitive times. In order to reap the benefits from the opportunities emerging internally as well as externally, the Government of India has been motivating the NRIs hard to upgrade their partnership in the country's development, apart from trying to attract FDIs to achieve a high growth rate and to increase the total capital base of the country. The global completion is fast intensifying which is posing dangers to the very survival of the small scale and tiny sectors. At the same time, certain companies are still facing the problem of labour surplus.

Despite the capacity of Indian workmen to be creative, innovative, and to perform wonderfully, we cannot achieve success unless the products/services are of high quality and are available at affordable price in the market. For large scale cost reduction, rightsizing may be required. Pertaining to the low cost of labour in the domestic market, business process reengineering (BPR) is largely the need of the hour in most of the Indian companies. It is also essential to bring operative efficiency in the informal sector by injecting better technology, improving skills, and arranging financial support and market access for SSI units. Progress on cross-border economic migration of natural persons would bring balance in the redistribution of human factor endowment (Nayyar, 2003). In the process, labour shortage economies would mainly gain, while the labour surplus transitional economies would get the needed relief.

In order to achieve the targets of the New Trade Policy, more emphasis should be accorded to development of infrastructure for which an investment of ₹ 14,50,000 crore would be required during the 11th Plan (Rajamni, 2007; 46). We also need to focus on development of the capacity to compete in the global market, overcoming unnecessary procedural delays, promotion of export and re-export activities. China has been able to generate huge employment opportunities by enhancing FDIs and exports. Against the target of 20 to 21 percent growth in Indian exports as stipulated in the new trade policy, Chinese exports have been growing at the rate of 35 percent. Implementation of the new policy initiatives with the fullest integrity, efficiency and better co-ordination may give better results. Every nation has to participate vigorously in the new world economic order, hence there can be no going back from the reform process.

However, concern for the poorer and the disadvantaged sections of society need to be given a heed. All the structural adjustments and economic reforms must have a human face, keeping in view the existing realities and requirements of the situation obtaining in a particular country. As Pope John Paul II (as quoted by Standing, 2002; 9), also remarked, "The rapid advance toward the globalization of the economic and financial system also illustrates the urgent need to establish who is responsible for maintaining the global common good and exercise of economic and social rights. The free market, by itself, can not do it, because there are many human needs that have no place in the market".

Therefore, for the stability of the new world order, a labour intensive but efficiency-promoting technology is required. In this connection, a final package with a revised arrangement for the organized sector; a strong beginning for strengthening the informal sector; the necessary legislative reforms; and a social security and welfare package of credible and sustainable kind, must emerge (Thakur, 2003; 648). It is very essential for the sustainability of the globalized economic order and free trade that some regulatory mechanisms led by committed professionals are evolved at the national as well as international level so that the malpractices to earn super profits by the corporate may be check-mated and the interests of the common man may be safeguarded.

References

Agarwal, Bina (1988): "Who Sows? Who Reaps?: Women and Land Rights in India," The Journal of Peasant Studies, Vol. 15, No. 4.

Amar Ujala (2006): "Tisri Badi Taqat" (The Third Big Power), Editorial (Hindi) October 25.

Ashwathappa, K. (1997): "Business Environment for Strategic Management", Himalaya Publishing House, New Delhi.

Banik, Niranjan (2000): "Analysis of Indian Exports during 1990s", Economic and Political Weekly, August 11-17; p. 4226.

Bhattacharya, B.B. & S. Sakthivel (2003): "Regional Growth and Disparity in India: A Comparison of Pre and Post Reform Decades", Discussion Paper Series No. 74/2003, Institute of Economic Growth. Delhi.

Bhattacharya, B.B. (1998): "Financial Reforms and Financial Development in India", Excel Books, New Delhi.

Brown, P. & Lauder, H. (2001): "Capitalism and Social Progress: The Future of Society in a Globalized Economy", Palgrave, New York.

Chand, Ramesh (2000): "Subsidies and Support in Agriculture", Economic and Political Weekly, August 11-17; 3015.

Chandrashekhar, C.P. & Ghosh, Jayati (2002): "The Market that Failed: A Decade of Neo-Liberal Economic Reforms in India", Left World Books, New Delhi (as referred by Thakur, 2003; 643).

Dreze, J. & Sen, A. (1995): "India–Economic Development and Social Opportunity", Oxford University Press, Delhi.

Fearn, Robert M. (1981): "Labour Economics: The Emerging Synthesis", Winthrop Publications, Cambridge.

Ghai, Yash (1999): "Rights, Social Justice, and Globalization in East Asia", in Bauer, Joanne R. and Bell, Daniel A. (eds.): "The East Asian Challenge for Human Rights", Cambridge University Press, Edinburgh.

Government of India (1991): "India's New Economic Policies", Ministry of External Affairs, New Delhi.

——(2001): "Report of the Task Force on Employment Opportunities", (July) Planning Commission of India, New Delhi.

——(2002): "Special Group on Targeting Ten Million Employment Opportunities Per Year", (May) Planning Commission of India, New Delhi.

Human Rights Watch, "Corporations and Human Rights", http://www.hrw.org/about/initiatives/corp.html/.

Hyman, R. (1999): "An Emerging Agenda for Trade Unions?" http://www.ilo.org/Public/english/bureau/inst/papers/1999/dp98/ ILO (1997-98): "World Labour Report", Geneva.

Jha, Praveen (2003); 'Workers in the Time of Economic Reforms: A Field Report', Indian Journal of Labour Economics, Vol. 46, No. 4, pp. 593-610.

Kannamma, Raman (2001): "Globalization, Transnational Corporations and Human Rights", Social Action, Vol. 51, No. 2 (April-June); pp. 175-91.

Karliner, Joshua (1997); "The Corporate Planet: Ecology and Politics in the Age of Globalization", Sierra Club Books, San Francisco.

Kloppenberg, Jack A. (1988): "First the Seed: The Political Economy of Plant Biotechnology", Cambridge University Press, New York.

Larrianga, Miguel de (2000); "(Re) Politicizing the Discourse: Globalization is a Shell Game", Alternatives, Vol. 25, No. 2 (April-June).

Majumdar, Bhasker (2003): "Labour in a Globalised World and Workers in a Localised Economy", Indian Journal of Labour Economics, Vol. 46, No. 4.

Mathew, Thomas (2001): "Uniting to Resist Globalization and Neo-facism", Social Action, Vol. 51, No. 1 (January-March).

Mehta, Balraj (2004): "Economic Development and Soaring Prices" (Hindi), Rajasthan Patrika, November 5, p. 8.

Nanda, M. (1995): "Trans-nationalization of Third World State and Undoing of the Green Revolution", Economic and Political Weekly, Vol. 30, No. 4.

Nayyar, Baldev Raj (2003): "Economic Globalization and its Advance from Shallow to Deep Integration", Economic and Political Weekly, November 8, pp. 4780-4782.

Noronha, Ernesto (2003): "Globalization: The Impact on Port and Dock Workers in India", The Indian Journal of Labour Economics, Vol. 46, No. 4, pp. 611-21.

Panda, A.K (2007): "Labour Market Reforms", Yojana, (May) Vol. 51, No. 5, p. 45.

Prasad, Gopal & Anand, Sunita (2007): "Employment: Recent Trends"; Yojana, Vol. 51, No. 5 (May), p. 48.

Portes, A. (2000): "Neo-liberalism and the Sociology of Development: Emerging Trends and Unanticipated Facts", in Roberts, J.T. & Hite, A. (eds.): "From Modernisation to Globalization: Perspectives on Social Development and Social Change", Blackwell, Oxford.

Rajamani, R.C. (2007): "Optimism on Growth, Caution over Inflation", Economic Survey 2006-07, Yojana (March), Vol. 51, No. 3.

Reddy, K. Kranthi Kumar & Reddy, P. Vijailakshmi (2001): "Globalization, Agriculture and Women", Social Action, 51; 4 (Oct-Dec), pp. 378-94.

Sarangi, Satinath (1998): "Corporate Violence in Bhopal", Paper presented at the International Conference on "Preventing Violence, Caring for Survivors, Role of Health Profession and Service in Violence", Organized by Centre for Enquiry into Health and Allied Themes, Nov. 28-30, Mumbai.

Sengupta, Chandan (2001); "Conceptualizing Globalization-Issue and Implications", Economic and Political Weekly, August 18-24.

Sethi, Prakash, S. (2000): "Human Rights and Corporate Sense", Far Eastern Economic Review, Oct. 13.

Shiva, V. (1988): "Women's Indigenous Knowledge and Bio-diversity Conservation", in Sen, Geeti (ed.): "Indigenous Vision, Peoples of India, Attitude to the Environment", Sage Publications, New Delhi.

——(1998): "Staying Alive: Women, Ecology and Survival in India", Kali for Women, New Delhi

Singh, Kavaljit (1998): "A Citizen's Guide to the Globalization of Finance", Madhyam Books.

Standing, Guy (2002): "Human Security and Social Protection" in Ghosh, Jayati and Chandrashekher, C.P. (eds.): "Age of Finance", Tulika, New Delhi.

Swaminathan, Madhura (2007): 'Food and Nutrition Insecurity', Yojana (May) Vol. 51, No. 5.

Tamara, Jack A. (1997): "Women's Work in Rural China: Change and Continuity in an Era of Reform", Cambridge University Press, Cambridge and New York.

Thakur, C.P. (2003): "Emerging Pattern of Industrial Relations:

From Reality Check to Some Speculations", Indian Journal of Labour Economics, Vol. 46, No. 4; pp. 637-49.

The Economic Times (2008): June 25, Lucknow.

Thasian, T. (2001): "Development Challenges in the 21st Century", Social Action, Vol. 51, No. 1 (January-March); pp. 46-60.

UNDP (2000): "Overcoming Human Poverty", United Nations Development Program, New York.

Venkat Ratnam, C.S (2001): "Globalization and Labour-Management Relations", Response Books, New Delhi.

Verma, M.M. (2009): "Globalization: Emerging Opportunities and Challenges for India", Convergence Asia (The Journal of Knowledge Economy Management), Vol. VIII, No.1 (October-March), p. 1-9.

Winston, Morton (1999): "Review of Human Rights and International Political Economy in Third World Nations: Multinational Corporations, Foreign Aid, and Repression", Human Rights Quarterly, Vol. 21, No. 3 (August).

Yojana (2007): "Poverty Check-Rural India Fares Better" Vol. 51, No. 5 (May).

2

Globalization: Myths and Realities

Arvind Singh

The period after 1950 was marked by the integration of national economies to a magnitude never witnessed earlier in the mankind's history. The current phase of integration is also strongly influenced by the developments in information technology [1] and the concomitant increase in the literacy levels worldwide. Technology has given impetus to innovation in telematics, computers, fiber optics, satellite and other communications; their convergence with television, electronic bourses for trading stocks, bonds, currency, commodities, future options and other derivatives; and the global explosion of e-commerce and the internet. The increasing access to education has ensured that literacy levels are increasingly on the rise, thereby affording opportunity to state and non-state actors to sell their ideas and perspectives with greater ease and speed.

At the economic level the wave of deregulation, privatization, liberalization of capital flows, opening of national economies, extension of global trade, and the export led growth policies that followed the collapse of the Bretton woods fixed currency exchange regime in the early 1970s, saw the interconnections of economic spaces. [2] The impending oil crisis [3] in 1973, fuelling inflationary pressures left many countries in the lurch, in Asia, Africa, Latin America and Europe.

Many developing economies, faced with the problem of mounting debt [4] and faltering on their debt service payments, had no option but to court IMF and World Bank. With crumbling of the socialist economies in the Eastern Europe and

Russia, with their emphasis on regulation and statism brought them to the heel of Washington consensus.

The present globalization [5] seems to be creating new horizons, and spaces of contestations for the nouvea rich elites, corporations and the Transnational Corporations. With the settling nuances of Financial Discipline being imposed globally by multilateral institutions such as WTO, IMF and World Bank the entrepreneurial juggernauts, and venture capitalists, having at their disposal Transnational Finances, have never had so easy to fulfil their goal of maximizing profits.

The economic forces of globalization have virtually rendered the National Policy makers and local affairs, grassroots lives and livelihoods as well as the natural ecosystem almost to the level of abstractness. [6] The ferocity with which the new forces are impinging on the Public Spaces seems to be triggering new risks and new inequalities. This may have the inherent potential to marginalize social groups, [7] indigenous peoples, and spurring a divide between rich and poor, and leading to an overall increase in poverty globally, as depicted in successive UNDP Human Developmental reports. [8] According to the living Planet Index assembled by the world wide fund for Nature and the New Economics Foundation, around 30 percent of Natures Productive Capacity has been lost, with in one generation.

Some other issues which have come to the fore are namely climate change, cross border pollution, desertification, and loss of biodiversity. These issues have gone beyond the pale of national government, and require global initiatives. Proliferation of weapons, trafficking, drugs trade, organized crime, nuclear and toxic wastes, epidemics and not to mention global terrorism cannot be addressed by nations on their own. Similarly dealing with refugees, immigrant populations, displaced peoples, and continued growth of mega cities – while maintaining safety nets requires massive public investments. Reactions to globalization, have in turn also included racial and religious responses in the form of jihadism [9] and ethnic identity formations.

Needless to mention that globalization has also accelerated time/space compression, [10] which has advanced democracy world wide, restrained the dictators, loosened oppressive regimes, and has advanced the cause of pluralism and respect for human rights. Concomitant by-product of this globalization has been the rise of new social movements, and an ever vigilant civil society, which has networked itself, towards a global presence effectively voicing its preferences and concerns. This has brought a new concern pertaining to issues of sustainable development [11] (without compromising the needs of the future generations) principals of social justice, citizen participation and ecological awareness.

The debate on globalization offers a spectacle of fissures, with many left social activists and scholars offering credible stances of data that seems to suggest that the past twenty five years have witnessed a divergence, rather than convergence, in levels of income between countries and among people. Economic inequalities have increased during the last quarter of a century as the income gap between rich and poor countries, between rich and poor people within countries, as also between the rich and the poor in the world's population has widened. Except for the countries in East Asia, South East Asia the incidence of poverty has increased in most countries of Latin America and Sub-Saharan Africa in the 1980s and in much of Eastern Europe during the 1990s. In the developing countries, employment creation in the organized sector continues to lag behind the growth in the labour force, so that an increasing proportion of workers are dependent on low productivity and casual [12] employment in the informal sector. Unemployment in the industrialized countries has increased substantially since the early 1970s, and remained at high levels since then.

The inequality pertaining to income and wages has witnessed an increase everywhere in the world. Symbiotic occupational structures of simple societies has seen an all round deterioration, with the result, alienation, violence, ethnicity, religious fundamentalism has registered on overall increase. Trade liberalization has led to a growing wage inequality between skilled and unskilled workers, not only in industrialized countries but also in developing countries (UNCTAD, 1997). During the period of globalization after 1990s, governments are increasingly obsessed with managing the inflation, in order to attract investment, thereby compelling the governments to pursue deflationary macroeconomic policies, consequently leading to squeeze in growth and employment. [13] The mobility of capital combined with the immobility of labour has changed the nature of employment relationship and has reduced the bargaining potential of the Trade Unions.

Financial liberalization which has meant a rapid expansion of public as well as private debt, has been associated with the emergence of a new class. The alliance of this new class and the *oligo polists* everywhere has led to unequal income distribution. Global competition has driven large international firms to consolidate market power through mergers and acquisitions, which has made market structures more oligopolist than competitive. [14]

Comparative Cost Advantage

Globalization enthusiasts are constantly endeavouring to create a hype of comparative cost advantage, which would afford goods at an affordable rates, also appears to be a smokescreen as natural resource based comparative advantage is easily turned upside down by technological developments which are more easily achieved by countries, at already relatively higher levels of development. The labour based advantage also often gets nullified by technological advantages of labour scarce capital abundant countries. Inequalities as a result of colonial structures that were implanted have not been entirely done away with, consequently leading to dependent relationship with the West. Thus globalization, as argued by the proponents, instead of being an equalizing factor, appears to have achieved the dubious distinction as another instrument of increase in disparities. [15]

Economic Growth and Poverty

While GDP increase has been the one side of the story sceptics are of the opinion that WTO engineered globalization has been causing entitlement failures and capability deprivations. [16] Nearly a quarter of the world's population continues to live in poverty with indications that the Plight of the poorest of the poor has deteriorated. Inequality has grown faster in the last 15 years than in the past 50. The series of United Nations Human Development Reports since 1990 establishes this very clearly. The income gap between top 20 percent of the world's population and the bottom fifth has more than doubled. By 1998, the top 20 percent consumed 86 percent of all goods and services. The bottom fifth had to manage with 1.3 percent. [17] Forbes, which uncovered some 140 billionaires on its list 20 years ago, found 470 on its second list three yeas ago. In 2006, it is a record 793 billionaires world-wide. The world's 793 richest people are worth a combined US$ 2.6 trillion. [18]

It is much more than the four times the total GDP of India, having more than a billion population. The wealth of the top 200 people is more than the combined income of the 40 percent of the global population. The number and percentage of people living on less than US$ 1 a day in Sub-Saharan Africa and the Middle East have increased while the percentage living on less than US$ 2 a day has increased in these regions, as well as in Latin America and the Caribbean. [19]. The apprehensions of Joseph Stiglitz (2002) seems to be turning prophetic: 'if globalization continues to be conducted in the way that it has been in the past, if we continue to fail to learn from our mistakes, globalization will not only succeed in promoting development but will continue to create poverty and instability. [20]

Developing Countries, Inflated Hypes

A recent paper published by the common wealth secretariat discusses the situation of the least developed and land locked countries in the global economic system. [21] It quotes WTO data to show that even after the removal of the systematic biases against trade and the dismantling of barriers since mid-88s, India's share in world merchandise trade increased by only 0.5 percent in 1983 to 1 percent in 2006. In 1948, soon after the conclusion of the GATT, India's share was much higher at 2.2 percent.

More generally the paper, by Stanford University visiting Professor T.N. Srinivasan, said the total share of world merchandise trade for Mexico, South and Central America, Middle East, Africa and Asia (excluding Japan) that together broadly covers the developing world, was 31.4 percent in 1948, 26.8 percent in 1983 and 35.4 percent in 2006. If South East Asia, which has been more open since 1960s, and China, which opened in 1978, are excluded, the share of the remainder of this group was 27.1 percent in 1948, 19.8 percent in 1983 and 19.6 percent in 2006.

It is also referred in this paper that World Bank data also suggests a similar trend. It is clear that although the period after 1980 is one of growing integration of the developing world with the World Trade—certainly it resulted in halting the decline and has in fact, raised the export share of the developing world—the gain in export share has largely been in China and South East Asia. Africa and South and Central America have experienced a steady decline in their share of world trade ever since 1948."

Here it would be pertinent to mention that advances made by some developing countries are because of their individual efforts to cut costs and increase global competitiveness, on the export front, rather than globalization-induced liberalization. [22] Chinas spectacular rise in the field of world trade, despite being a late and rather-reluctant adherent to the principles of free trade, can be ascribed mainly to the unequalled productivity gains achieved by that country in the last few years.

Multilateral Institutions, IMF and the World Bank

The IMF and the World Bank were entrusted with the twin responsibility of financial stabilization and development. Since the debt crises broke in 1982, when Mexico first declared a moratorium on its international debt payments, the IMF and World Bank have been commissioned and dispatched to the frontiers of the global economy to exact payments from and supervise the credits to the third world. In this capacity they have been able to profoundly affect the organization of production and trade in the periphery to the benefit of the core of the world capitalist system.

To be fair, these international institutions were catapulted into the role of debt collector by force of historical circumstances rather than design. The privatization of the world's financial markets which began in the 1970s, and the concomitant rise of private lending to the third world, in that period, ruled out direct government intervention on the part of the leading industrial nations. Karlotto Pohl, IMF governor for the Federal Republic of Germany in 1982, Summed up the bankers position during a visit to Buenos Aires.

"The IMF is our only hope. It is only institution that can lend many and impose conditions for doing so. No government can do this, nor any bank. [23]

In all debt rescheduling exercise in the 1980s it has been the seal of approval of IMF/World Bank, as expressed in official memoranda of agreements and letters of intent exchanged between them and the debtor countries which has released, in complex and interactive packages, official and commercial credit flows. [24] There were basically two groups of seriously indebted countries. On the one hand, there were the 15, so called Baker Countries. These were the middle income countries, mostly in Latin America, Plus Nigeria, the Philippines, and former Yugoslavia. On the other hand, there was a group of some 20 least developed countries, mostly in sub-Saharan Africa. The difference between the two groups, apart from the size of the debt and level of economic development, lay in the composition of the debt.

The former group incurred their debt mostly through, private lending, the latter mostly through 'official' credits. Yet the terms and conditions of the rescheduling packages have been remarkably similar, weather introduced under IMF stabilization agreements (as in the case of the former) or under IMF/World Bank structural adjustment facilities (as in the case of the latter). In both cases the scope and detail of the combined IMF conditionality rules and the World Bank's structural adjustment contracts have amounted to a degree of economic intervention in the debtor countries which matched, perhaps even, exceeded, the direct administration of bygone colonial governments. Inside the ruled countries the IMF came to be known as the 'International Ministry of Finance'.

Structural adjustment is the generic term used to describe a package of measures which the IMF, the World Bank and individual western aid donors have persuaded many developing countries to adopt during the 1980s, in return for a new wave of loan. And Adrian Leftwich, writes, the aim of adjustment was to shatter the dominant post-war, state led development paradigm and overcome the problems of developmental stagnation by promoting open and free competitive market economies, supervised by minimal states. [25] Between 1980 and 1990, World Bank structural adjustment loans increased from 7 to 187 in 60 countries. [26] The inventory of IMF/WB prescriptions is by now well known. It includes currency devaluation, deregulation of prices and wages, reduction of public spending on social programmes, and state bureaucracies removal of food and other subsidies on basic necessitates, trade liberalization, privatization of state enterprises, and the expansion of the export sector, the latter in the case of agriculture–often at the expense of food production. The officially stated aims of these policies was to stabilize domestic economies, to stimulate economic growth and to ensure the country's ability to earn the foreign exchange needed to service its foreign debts.

Global Growth Patterns

A World Bank Study, Global Economic Prospects: managing the next wave of globalization contains information about much of the upside of globalization. Driven by globalization, since 1974, exports have doubled as a proportion of world economic output to over 25 percent and on existing trends will rise to 34 percent by 2030. World income has doubled since1980, and almost half a billion people have climbed out of poverty since 1990. On present trends, the number of people living on under one purchasing power dollar a day will halve from today's one billion by 2030. This will result from growth in South and East Asia, whose share of the poor will halve from 60 percent while Africa's will rise from 30 percent to 55 percent. Of course, a linear extrapolation from today's trends could prove wrong with rise of protectionist measures, pandemic diseases, or environmental limits to growth.

The scale, the benefits of globalization can all prove to be exaggerated, if we look into the data's available regarding growth. [27] Compared to the immediate post-War period, the average rate of growth has steadily slowed down during the age of globalization from 3.5 percent per annum in the 1960s to 2.1 percent, 1.3 percent, and 1.0 percent in the 1970s, 1980s and 1990s respectively. [28]

The growing economic interdependence is highly asymmetrical: the benefits of linkages and the costs of delinking are not equally distributed. Industrialized countries (the European Union, Japan and USA) are genuinely and highly interdependent in their relations with one another. But developing countries are largely independent in economic relations with one another, and highly dependent on industrialized countries.

Globalization creates losers as well as winners, and entails risks as well as providing opportunities.

Labour

Globalisation has not been without attendant ramifications to labour, world wide. Most explicit consequences for labour have been unpalatable. Wage shares have fallen while profit shares have risen. Capital mobility alongside labour immobility has reduced the bargaining power of organized labour. The rise in unemployment and accompanying casualisation of the work force, with more and more people working in the informal sector, has generated an excess supply of labour and depressed real wages. [29] The rapid growth of global markets has not seen the parallel development of social and economic institution to ensure their smooth and efficient functioning, labour rights have been less assiduously protected than capital and property rights, and the global rules on trade and finance are unfair to the extent that they produce asymmetric effects on rich and poor countries. [30] Most states are contracting their public welfare services to the private sector, shifting the state's role to that of a facilitator. As states retreat from their traditional role as protectors of formal labour, work is becoming increasingly insecure and degraded.

WTO and Doha Round

The deepening of poverty and inequality—prosperity for few and marginalization and exclusion of many has wider implications for social and political stability of many nations. Doha round which began in 2001, was supposed to be about trade led and trade facilitated development of the world's poor countries. [31]

After five years of negotiations, the talks collapsed because of unbridgeable differences among the EU, the U.S. and developing countries led by India, Brazil and China. From the developing countries perspective, the problem is that the rich countries want access to the poor countries, resources, markets, and labour forces at the lowest possible price. [32]

Some rich countries were agreeable to deep cuts in agricultural subsidies but resisted opening their markets, while some others reversed this. Developing countries are determined to protect the livelihood of their farmers because farmers suicides have been a terrible human cost and a political problem for state and central governments in India for some years already—and rural development. [33] The rich countries pledges of flexibility failed to translate, as they were bent on protecting the interests of the tiny agricultural minorities. By contrast, in developing countries, farming accounts for 30-60 percent of GDP and up to 70 percent of the labour force. This is why labour rights protection is at least as critical for developing countries as intellectual property rights protection is for the rich, it is also to be borne in mind that Western Countries for centuries relied on public regulation, social investments, in order to protect the interests of vulnerable caused by the market failure.

Environment

National barriers to trade and investment have been dramatically reduced around the world in the past 20 years. As a result, FDI by transnational corporations in developing countries grew twelve fold between 1970 and 1992 (World Investment Report 1996). If then trebled between 1992 and 1997, rising to US$ 149 billion out of a world wide FDI total of US$ 400 billion—(World Investment Report 1996, and 1998) the opening of markets world wide to foreign imports and the promotion of exports has caused a similar explosion in the volume of world trade, whose value has grown from US$ 380 billions in 1950 to US$ 5.86 trillion in 1997: a fifteen fold increase. [34]

The boom in world trade and investment due to economic globalization has contributed variously to ecological problems. If the trade has to be sustained then it requires huge infrastructure for transportation. Transportation driven by fossil fuels, combustible gases release harmful gases into the air leading to greenhouse effect, thereby leading to global climate changes. The same logic also holds true to increased bio-invasion—a primary cause of species extinction by which species from distant ecosystems are transported in the cargos, ships etc. with often catastrophic results for local biodiversity. Similarly the removal of border controls has seriously hindered the task of preventing illegal traffic in endangered species. The removal of barriers have also aided the destruction of biodiversity by providing twin advantages to corporations, who can access new markets of consumers with their advertisements and can exploit the natural resources to meet their production needs. [35]

Today products, technologies and life styles that were previously confined to industrialized countries and that, when used or followed are often highly polluting, are now exported and sold world wide. That is the case for example, of the motorcar, whose numbers have increased from a few thousand worldwide in 1900 to 501 million today. [36] The result is crippling air pollution, leading to climate change. Trade liberalization has led to unceasing exploitation of the natural resources. Thus metals must be mined from the ground to be converted into cars, trees must be felled to be converted into paper, packaging and furniture; oil and coal must be mined to be converted into electricity; fisheries are exploited for fish products; and soils are mined for cash crops. Thus there has been a eighteen fold increase in the global consumption of materials (including minerals, metals, wood products and fossil food based materials) since 1900. [37]

Mining now strips more of the earth's surface each year than natural erosion by rivers. [38] Global fish stock depletion and deforestation have reached devastating levels, with over fishing now threatening most major commercial fishing grounds, and logging for wood products threatening more than 70 percent of the worlds large intact virgin forest. The production of cash crops for export is also causing severe and unsustainable ecological damage, including soil erosion, land degradation from overgrazing, desertification, water depletion, chemical contamination, biodiversity loss and deforestation when the corporations find the resources, depleted, they simply move on to another area leading to massive and often permanent ecological damage.

Agriculture

In 1995 the WTO Agreement on Agriculture (AOA) was introduced. A major element of AOA discipline was substantial reduction in the level of subsidies granted by the WTO members. [39] It is alleged that developed countries provide domestic support of the order of US$ 320 billion to their farmers, thus enabling them an unequal bargaining power against farmers of developing countries. Rich countries comprise only 3-5 percent of population in developed countries and receive huge domestic and export subsidies. This is in contrast to the millions of resource poor farmers (who constitute the bulk of the population) in developing countries for which agriculture is the only means of sustaining their livelihoods. Further, developed countries subsidies keep the global agricultural prices suppressed and make farm activity in the developing countries non-remunerative. Therefore, it is not surprising that the developing countries are not able to compete with the developed countries even in the agricultural sector where they have natural competitive advantage, just because the developed countries are artificially sustaining uncompetitive agriculture in their economies by creating distortions in the world economy through the channel of subsidies. [40]

The globalization of food and agricultural systems, in effect, means the corporate takeover of the food chain, the erosion of food rights the destruction of the cultural diversity of food and the biological diversity of crops and the displacement of millions from land based rural livelihoods. Global free trade in food and agriculture is the biggest refugee creation programme in the world, for exceeding the impact of Kosovo. It is equivalent to the ethnic cleansing of the poor, the peasantry, and small formers of the developing world. [41] Thus globalization has led to a dramatic transformation of agriculture in India, which has had a devastating impact on peasant farmers. The policies have brought about following changes:

- A shift in production from food to export crops that has reduced food security.
- A flood of imports that have wiped out local business and diversity.
- An opening for global corporation to take over the control of food processing.

A cursory glance at the plight of the farmers in the four states of South India, is an eye opener. Poverty deaths and spate of suicides (According to official statistics there were 8900 suicides by farmers between 2001 and 2005) in South India, (Andhra Pradesh, Karnataka, Kerala and Maharashtra) [42] is increasingly as a result of shift to cash crops.

The new patent regime has exposed the third world agriculture to Bio-piracy theft of the indigenous knowledge of the third world countries. TNCS are using the WTO to take away biodiversity from the people of developing countries. By treating seeds, plants, cells etc. as human inventors they are being patented. Patents on biodiversity imply that the TNCS who own patents get exclusive rights to the production and sale of seeds, livestock and medicine. This establishes monopolies on food and health, makes illegal for farmers to save and exchange seeds (due to the development of technologies like terminator and germinator due to which the seeds developed become sterile after one season). By obtaining patents: World Grace and Co. for rice, TCC for basmati rice—they have deprived the rights of Indian farmers.

Financial Liberalization and Global Capital

Financial markets globally have become more and more

instable due to globalization. Small developing countries are most vulnerable to the instability of financial markets. With the crippling of Govt's authority to intervene, they have turned out to be merely mute spectators in the casino game played by Foreign Investors. Thus, the Russian, Mexican, and South East Asian Financial crisis had a telling effect on the economies of these countries, as wealth simply melted away due to pressures on the exchange rates. The floating exchange rates have proved to be a boon to speculators who have minted money and left domestic investors high and dry.

It is estimated variously that between 2 and 10 percent of global financial transactions are directly related to production and trade in the 'real economy'. The rest, the overwhelming, majority is speculative.

Conclusion

The force of globalization with their attendant deleterious effects seems to be transforming the world towards centralization, monopolies, and monocultures. Free trade is not leading to freedom. It is leading to slavery. Diverse life forms are being enslaved through patents on life, farmers are being enslaved into high-tech- slavery, and countries are being enslaved into debt and dependence, and destruction of their domestic economies.

We want a new millennium based on economic democracy, not economic totalitarianism. The future is possible for humans and other species only if the principles of competition, organized greed, codification of all life, monocultures and monopolies, and centralized global corporate control of our daily lives enshrined in the WTO are replaced by the principles of protection of people and nature, the obligation of giving and sharing diversity, and the decentralization, and self organization enshrined in our diverse cultures.

Notes

1. N. Woods, (1998), "Globalization: Definitions, Debates and

Implications; in N. Woods (ed.), Globalisation; Special Issue, Oxford Development Studies, 26, 1, pp. 5-16.
2. J. Timmons Roberts & Amy Hite, (2000) "From Modernization to Globalization", Blackwell Publishers, pp. 302.303.
3. Ibid, pp. 240-242.
4. J. Dunning, (1998), "Globalisation and the New Geography of Foreign Direct Investment", in N. Woods (ed.) Globalisation Special Issue, Oxford Development Studies, 26, 1, pp. 47-70.
5. Ankie Hoogvelt, (1997), "Globalisation and the Post Colonial World, Macmillan Press Ltd., pp. 242-243.
6. S. Prabhu, (1997), "Promotional and Protective Social Security during Economic Reform", Review of Development and Change, 11, 1, pp. 24-51.
7. Ibid. p. 39.
8. UNDP, (1997), Human Development Report.
9. Ankie Hoogvelt, (1997), "Globalisation and the Post Colonial World", Macmillan Press Ltd. pp. 188-95.
10. M. Duffield, (1999), "Globalisation and War Economics: Promoting Order or the Return of History", Fletcher Forum of World Affairs, 23, 2, pp. 21-36.
11. Hans-Peter Martin & Harold Schumann, (1997), "The Global Trap, Zed Books Ltd. pp. 214-216.
12. Ibid. p. 64.
13. J. Stiglitz, (2000), "What I learned at the East Asian Crisis," The New Republic, 17, April.
14. O'. O Neill, (1999), "Hunger Needs and Rights", in Harris White and Hoffenberg (ed.), pp. 217-32.
15. T.R. Papola, (2007) "Social Dimensions of Globalisation", IASSI, Quarterly, Vol. 25, No. 3.
16. A.V.V.S.K. Rao, (2007) "Globalisation: New Challenges for India," Mainstream, April 6-12.
17. P. Sainath, (2004), "The Globalisation of Inequality", Seminar, India 2003, January.
18. Hindu, (2006), March, 11.
19. Hori Wallach and Debora James, (2006), "Why the WTO Doha Round Talks have Collapsed—and a Path Forward", http//www.globalexchange.org/campaigns/wto/4257.html August, 14.
20. Joseph Stiglitz, (2002), "Globalisation and its Discontents, Penguin, p. 248.

21. The Economic Times, (2008), August, 20.
22. Ibid.
23. Quoted in S. Bransford and B. Kucinski, (1988), "The Debt Squads, Zed Books, p. 18.
24. In 1989 the IMF announced a change in policy. It now no longer insists that countries be current on their debt to private creditors before drawing on its resources. However, the guidelines for the implementation of this new policy are strict and include the Fund's satisfaction with the concerned country's medium term adjustment strategies. And even where the commercial credits have been resumed independent of such packages, the international Banks and other financial institutions have wished to reassure themselves that IMF supervision is firmly on place.
25. A Heltwich, (1993), "Governance, Democracy and Development in the Third World", Third World Quarterly, 14 (3), pp. 607.
26. Ibid, p. 608.
27. Ramesh Thakur, (2007), "Globalisation and Trade for development", The Hindu, January, 12.
28. Ibid.
29. C. Tilly, (1995), "Globalization Threaten's Labour Rights", International Labour and Working Class History, 47, pp. 1-23.
30. A. Satpathy, (2004), "Size, Composition and Characteristics of informal sector in India. In National Labour Research Institute Research Studies Series, New Delhi, V.V. Giri National Labour Institute.
31. Rajendra Kumar, (2007), "Failüre of the Doha Round—Looking back to look ahead", South Asian Politics, January, No. 9.
32. Ibid.
33. Briefing by Agricultural Ministry Officials in Hyderabad on April 10, 2006, DNA, April 11, 2006.
34. World Economic Outlook, October 1997, 1997; see also Financial Statistics year Book, 1997.
35. Edward Gold Smith and Jery Mander, (2001), "Impacts of Globalisation", London, p. 191.
36. Brown and Flavin, (1999), "State of the World", p. 6.
37. Gardner and Sampat, (1999), "State of the World", pp. 43-44.
38. Ibid.
39. V. Mathew Kurien, (2006) "AOA, TRIPS and the Third World Agriculture", Mainstream, Dec. 22-28.
40. Rajendra Kumar, "Failure of the Doha Round–looking back to

look ahead, "South Asian Politics, January, No. 9.

41. Vandana Shiva, (2001), "Impacts of Globalisation", Earthscan Pub., p. 204.
42. Briefing by Agricultural Ministry Officials in Hyderabad on April 10, 2006, DNA, April 11, 2006.

3

ASEAN-India Free Trade Agreement

Swami Prakash Srivastava

Over the past years, ASEAN-India functional cooperation has deepened and broadened. In terms of sectors, Asean-India cooperation covers wide ranging areas: trade, investment, tourism, human resource development, science and technology, and people to people contacts. Recently, several new areas have been included in the cooperation such as health, transport and infrastructure, small and medium enterprises, information and communication technology (ICT) and agriculture. India supports ASEAN's efforts to build an Asean Community by 2015. Asean-India bilateral trade had already reached US$ 30 billion, and looked forward to achieve the target of US$ 50 billion by 2010. An ASEAN India Free Trade Area (AIFTA) has been established and would anchor the strategic engagement between both sides and sustain the momentum of the relationship. As part of its "Look East" policy, which involved developing closer relation with the ASEAN with fast growth in trade and investment relations, India has also been fostering bilateral relations in a wide range of areas with almost all the ASEAN member countries, At the same time there is great interest among ASEAN countries to forge stronger economic and technological relationship with India.

Introduction

The origin of ASEAN lies in Association of Southeast Asia (ASA) proposed by Malayan Prime Minister Tunku Abdul Rahman in 1959. The ASA was short-lived because of territorial and political disputes among the member countries.

Concrete efforts for regional economic cooperation were further revived by the ASEAN Deceleration of 8th August 1967 which states that one of the aims of ASEAN is "to accelerate economic growth in the region through joint endeavours in the spirit of equality and partnership in order to strengthen the foundation for a prosperous and peaceful community of Southeast Asian nations" The ASEAN, initially had Indonesia, Malaysia, the Philippines, Singapore and Thailand as original founding members. Subsequently, after the end of Cold War, the grouping was joined by Cambodia, Lao PDR, Myanmar, Vietnam and Brunei Darussalam. ASEAN has four Summit level Dialogue Partners, i.e. China, Japan, ROK and India. In addition, it has a number of dialogues and sectoral Dialogue Partners as well. The ASEAN summit is the highest forum for ASEAN cooperation. Its meetings are held once every three years. The ASEAN Ministerial Meeting (AMM) is the next highest decision making body.

The ASEAN land area and population are larger than the 15 nation European Union. It represents the most longstanding and successful regional grouping for economic integration and peaceful coexistence. The recent move of ASEAN Free Trade Area (AFTA) and ASEAN Regional Forum has shown its zeal towards global integration. The process of reform and economic development in eighties and nineties in the ASEAN economies has facilitated the integration of their economies in the global set up. Outward looking growth strategies based on Foreign Direct Investment (FDI) has helped their fast progress and prosperity.

Review of Literature

Suparna Karmakar (2005) analyses the economic scenario in the Asia-Pacific region. She takes a macro overview of the potential of an agreement on trade in services between India and the members of ASEAN in the context of the ongoing attempts at multilateral liberalization and the proliferation of bilateral/regional comprehensive new-age free trade agreements.

Laurence Henry (2007) suggests that the development of trade and economic arrangements between India and Southeast Asia must be rooted within the larger processes of economic and diplomatic exchanges in Asia.

Mukul Asher and Amitendu Palit (2008) explore India's Look East Policy, initiated in 1992, which is all set to enter a new phase with the signing of the India Asean FTA.

Aekapol Chongvilaivan's (2008) suggests that the landmark agreement between India and Asean states is expected to constitute a tremendous free trade bloc, a large market of 1.5 billion people, with a combined GDP of US$ 1.2 trillion.

Pal and Dasgupta (2008) the authors analyzed the tariff structure of ASEAN countries in more detail and came to the conclusion that India is unlikely to gain too much market share in the ASEAN because of the AIFTA deal.

Kawai and Wignaraja (2009) "increasingly, policymakers have realized the need for stepping up the pace of the integration to improve international competition by exploiting economies of scale and strengthening their bargaining power through a collective voice on global trade issues."

Kumar (2005) suggest that India's inclusion in ASEAN plus Japan, China and South Korea grouping would generate additional welfare gains of US$ 48 billion.

Sen (2006) after the recent deadlock in WTO talks, it has already been indicated by Indian policy makers that bilateralism is likely to emerge as one of the key instruments of its commercial trade strategy.

Thomsen (1999) the Asian countries are one of the first recipient of global relocated capital and foreign direct investment has played a major role in promoting exports in these countries.

Kawai and Wignaraja (2009) believe that policy makers have realized the need for stepping up the pace of integration to improve international competitiveness by exploiting economies of scale and strengthening their bargaining power through a collective voice on global trade issues.

Need of FTA for India and ASEAN

ASEAN has embarked on an ambitious integration process, which will culminate in the creation of an ASEAN Economic Community (AEC) by 2015. This means a single market and production base, a highly competitive economic competitive economic region, a region of equitable economic development and a region fully integrated into the global economy. ASEAN is very diverse that it has everything for everyone. For business, it has more developed economies, which offer high value added business opportunities, and lesser developed economies, which have cheap and productive labour. There are a number of reasons for such scepticism.

First, India runs a major trade deficit with the ASEAN countries. For the last five years, India had negative trade balance for every year vis-à-vis ASEAN. For example, in 2007-08, the latest complete year for which data are available, India had a trade deficit of more than US$ 6 billion with ASEAN. In 2006, the GDP of ASEAN grew by 6.0 percent, much higher than expected. FDI into ASEAN grew by 17 percent in 2005 to US$ 41 billion from US$ 35 billion in 2004.

ASEAN continued to sustain positive trend for its trend for its trade performance as total exports for 2005 increased by 13.5 percent from US$ 569.4 billion in 2004 to US$ 646 billion in 2005. There were more than 2 million tourists from India visiting ASEAN this year and 2,80,000 ASEAN tourists to India. There is huge potential for further growth and expansion. India's Proposal is to set a target of 1 million tourist arrivals from ASEAN to India by 2010. ASEAN countries are much more dependent on trade than India. Singapore for example, has a trade to GDP ratio of more than 185 percent (according to 2007 data). Other ASEAN countries also have a much higher export to GDP ratio than India (Table

3.1). The recent financial crisis and the loss of market in developed countries have hurt these countries significantly.

Consequently, it can be expected that these countries will be pursuing export opportunities in new markets quits vigorously. India, with its high growth rate and large domestic market, can be a possible alternative for these countries. The ASEAN countries are the world's leading exporters of light manufacturing products and some agricultural items. It will not be surprising if Indian producers of these sectors come under pressure because of the AIFTA.

Table 3.1: Export GDP Ratio of Selected ASEAN Countries and India

ASEAN Countries	GDP Ratio
Malaysia	94.7
Vietnam	68.4
Thailand	61.5
Cambodia	47.3
Philippines	34.2
Indonesia	27.3
Lao PDR	22.6
India	14.5

Source: Asian Development Bank, based on data for 2007.

Secondly, one of the possible benefits from Regional Trade Agreement comes from the advantage associated with economies of scale. If the domestic market size of a country is not large enough, then a bigger market accessed through regional trade agreement can help industries take advantage of economies of scale. For example, while discussing the merits of Asian FTAs, While this is a valid arguments with Singapore and Thailand. And these two countries account for about 60 percent of India's exports to ASEAN 10. also, India has a trade agreement with Myanmar through the Bay of Bengal Initiative for Multi-Sectoral Technical and Economic Cooperation (BIMSTEC) mechanism.

Given these existing trade relations, the AIFTA essentially boils down to having improved market access to Indonesia, Malaysia, Philippines and Vietnam. Given the low applied tariffs in most of the ASEAN countries and also due to a much stronger trade relationship between these countries and china (which, incidentally, already has an FTA with ASEAN), it is doubtful how much incremental market access is limited, then the expected gains through economies of scale will also not be realized. On the other hand, if access to the Indian market further improves economies of scale for producers from ASEAN, then Indian domestic producers may face even tougher competition from these countries.

The area where the Indian industry is likely to gain from the AIFTA is cheaper availability of intermediate goods from the ASEAN region. For some companies operating in India and ASEAN countries, this agreement will lead to improvement in their-intra firm production networks. There are reports that some major auto mobile manufacturing companies of this region are planning more intra-firm and intra-industry trade to take advantage of tariff reduction under the AIFTA.

India-ASEAN Free Trade Agreement

India and the Association of South East Asian Nations (ASEAN) on August 13, 2009 signed a Free Trade Agreement (FTA). The agreement, which relates only to goods, took nearly six years to negotiate. The agreement was signed by Union Commerce and Industry Minister and his ASEAN counterparts at a ceremony in Bangkok, Thailand after the two sides held annual consultations. The accord, India's first with a trade bloc, will cover 11 countries with a combined Gross Domestic Product (GDP) of over US$ 2 trillion. The combined population of the region is of the order of 1.6 million. The Indian economy is of similar size to China, Japan and South Korea, countries with which Asean has already signed FTAs. Under the agreement, Asean members and India will reduce import tariffs to zero for more than 80 percent of their total imported goods between 2013-2016, while import tariffs for sensitive goods will be reduced to 5 percent by 2016.

Nine members of the 10-nation regional trade bloc signed the pact. Vietnam, the 10th member nation, would do so after its formal recognition by India as a "market economy". According to an official report, India and Vietnam had already agreed to sign a memorandum of understanding on this issue. The implementation of the FTA, would therefore takeoff from January 1, 2010.

The FTA negotiations with the 10 nation's South East ASEAN bloc began in 2001 but went through several rough patches. The pact has been delayed several times due to the differences over issues such as restricted list of goods, duty cut in farm products like palm oil and rules related to value addition. While the negotiations were concluded in the second half of 2008, differences arose on the methodology of breaking the customs barriers. The Agreement provides an array of business opportunities that will brighten the economic sentiment of the ASEAN business community. In fact, with this engagement with India, an emerging giant, ASEAN has now completed the creation of the largest economic space for ASEAN businesses to operate taking into account the successful FTAs with China, Japan, Korea and Australia and New Zealand. The ASEAN-India FTA is the fifth ASEAN wide FTA. The signing marks the end of protracted negotiations that spanned almost six years following the signing of the ASEAN-India Framework Agreement on Comprehensive Economic Cooperation in 2003.

India has agreed to special and differential treatment to ASEAN group and align its peak tariff levels. India will reduce its tariff for Brunei, Cambodia, Laos, Indonesia, Malaysia, Singapore, Thailand and Vietnam in 2011. Correspondingly, while Brunei, Indonesia, Malaysia, Singapore and Thailand will reduce their tariff for India in 2001, the new Asean members like Cambodia, Laos, Myanmar and Vietnam

(CLMV) will do so in 2016. Philippines which has expressed its reservations to the FTA has agreed to eliminate its tariff on reciprocal basis for India by 2016. India will unilaterally extend concession on 11 tariff lines to CLMV.

The Economic Ministers from ASEAN Member states and India signed the following agreements to effect the free trade in goods among them when they met for their 7th AEM-India Consultations in Bangkok, Thailand on 13 August 2009.

- Protocol to Amend the Framework Agreement of Comprehensive Economic Cooperation between ASEAN and India.
- ASEAN-India Trade in Goods (TIG) Agreement.
- Memorandum of Understanding on the Basel Convention on the control of Trans boundary Movements of Hazardous Waste and Disposal.
- ASEAN-India Agreement on Dispute Settlement Mechanism.

Advantages of FTA

Domestic opposition persists against India's FTA with ASEAN although it might well result in a boom in bilateral trade that can easily cross US$ 50 billion by 2010. ASEAN's GDP of US$ 1.5 trillion is not very different from that of India's GDP of US$ 1.2 trillion. The FTA is bound to open a huge market for our goods. India can benefit from services trade with ASEAN. This FTA, thus, is likely to be our most ambitious trade agreement as it will spur India Inc's drive eastwards. On the other hand reactions from different chambers of commerce like Federation of Indian Chamber of Commerce and Industry and the Confederation of Indian Industries indicate that segments of the manufacturing sector seems to be more positive about the FTA.

By locking in its demand on tariff reductions through a multilateral FTA like the ASEAN, India now has more trade allies and a stronger footing for an informal industrial ministerial meeting of the World Trade Organization (WTO).

This agreement was well balanced and was in harmony with India's look East Policy. The negotiators have ensured that our sensitive areas where we had concerns are fully addressed. The whole debate of the CECA adversely impacting domestic planters was based on "uninformed speculations' The implementation of the FTA would, therefore, take off from January 2010, as now agreed upon.

Disadvantages of FTA for India

Theoretically, trade liberalisation, which is based on comparative advantage and inter-industry leads to winners and losers. To ensure an increase in total welfare, the government needs to redistribute some of the increased wealth from the gainers to the losers. The AIFTA shows signs in such inter-sectoral trade-offs. From the analysis of India's commitment schedule as well as looking at the production structure of the ASEAN countries, it can be said that agricultural sector in India, particularly plantation sector like tea, spices, coffee and rubber will be negatively effected. Marine products, textiles and garments, and the auto components industry are also likely to be faced increased competition due to AIFTA.

Large Trade Deficit: Though India has a negligible stake of one percent in ASEAN trade, the overall trade with the bloc has expanded from US$ 7 billion in 2001 to US$ 39 billion in 2007. This dramatic increase in trade is one argument being routinely, it is clear that India is emerging as the loser from the agreement, because imports into India far exceed exports to ASEAN countries. This imbalance, known in economic parlance as a trade deficit, has spiked from US$ 3.5 billion to US$ 14.5 billion during the same period, and now accounts for roughly 15 percent of India's total trade deficit. Between 2005-06 and 2006-07, while India's exports to the ASEAN countries grew by about 21 percent, its imports from those countries went up by a whooping 66 percent. To bridge this rising trade deficit, one of two things must happen-either a lot fewer goods must be imported into India (and this can be achieved by placing higher tariffs on such imports), or exports from India into ASEAN should triple. Neither of these is likely, however, and the reasons are not difficult to figure out.

India's average applied tariffs in agriculture and non agriculture during 2007 (34 and 12 percent respectively) are higher than ASEAN tariffs (12 and 7 percent respectively). Conventional wisdom would suggest that in such a scenario India's exports ASEAN should rise, and correspondingly its imports from those nations ought to shrink. But this did not happen; i.e. despite the advantage in tariffs, Indian has been unable to match imports from ASEAN countries with its exports. With the FTA just signed, import tariffs on around 4000 items will fall to zero, creating an even greater impetus for ASEAN exports to India. For the foreseeable future, we must expect the trade deficit to further widen.

The centre has been eager to point to the 'negative list' of 489 items, which will not undergo any tariff cuts and will therefore remain protected from imports as before whereas for products that do not figure on the negative list , duties will be reduced in a phased manner and brought down to zero by 2019. But the list of items not on the negative list is much larger than those on this list. For instance, import tariff on 60 percent of agriculture tariff lines will be brought down to zero.

Curiously, while the government is highlighting the virtues of India's negative list, it is absolutely silent on the list of sensitive and highly sensitive items of ASEAN. Although this list has not been put in the public domain, Asean has maintained that for India will be the same as what exist under its FTA with China.

The cumulative 'sensitive' and 'highly sensitive' list of the 10 ASEAN member countries has 2200 items-more than 4 times the number of items in India's list. Thus, it appears that India has received the worse of this deal. While ASEAN will continue to safeguard its market, India has decided to open the floodgate for cheap imports.

India's Agreement on Trade in Services and Investment with ASEAN

India and ASEAN are currently negotiating Agreements on trade in Services and Investment, which were to be concluded by December 2009. The current Agreement in goods will provide an impetus to the negotiations in service pact. India's total trade in services was US$ 137.5 billion in 2006 compared to US$ 280.9 billion for ASEAN. Similarly, FDI attracted by India in 2007-08 was US$ 24.6 billion whereas ASEAN countries attracted FDI US$ 60.5 billion in 2007. Singapore is the largest investor in India among the 10 ASEAN countries with its investments rising from ₹ 1,416.9 crore in 2005 to ₹ 15,775.9 crore in 2008. Malaysia ranks second, with its investments in India going up from ₹ 21.3 crore in 2005 to ₹ 453.8 crore in 2008, according to the report of the Federation of Indian Chambers of Commerce and Industry (FICCI). The signing of the agreement signals India's firm commitment to its "look east policy" of building upon its historical links with the countries of the South East Asia region and further deepening and widening this partnership.

One reason the Government of India has been eager to close this deal is that it anticipates likely gains for India in the services sector, for which negotiations with ASEAN are yet to begin. India is among the top ten services exporting nations globally, while ASEAN is a major importer. At US$ 150 billion, ASEAN's imports in this sector are almost half as large as that of the USA. That is the gain which the centre is eyeing, even as it now makes huge concessions in agriculture. But this trade off is not something India can afford to make casually; in the Indian economy, communities do not easily move between different professions and such deal making is risky. India has historically been unable to muster strong negotiating teams in trade discussions, and this has been made worse by routine disregard for the negative impacts on some communities from trade deals. This FTA continues in the same vein. The pain of Kerala farmers is likely to be significant.

And the gains in the services sector, even if they materialize one day, will do noting to help the farmers who will lose to.

ASEAN-India: Trade in Goods Agreement

The signing of the ASEAN-India trade in Goods Agreement paves the way for the creation of one of the world's largest free trade areas (FTA) market of almost 1.8 billion people with a combined GDP of US$ 2,75 trillion. The ASEAN-India FTA will see tariff liberalization of over 90 percent of products traded between the two dynamic regions, including the so-called 'special products' such as palm oil (crude and refined), coffee, black tea and pepper. Tariffs on over 4,000 products lines will be eliminated by 2016, at the earliest. The ASEAN-India TIG Agreement will enter into force on 1 January 2010 once India and at least one Asean members state notify completion of their internal ratification process.

The mutually agreed tariff liberalization would gradually cover 75 percent of the two-way trade, beginning from January 2010. India-ASEAN trade was of the order of US$ 40 billion in the 2007-08 accounting year. As of now, the regional bloc is India's fourth largest trading partner and it currently accounts for about 10 percent of its global trade. Under the ASEAN-India FTA, the ASEAN member countries and India will lift import tariffs on more than 80 percent of traded products between 2013 and 2016. According to the Federation of Indian Chambers of Commerce and Industry (FICCI), the agreement would provide access to the large ASEAN market to India. It will give Indian business access to the large ASEAN market; Indian industry does not have many concerns and sensitiveness on agricultural products have been taken care of.

The agreement has provided flexibilities to India and ASEAN countries to exclude some of the products from tariff concessions or eliminations to address their respective domestic sensitivity. India on its part, has excluded 489 items from the list of tariff concessions and 590 items from the list of tariff elimination to address sensitivities in agriculture, textiles, auto, chemicals, crude and refined palm oil, coffee, tea, pepper, etc. The ASEAN member countries have also maintained similar exclusion lists from the proposed tariff concessions or eliminations.

The exchange of tariff concessions between India and the ASEAN member countries would lead to growth in bilateral trade investments resulting in economic benefits to both the sides. Indian exporters of machinery and machine parts, steel and steel products, agriculture products such as oil cake, wheat and buffalo meat, auto components, chemicals and synthetic textiles would gain additional market access as a result of tariff liberalisation by ASEAN. Indian manufacturers would also be able to source products at competitive prices from the ASEAN countries The agreement also provides for bilateral mechanisms to address sudden surge in imports after the agreement comes into effect.

In such an eventuality if it hurts domestic industry, safeguard measures like the imposition of safeguard duties may be put in place for a period of up to four years. The flexibility to invoke safeguard measures will remain available for both the sides for a period of seven years to 15 years from the date of the agreement comes into force. As per the recent Indo-Asean pact, negotiations for free trade area in goods are slated to be finalized by June 30, 2005 and that for services and investments the negotiations are slated to begin in 2005 and conclude in 2007. Negotiations on exchange of tariff concessions under EHS will begin from November 1, 2004. A trade negotiating committee will begin framing the rules of origin, modalities for tariff reduction and FTA in January 2004.

It is also not clear whether it makes strategic sense to sign the TIG agreement without finalising an agreement on liberalisation of trade in service between India and ASEAN. Most projections before the AIFTA suggested that there is significant complementarity between India's service-oriented economy and ASEAN's light manufacturing-driven economy. The recommendations of these studies were that an Indo-ASEAN FTA should thrive to balance these complementarities and bring out a mutually beneficial deal covering both goods and services. One wonders whether signing of the TIG agreement will weaken India's negotiating position while discussing opening up of trade in services.

Finally, in an increasingly integrated world, one should be careful about signing FTA'S. But one needs to keep in mind that the ASEAN countries are one of the first recipients of global relocated capital and foreign direct investment (FDI) has played a major role in promoting exports in these countries (Thomson, 2009). Therefore it is possible that in many cases, that preferential tariff rates of the ASIAN-India FTA will actually help a developed country (e.g., a Japanese or a US firm) based in one of the south-east Asian countries. Indian policy makers should ensure that the AIFTA does not become a conduit for firms from developed countries so that they can avoid the MFN tariff rates by deflecting their exports through the AIFTA route using their subsidiaries in the ASEAN region.

Items of Trade

India's exports to ASEAN member countries include oil meals, gems and jewellery meet and meet preparations, cotton yarn, fabrics, machinery, rice, drugs and pharmaceuticals, chemicals, etc. India's imports mainly consist of artificial resins, plastics material, natural rubber, wood and wood products, electronics goods, organic chemicals, particularly, Malaysia, Singapore and Thailand, are also increasingly investing in India in sectors such as telecommunications, fuels, hotel and tourism, services, heavy industry, chemicals, fertilizers textiles, paper and pulp and food processing.

Domestic planters under the trade pact, India has included 489 items from agriculture, textiles and chemicals in the negative list, meaning these products will be keep out of the duty reduction. The bulk of trade between the two regions include textiles, steel, processed food, plantation crops, iron and steel, ready made garments and chemicals. Black tea, coffee, pepper and rubber have been included in the sensitive list, which could mean duties will be cut by 2019 only. However, duty on these items at no time will be eliminated.

Impact of FTA on Indian Agriculture and Fisheries

Since Kerala and ASEAN countries both produce several similar items, competition from the latter is a cause of worry in the farmer. But the centre has over ridden the state's objections to the free trade agreement. Notwithstanding this, Prime Minister Manmohan Singh secured the approval of the Union cabinet on July 23 and thc dcal was signed on August 13, 2009 at Bangkok. A cabinet sub-committee will hold detailed talks with the Kerala Government over India's recently signed free trade agreement with the ASEAN.

Agriculture: Farmers in South India, especially Kerala, fear lower duty on plantation crops like coffee and pepper would lead to dclugc of imports from ASEAN members like Indonesia, Malaysia, which could leave domestic farmers vulnerable to competition. For a state that exports 80 percent of its agricultural produce, Kerala's concerns must not be trivialized. The central government notes that five items- tea, coffee, pepper, crude palm oil and refined palm oil-are on the 'highly sensitive' list and will undergo only partial duty cuts in 2019. In the case of palm oil, where the applied tariff for crude palm oil is zero, and that for refined palm oil is a very low 7.5 percent. These low import tariffs are hurting coconut farmers in Kerala.

The government argues that under FTA, these rates can be increased to 37.5 and 45 percent respectively in the event of an import surge, but even this higher rates are far lower than the rates allowed under the WTO to protect against such surges- the global trade body allows surge protection rates for palm oil to be set as high as 300 percent. Ironically, the Indian government sought and obtained this higher protection in the

WTO, to now dilute it in a different trade agreement defies logic. Similarly, tariffs on tea and coffee are being reduced from 100 to 45 percent, and that for pepper from 70 to 50 percent, and the government claims that these items are protected as a result. But the difference in productivity of these crops between Kerala and the ASEAN bloc is vast, and even 50 percent tariffs are not sufficient to overcome this.

Productivity in pepper in Kerala is around 320 kilogram per hectare (kg./ha.), while Vietnam produces 1.2 tonnes and Indonesia 2.3 tonnes from the same area. Cheap pepper imports meant for oleoresin extraction will easily find their way into the open market, and depress prices. Similarly productivity of coffee in India stands at 765 kg./ha. while Vietnam produces 1.7 tonnes/ha. This year coffee exports from India have dipped by 20 percent over the preceding year on account of higher price of Indian beans. Aggressively priced coffee Vietnam can easily displace Indian coffee from domestic markets too, if one factors in the high cost of cultivation in Kerala as compared to Vietnam or Indonesia, in State Government's fears of trade diversion due to cheap imports are very real.

Planters of tea, coffee and spices in southern India are seeking financial support from the government to counter cheaper imports under the FTA India signed with the ASEAN. Under the pact that comes into force Jan 1, 2010 import tariff on tea and coffee will be reduced to 45 percent from 100 percent, and to 50 percent from 70 percent on pepper over the next 10 years.

While the government is highlighting the virtues of India's negative list, it is absolutely silent on the list of sensitive and highly sensitive items of ASEAN. Although this list has not been put in the public domain, ASEAN has maintained that for India it will be the same as what exists under its FTA with China. The cumulative 'sensitive' and 'highly sensitive' list of the 10 ASEAN member countries has 2200 items-more than 4 times the number of items in India's list. Thus, it appears that

India has received the worse of this deal. While ASEAN will continue to safeguard its markets, India has decided to open the floodgates for cheap imports.

Fisheries: India's free trade agreement with the ASEAN will not adversely affect the country's fisheries sector. India will have to strike a balance between modernization and the interests of the traditional fishing community while making the sector internationally competitive. India exported 541,701 metric tones of fish and fish products, with a value of ₹ 7620,92 (in crore) during the year 2007-08 (MPEDA, 2008). India ranks 27th in the world, in terms of value, and 23rd in terms of quantity (FAO, 2008).

The government of India in its 11th Five Year Plan period (2007-2012) has set up a target to increase fisheries exports from ₹ 6000 crore to ₹ 14000 crore. Seafood exports are an important component of food exports, as they constitute more than 70 percent of the food exports. Fish and fish products (Tariff Code 03) contributed to nearly 1 percent of India's total export value in 2007-08. Countries importing Indian fish and fish products include Japan, US, European Union (Spain, Belgium, United Kingdom, Italy, France, Germany, Portugal, Netherland), China, Hong Kong, United Arab Emirates, Canada, Singapore and Thailand.

India's major importing fish and fish products are fresh or chilled fish, and feed from aquatic products. These products are mainly imported from countries such as Bangladesh, Japan, Pakistan besides some from USA, Norway, China, Singapore, Thailand and Korea RP. Fish feed is imported from countries such as Thailand, Chile, Peru, Myanmar and Taiwan (during the year 2007-08).

Non-tariff Measures: Besides tariffs, Indian fish and fish products are subject to a number of non tariff measures imposed by some of these countries. Phyto-sanitary measures are one of the important non tariff barriers. One of the standards, is to monitor the presence of certain antibiotics in fish exports from India, such as chloramphenicol, nitrofurn, besides this, presence of Parahaemolyticus also leads to reject of exports. The Japanese exports require a health certificate issued by Exports Inspection Council of India.

In the case of US, exports are subject to inspections under the Public Health Security and Bioterrorism and Response Act of 2002. Mandatory labelling of country of origin/whether 'farm raised 'or 'wild' for fresh fish and shellfish is mandatory under Public Law in the United States of America.

Other Trade Agreements that include Fisheries and Fish Products

Besides this, India has also signed a number of bilateral and regional trade agreements (preferential and free trade agreements), that includes fish and fish products as one of the components.

India has been a member of WTO since 1995, and has been active in all its negotiations. In the recent negotiations on the Doha Development Agenda, India has been active in the NAMA negotiations and in the negotiating committee on rules especially on fisheries subsidies.

India's Trade with ASEAN 10

Compared to other regional groupings, ASEAN is the fifth most important market in the world in terms of Indian exports and fourth in terms of imports. India's sustained endeavours to engage with ASEAN in the past one decade have shown fruitful results.

ASEAN-India trade in 2003-04 was about US$ 15 billion, an increase of approximately 350 percent over the 1993-94 trade figures.

During this period, India's exports to ASEAN were US$ 5.8 billion while imports about US$ 7.4 billion in this period; balance of trade was in favour of ASEAN, and still it continues to remain in favour of ASEAN. There remains significant potential to further expand these ties. For a total population of approx. 1.5 billion people and with a combined GDP of US$

1.5 trillion, a trade turnover of approximately US$ 15 billion is grossly inadequate. The trade with India is expected to increase to US$ 10 billion after the agreement goes in to effect next year. Trade between ASEAN and India is expected to increase to US$ 60 billion dollars after the agreement goes in to effect next year. ASEAN India bilateral trade amounted to US$ 47 billion in 2008. Table 3.2 shows the India-ASEAN trade from 2000-01 to 2008-09 (April-February).

Table 3.2: India-ASEAN Trade (April-February)
(Million US Dollars)

Year	Export	Import	Total Trade
2000-01	2,913.78	4,147.48	7,061.26
2001-02	3,457.02	4,387.22	7,844.24
2002-03	4,618.54	5,150.17	9,768.71
2003-04	5,821.74	7,433.16	13,254.90
2004-05	8,425.89	9,114.66	17,540.55
2005-06	10,411.30	10,863.68	21,294.98
2006-07	12,603.86	18,089.64	30,693.50
2007-08	16,376.24	22,663.48	39,039.72
2008-09 Apr-Feb	18,893.10	23,378.87	40,271.97

Source: Ministry of Commerce, Government of India.

In the Indian context, ASEAN is emerging as an important trade partner. India's bilateral trade with ASEAN has risen sharply from US$ 7.0 billion in 2000-01 to US$ 38.4 billion in 2007-08. A review titled "The Indian Foreign Trade Report 2008-09 reflects upon ASEAN as a major production base in the world market accounting for 6.3 percent of world exports and 5.5 percent of world imports in 2007. ASEAN's exports to GDP ratio is 69.9 percent and imports to GDP ratio is 60.9 percent. Being a major trade block, ASEAN aims to create its own single market or ASEAN Economic Community by 2015.

ASEAN accounts for 9.6 percent of India's global trade. India's exports, which significantly depend on the developed markets of the US and Europe have been shrinking for the last six months on slowdown in demand for merchandise in these recession hit markets. The country's exports managed a meagre growth of 3.4 percent in 2008-09 at US$ 168 billion. India's exports to ASEAN were about US$ 17 billion (₹ 81,770 crore) in 2007-08 and imports were US$ 23 billion. For about 89 percent of its tariff lines, India has made significant tariff reduction commitments. Among these tariff lines, 74 percent are under the Normal Track (NT) and 15 percent are under the Sensitive Track (ST).

Given such generous tariff reduction commitments by India, there are apprehensions whether the AIFTA agreements is favouring the ASEAN countries more. There are a number of reasons for such scepticism. First, India runs a major trade deficit with the ASEAN countries. For the last five years, India had negative trade balance for every year vis-à-vis ASEAN. For example, in 2007-08, the latest complete year for which data are available, India had a trade deficit of more than US$ 6 billion with ASEAN. As edible oil (HS-15) and mineral oil (HS-27) figure prominently in the trade between India and ASEAN, it is worthwhile to check how India's trade balance with ASEAN behaves for non-oil trade.

Even without taking edible oil or mineral oil trade into consideration, India had a trade deficit with ASEAN for the last three years. If India is further liberalizing its tariff rates vis-à-vis these countries, then unless there is a major gain in market share in ASEAN, India's trade balance is expected to deteriorate due to AIFTA. So India is unlikely to gain too much market share in the ASEAN because of the AIFTA deal. Table 3.3 shows the India's Trade with different ASEAN countries in 2008-09 (April-February).

India's trade with ASEAN mainly concentrated in Singapore, Malaysia, Indonesia and Thailand. Singapore continues to remain the largest market in ASEAN for India's merchandise exports. India's trade relations with the ASEAN region have the specific advantages of geographical proximity and a large population of Indian origin within the region. India's economic structure is also largely complementary (service oriented) to ASEAN economies (light manufacturing) with significant areas of mutual gain.

Table 3.3: India's Trade with Different ASEAN Countries in 2008-09 (April-February) (Million US$)

Country	Exports	Imports	Total trade
Brunei	14.77	274.23	289.00
Cambodia	42.19	2.61	44.80
Indonesia	2187.90	6052.82	8240.72
Laos	4.59	0.47	5.06
Malaysia	3256.84	6653.78	9910.62
Myanmar	204.46	808.98	1014.44
Philippines	657.67	187.61	845.28
Singapore	7490.23	6627.58	14117.81
Thailand	1658.83	2415.18	4074.01
Vietnam	1374.63	355.61	1730.24

Source: Ministry of Commerce, Government of India.

India's Tariff Commitments with ASEAN

India has made significant tariff reduction commitments. Among these tariff lines, 74 percent are under the Normal Track (NT) and 15 percent are under the Sensitive Track (ST). Given such generous tariff reduction commitments by India, there are apprehensions whether the AIFTA agreement is favouring the ASEAN countries more. The FTA will liberalize tariffs on about 40,000 items accounting for nearly 80 percent of trade between India and ASEAN. Electronic goods, chemicals, certain capital goods and some categories of textiles are among the items covered. When the agreement becomes effective, from January 1, 2010, tariffs on the products covered will sink to zero between 2013 and 2016. A bilateral safeguard mechanism will address any sudden surge in imports with "safeguard tariffs" to protect domestic industries for a period of four years.

India on its part, has excluded 489 items from the list of tariff concessions or eliminations to address sensitivities in agriculture, textiles, auto, chemicals, crude and refined palm oil, coffee, tea, pepper, etc. the ASEAN member countries have to also mentioned similar exclusion lists from the proposed tariff concessions or eliminations. The exchange of tariff concessions between India and the ASEAN member could lead to growth in bilateral trade investments resulting in economic benefits to both sides.

Table 3.4 shows the break up of India's tariff schedule for the different reduction schedules. From the table it can be seen that about 74 percent of India's tariff lines will be under "Normal Track (NT)" reduction commitments. About 15 percent of India's tariff lines are schedule under the "Sensitive Track (ST)" tariff reduction schedule. Tariff Rates for these products are to be reduced to 5 percent by a certain date, which depends upon the specific country schedules. Further reductions to 4.5 percent and 4 percent are also planned for specific countries.

Table 3.4: Break-up of India's Tariff Schedule for ASEAN

	(Number of tariff lines at HS-8 digit level
Exclusion list (EL)	1,297
Sensitive track (ST)	1,805
Special products(SP)	40
Normal track (NT-2)	1252
Normal track (NT-1)	7775

Source: India's Tariff schedule to ASEAN 5 and CLMV.

The ASEAN-India FTA or AIFTA classifies the tariff lines into four broad heads. These are:

1. **Normal Track (NT):** The applied MFN rates will be reduced and subsequently eliminated. This is divided into 2 sub categories called normal track 1 (NT-20) and normal track 2 (NT-2). The difference between the two is that NT-

2 has a longer implementation period (till 2020) than NT1 (till 2018).

2. **Sensitive Track (ST):** For the first stage of implementation, applied most favoured nation (MFN) rates that are above 5 percent in accordance with the country specific reduction schedules.
3. **Special Products (SP)**: These refer to the some select products for which India ha decided to reduce tariff rates at a much more gradual pace than either the normal track or sensitive track.
4. **Exclusion List (EL):** For these products no reduction commitments have been made. But it has been mentioned in the agreement that the exclusion list shall be subject to an annual tariff review with a view to improving market access.

For India, the AIFTA allows certain "special products" for which the tariff reduction schedule is spelled out in the agreement. These products are Crude and Refined Palm Oil (CPO and RPO, respectively), coffee, black tea and pepper. At HS-8 digit level, there are 40 tariff lines listed under 'Special Products". Tariff rates for these products will be reduced by an average annual rate of 6.8 percent between now (base rate) and 2019, except those for pepper and Refined Palm Oil (RPO), where the tariff rates will be reduced by 3.3 percent and 5.8 percent, respectively, during the same period.

Further analysis of these tariff lines helps us identify the sectors where India wants maximum protection. Classification of the tariff lines according to broad HS groups shows that a large umber of products in agriculture, fish and marine products and textiles and garments have been put under the Exclusion List (EL) (Table 3.5). This table is also illustrative of the sectoral threat perception India has from the AIFTA.

The present level of protection for the tariff lines covered under the EL shows wide variations. For about 160 tariff lines (at HS-8), the level of existing protection is very high (base MFN tariff rates for these tariff lines are 100 percent or more).

However, for 568 tariff lines, base MFN rates are quite low - 10 percent or less.

Table 3.5: Sectoral Distribution of items in the 'Exclusion List' of India

	At HS-6 digit	At HS-8 digit
Agricultural products (HS 01-24, except HS 03)	268	626
Fish and Marine products (HS 03)	33	51
Mineral Oil (HS 27)	13	31
Organic Chemicals	13	48
Plastic and Rubber items (HS 39–HS 40)	15	89
Textiles and garments (HS 50-63)	83	226
Machinery (HS 84-85)	22	57
Motor vehicles (HS-87)	26	93
Others	24	77
Total	496	1,297

Source: India's Tariff schedule to ASAN 5 and CLMV.

India's Free Trade Agreement with Thailand

India and Thailand signed an Early Harvest Programme (EHP) which was supposed to be followed by a full fledged free trade agreement (FTA) in 2004. Under the EHP, the two sides eliminated duties on 82 items, both agricultural and industrial, like television tubes, mangoes and apples, grapes and some metals. The FTA was however, not signed because of disagreements related to the rule of origin (the rules which determine which products are to be considered as originating from the partner country and which are to be considered as originating from a third country) and political instability in Thailand. However, Thailand now seems confident about concluding a comprehensive agreement soon. Thailand is also a part of ten member ASEAN group which signed a free trade agreement on goods with India this year.

A free trade agreement between India and South East Asia will be signed at the upcoming summit of the Association of South East Nations (ASEAN) if the Thai parliament approves the pact. FTA is still subject to the approval of the Thai parliament as well. Under Thailand's new 2007 constitution all international agreements must first be approved by the parliament before going into effect. All the other members of Asean have already agreed to FTA. India and Thailand are planning to expand their limited free trade agreement (FTA) including just 82 items to services and investments. At present both the countries are engaged in lifting the free trade agreement into a comprehensive pact to include services and investments. Expanding commercial ties could push up bilateral trade from US$ 6 billion at present to US$ 10 billion in 2011.

India Inc's diffidence has been fuelled in large measure by the skewed trade balance in favour of Thailand after the FTA came into effect in September 2004. Much of the gains have, in fact, accrued to Thailand for the 82 items that secured tariff concessions under the Early Harvest Scheme(EHS), which includes items like colour picture tubes, auto parts and electronic goods. From 2004-05 to 2007-08, Thailand exports to India under EHS tripled to US$ 470.5 million while India's exports to Thailand rose by only 87 percent to US$ 90.7 million. This bilateral trade pattern marks a sharp reversal from an earlier situation when India registered an over all trade surplus with Thailand till 2004-05.

Under these circumstances, doubts are being fanned whether such agreements benefit India. Apex chambers like FICCI noted that in Thailand power was cheaper. Cost of capital, too, is lower. Inputs like glass parts for colour TV picture tubes can also be imported duty free while they attract a duty of 15 percent in India. Unless these disadvantages are corrected, imports from Thailand will surge while India's exports languish.

India Inc. has similar concerns over the CECA with

Singapore and fears that China will misuse such agreements as a staging ground for cheaper exports to India. It considers the city-state to be mainly a trading rather than a manufacturing hub, although it hosts 7,000 plus MNCs. Although the CECA allays these concerns with clearly laid out rules of origin norms, Indian industry's doubts nevertheless persist although there are huge potential gains from using Singapore as a base to expand in Asia.

ASEAN China Investment Agreement

China and the ASEAN signed an important investment pact at a meeting in Bangkok, Thailand on August 15, 2009. The pact provides guarantees against nationalization, riots and disputes and is expected to boost investment. The ASEAN-China Investment Agreement is expected to boost bilateral investments by 40-60 percent over the next two years.

China is currently the eighth largest investor in South East Asia with US$ 5.6 billion in cumulative investments as of 2008. Investments in China from the 10 members of the ASEAN grouping amounted to US$ 6.1 billion as of 2008-09. The new investment agreement provides Chinese and ASEAN investors guarantee which are not necessarily preferred to other countries. For instance, the agreement will guarantee compensation for investors in case of nationalization and riots. The association agreed to set up a dispute settlement body soon to resolve legal problems that might arise between investors and the respective states. It may be mentioned here that the Asean has already signed a partial free trade agreement with China, which covers trade in goods. China was the fourth largest export market for ASEAN between January and September 2008 when the region's exports to China amounted to US$ 85.6 billion. China's exports to the region during the same period was US$ 107 billion.

Oppositions to the FTA

Many Indian organizations opposed the deal because of

India's trade deficit with most ASEAN countries. Domestic manufacturers, for their part, distrust these bilateral pacts due to the handicap of inverted duty structures where the duty on the finished product is lower than on raw materials. This acts as a disincentive as finished products can be imported at lower duties.

Opposition from the states in India, for example: Kerala and Karnataka states feared that their farmers would be hurt by an influx of goods such as coffee, tea and palm oil from ASEAN. After strong lobbying by India's farm sector, the terms of the FTA let India exclude 489 products, mostly commodities including rubber, from tariff cuts. Tariffs on a much smaller list of "highly sensitive" products, including palm oil and coffee, would be reduced over about 10 years, but only modestly. For some of the most sensitive products like tea, coffee and pepper, the tariffs are being phased down gradually from 70-100 percent tariff levels.

The FTA also does not include software and information technology in which India is a world leader. A service trade agreement, which is of enormous interest to India and it exports-oriented software and information technology sector, has been postponed until December 2009. To be sure, economists are sceptical whether these FTA's have anything to do with free trade. Far from it, as they form an unruly mass of crisscrossing strings that Professor Jagdish Bhagwati of Yale University called a "spaghetti bowl" that hampers rather than facilitates free trade for those left out. Even if these are considered second best options to a multilateral World Trade Agreement, the basic point is that India is unlikely to derive much benefit from them if there is a sense of ambivalence regarding the potential gains among stakeholders like farmers and India Inc.

Comprehensive Economic Partnership Agreement (CEPA) with South Korea

India is taking real steps to further its Look East Policy

towards Southeast Asia. The FTA signing with ASEAN marks India's first major multilateral FTA. A few days before the ASEAN FTA signing, India signed a Comprehensive Economic Partnership Agreement (CEPA) with South Korea. CEPAs are lighter versions of FTAs, in which the tariff removal rate occurs on a much slower pace than with regular FTAs. Before South Korea, India's only other comprehensive economic partnership agreement was with Singapore in 2005. This FTA is an aggressive move on the part of India in competing primarily for influence with China in ASEAN. Further, it give ASEAN countries another reason to promote themselves as a location for a factory or regional office as the ASEAN-India FTA agreement gives claim that locating in their country opens up a market of nearly 1.6 billion people which is larger than even China's population or market.

Conclusion

The ASEAN group has undergone a long transition period of accumulation which has sewed as a pathway to economic transformation and progress. Market forces has played a contributory role in promoting ASEAN economic cooperation, SAARC must learn this lesson from the ASEAN experience. The ASEAN by and large encourages global approaches to international economic issues and problems.

Curiously, while the government is highlighting the virtues of India's negative list, it is absolutely silent on the list of sensitive and highly sensitive items of ASEAN. Although this list has not been put in the public domain, ASEAN has maintained that for India will be the same as what exist under its FTA with China. The cumulative 'sensitive' and 'highly sensitive' list of the 10 ASEAN member countries has 2200 items-more than 4 times the number of items in India's list. Thus, it appears that India has received the worse of this deal. While ASEAN will continue to safeguard its market, India has decided to open the floodgate for cheap imports.

Given such inter-sectoral trade-offs, the role of the

government becomes important. The total welfare gain from such a agreement will critically depend upon the government's ability to adopt the policies for alleviating the burden falling on those adversely affected. As redistributive measures are generally weak in India, it is not surprising that AIFTA is facing opposition from sectors where Indian producers are expecting increased competition from the ASEAN countries.

India's active participation and frank discussions at the various India-ASEAN Summit as well as individual bilateral meetings with ASEAN member countries and member countries of the East Asia Summit reflects the maturing of relationship based on mutual interest and deep understanding. The signing of the agreement signals India's firm commitment to its "look east policy" of building upon its historical links with the countries of the South East Asia region and further deepening and widening this partnership. India and ASEAN are currently negotiating agreements on trade in Services and Investment, which are to be concluded by December 2009.

One reason the Government of India has been eager to close this deal is that it anticipates likely gains for India in the services sector, for which negotiations with ASEAN are yet to begin. India is among the top ten services exporting nations globally, while ASEAN is a major importer. At US$ 150 billion, ASEAN's imports in this sector are almost half as large as that of the USA. That is the gain which the centre is eyeing, even as it now makes huge concessions in agriculture. But this trade off is not something India can afford to make casually; in the Indian economy, communities do not easily move between different professions and such deal making is risky. India has historically been unable to muster strong negotiating teams in trade discussions, and this has been made worse by routine disregard for the negative impacts on some communities from trade deals. This FTA continues in the same vein. The pain of Kerala farmers is likely to be significant. And the gains in the services sector, even if they materialize one day, will do noting to help the farmers who will lose to.

References

Aekapol Chongvilaivan, "India's Ties to ASEAN Must Look beyond Trade in Goods," The Nation, 4 November 2008.

Asher, M.G. and R. Sen (2005), "India-East Asia Integration: A win-win for Asia", Economic and Political Weekly 60 (36): 3932-41.

Association of South East Asian Nations (2005), ASEAN Statistical Yearbook, Manila: Philippines, ASEAN.

Bhupesh Bhandari, "PM in Singapore: suggests South Asia 'Arc of Advantage' Business Standard, November 22, 2007.

Competition Success Review, October 2009, p. 26

Harish Khare, "PM admits to difficulties in concluding FTA", The Hindu, November 20, 2007.

Mithani D.M. International Economics, 2007, pp. 386-387.

Monthly Review of the Indian Economy, September 2009, pp. 119.

Reintegrating India with the World economy, T.N. Srinivasan and Suresh Tendulkar, Oxford University Press, (2003), p. 48.

Rupa Chanda and Sasidaran G, "Understanding India's Regional Initiatives within Asia," ISAS Working Papers, No. 373, 2008.

Sasatra Sudsawasd and Prasopchoke Mongsawad, "Go with the Gang, ASEAN" ASEAN Economic Bulletin, ISEAS 24, no.3 (2007): 339-356.

The Economic Times, October 8, 2009.

The Hindustan Times, November 21, 2007.

The Hindustan Times, October 9th, 2009, p. 8.

The political economy of the World Trading System: The WTO and Beyond, Bernard M. Hoekman and Michel M. Kostecki, OUP, 2nd ed. (2001).

Third Concept, December 2007, pp. 8-9.

Third Concept, January 2008, pp. 7-8.

4

Global Climate Change and its Impact on Indian Economy

Swami Prakash Srivastava

The industrialized nations are primarily responsible for the high volume of carbon emissions. Hence, they should share a certain percentage of their GDP with developing nations to enable access to green technology. But as usual, industrialized nations have been shrinking any commitment regarding reduction in carbon emission. Instead, they have been demanding action from developing countries like India. If carbon emissions continue to increase at the current rate of 3 percent per year, then we would overshoot the threshold limit for climate change catastrophe in the next 20 years, in half the time that was projected earlier. Such a disaster scenario would play out, say researchers, only if there is no abatement of emission worldwide and if we assume that no scientific method would be employed to remove excess carbon from the atmosphere.

This is the first time that India has accepted a reference to 2 degree C as a possible threshold guiding global action, but this is entirely in line with our stated position on global warming" Prime Minister Dr. Manmohan Singh said, "The rich world has already made a political pledge on green house gas reduction. But some say it is too little, too late-with a drop of just 7-14 percent below 1990 levels by 2030, India has demanded a 40 percent reduction".

Some experts believe that the Indian pledge to hold the 2degree C line, combined with the rich nations' reluctance to vacate carbon space, could lock India into unsustainably low emission levels for good. "The industrialized countries have attempted to corner us," explains one climate observer. "They have already said they shall not empty the space but they have also made us agree that the room is bound to get smaller. Which simply means that the poor Indians, already cramped for space, will have to now recede further into the corner." The rich nations are also not ready to share green technology for free or nearly free and not do they want to compensate the developing world for the disproportionate share of carbon space they hold. Clean technology and/or compensation could have helped poorer nations search for alternatives to fossil fuels.

Introduction

The World bank, in a presentation based on preliminary results of a modelling study, has pointed out that power consumption and, therefore, , the GHG emissions in India are bound to increase 3.5 times the 2007-08 levels by 2031-32 due to increasing urbanization, electrification and household incomes. This could be brought down to 2.7 times the 2007-08 levels with stringent energy efficiency measures, the study results show. The World Bank modelled what are technically called marginal abatement cost curves-statistical projections of how much it would take to reduce GHG emissions from different sectors of the economy. While the report is still to be finalized, the figures from the bank come as scientific evidence in favour of the Indian government's International position. India has long contended that taking severe emission reduction targets can only come at the cost of its poor and that India which already has an extremely low per capita emission needs the carbon space to pull its people out of poverty and provide basic amenities like power, sanitation and water to all.

India's energy demand is likely to increase threefold by 2030, a substantial portion of which will be met through fossil fuel, which will cause emission of greenhouse gasses to go up sharply, says a report by management firm McKinsey & Co. Suggesting initiatives such as expanding programmes to increase energy efficiency, developing clean sources of power generation and creating energy efficient infrastructure, the report, "Environmental and Energy Sustainability" narrates:

According to official estimates, currently, the transport sector accounts for a major consumption of fuel and contributes almost 15 percent of the total carbon dioxide emissions. The sector is expected to grow by 25 percent in next three years. Similarly, 80 percent of the country's total coal production goes into the power sector. The National Action Plan on climate change (NAPCC) also lists nine energy intensive sectors–thermal power plants, fertilizers, cement, iron and steel, chlor alkali, aluminum, railways, paper and pulp and textiles.

India merely said it would keep its per capita emissions at below the developed world average. India's per capita annual emission (PCE) is about 1.1 tonne. The US's per capita carbon emission is over 18 tonnes and the world PCE average is around five tones. So India still has scope to increase its per capita emissions by about four times and yet remain below the current world average. However, the western governments are in no mood to allow India go up to the world average level of emissions, and they want caps on emissions put in a manner that it will become difficult for India to meet the basic energy needs of the people using local resources. For instance, India's per capita annual electricity consumption is only 500 units compared to 8,000-10,000 units per capita consumed by the western societies.

Look at the yawning gap. It is morally shocking. Also, nearly 800 million Indians must be consuming less than units per capita every year. This is simply because in Uttar Pradesh and Bihar, with population of over 300 million, there is no electricity on average for 8 to 10 hours a day, apart from a large number of villages all over which are not connected to the grid at all. So, it is quite reasonable to expect that India's per capita electricity consumption will go up from the present 500 units to at least 3,000 units in the next 10 years.

However, India will still consume less than half of the present per capita electricity consumed by the west. This difference of magnitude is what the west needs to appreciate. Now much of the incremental electricity has to be coal fired because India has over 250 billion tones of coal reserves. The G8 is currently talking about two broad parameters which are likely to become the basis of undertaking emission cuts by all countries. One, overall emission must be reduced by 50 percent from current levels by the year 2050. Two, the world must limit the global warming up to 2 degrees from pre industrial levels. However, according to the Fourth Assessment Report of the IPCC, only an 85 percent reduction in emissions (from 2,000 levels) can possibly prevent a global warming of 2 degree and more.

Review of Literature

1. **Adam David (2009):** An increasing number of climate change Scientists feel the earth may have already tipped over the edge.
2. **Lovejoy (2009):** There is also the view that "since there are already threshold changes in ecosystems and ocean acidification...dangerous change is likely to appear before 2 degrees Celsius.
3. **Li (2008):** It is moot whether de-carbonization can proceed "faster than the rate of depreciation of long lasting fixed assets.
4. **Aggarwal P.K. (2008):** There are vibrant struggles against forced displacement from industrial projects, special economic zones and dams etc, which directly or indirectly relate to global warming.
5. **Reilly (2000):** The CO2 fertilization effect is an important factor. Inclusion of the effect in yield studies significantly raises the estimates of climate effected yield of many crops.
6. **McCarl and Reilly (1999):** There is also a need to develop estimates on how non-agricultural water use might

change in the face of climate change.

7. **Hohmann and Kane (1994):** Climate change is likely to shift the comparative advantage of agricultural production region. Such shifts are likely to alter the places in which specific crops are grown, both within countries and internationally, altering patterns of trade in agricultural commodities among regions and countries.
8. **Ziska (1997):** The protein content of the grain decreases under combined increases of temperature and CO2.
9. **Rosenzweig and Iglesias (1994):** The effects of changes in temperature, precipitation and carbon dioxide concentrations on crop productivity have been studied extensively using crop stimulation models. The combined effects of climate change have been found to have implications for dry land and irrigated crop yield as well as irrigation water use.

India's Stand on Emission Cuts

India's stand is not difficult to understand. India can not compromise on its ambition of ensuring a decent life for its citizens, especially when teeming millions are still very poor. It has to make the obvious choice between livelihood needs of millions today and a climate crisis, say 50 years hence. Historical responsibility for the current crisis lies with developed countries and they should finance the Developing countries to adopt mitigation measures and assist them by way of transfer of technology. The Developing Countries can at the most be held liable for their current carbon emissions and India is already undertaking voluntary action under its National Action Plan for Climate Change. India accounts for around 4 percent of global emissions, as against 20 percent each for the US and China and 15 percent for EC. India's per capita emission of 1.8 tonnes/annum, are much lower than 20 tonnes/annum of US. India has committed to not allow its per capita GHG emissions to exceed the average per capita emissions of Developed countries. This effectively puts a cap on India's emissions, which will be lower if developed countries choose to be more ambitious.

Together, the US and China account for 40 percent of the world's green house gas emissions; hence the need for more concerted action. The US and China are presenting a positive and united approach without a specific action plan could mean that the Copenhagen summit will achieve little more than getting the representatives of 192 member countries to visit Denmark at the further expense of the planet. The proposed US legislation, however, is not developing world friendly as it penalizes it in terms of trading rights. As for the negotiations building up to what is meant to be the next major milestone in the climate change regime. There was as yet no clarity on targets and the scale of funding and technology transfer for mitigation and adaptation. This was despite the fact that US, which was not part of the Kyoto Protocol of 1977, rejoined climate change negotiations at Bonn.

Since emissions from the developing countries are on the whole lower than those of the developed world—and will need to continue to rise in the short term as they maintain economic growth and address poverty—it has been proposed that developed countries cut emissions by at least 80 percent relative to 1990 by 2050, with major steps towards this goal over the next decade. Developing countries will also need to play their part, significantly slowing and peaking emissions growth in the coming decades. For the US, such commitments would mean cutting emission to around one-tenth of today's per capita level, while for China it had mean creating a new low carbon model of economic development. For all countries, this is a major challenge-a revolution that implies a huge shift in policy.

India will not accept any legally binding obligation to cut emissions, India's per capita emission of green house gases is less then one-tenth of the average of developed countries. The climate changing damage was done the last couple of centuries essentially by the advanced countries during their phase of industrialization. India needs to increase its per capita energy consumption significantly, to achieve a standard of living a little removed from subsistence poverty. So India will increase energy consumption and therefore register increase in emission as well. However, India is determined to reduce the energy intensity of growth. India has undertaken eight missions aimed at mitigation and adaptation of climate change. These will raise India's energy efficiency by 20 percent by 2020.

Role of NCCMA in Mitigating Global Warming

In continuation of India taking a broader perspective on measures to reduce the phenomenon of global warming, Prime Minister Manmohan Singh has said that the government proposes to set up a National Climate Change Mitigation Authority (NCCMA).

This body would assign and monitor aspirational green targets to be achieved by the year towards reducing India's green house gas emissions. The NCCMA's guidelines would complement or get include in the proposals spelt out in the Prime Minister's National Action Plan on Climate Change (NAPCC) formulated in 2008. Although many aspects of the NCCMA's proposals find mention in the NAPCC by instituting an authority dedicated to encouraging and monitoring green initiatives as well as suggesting model emissions targets, the government of India is demonstrating its green commitment in tune with the prevailing international sentiments on an inclusive agenda for all.

India's Energy Demand

India's energy demand is likely to increase threefold by 2030, a substantial portion of which will be met through fossil fuel, which will cause emission of greenhouse gasses to go up sharply , says a report by management firm McKinsey & Co. Suggesting initiatives such as expanding programmes to increase energy efficiency, developing clean sources of power generation and creating energy efficient infrastructure, the report-Environmental and Energy Sustainability: An Approach for India-argues that India could reduce emissions by 45 percent and lower energy consumption by 22 percent by 2030. This is significant saving considering that India imported 84 percent of its crude oil requirement at a cost of US$ 100 billion in 2008.The report says that India's GDP could increase four fold to US$ 4 trillion by 2030. Nearly 80 percent of the energy requirement for this growth would be met through fossil fuels. As a result, the emission of green house gases could increase from roughly 1.6 billion tones carbon dioxide equivalent (CO2 e) in 2005 to 5.0 billion to 6.5 billion tones (CO2e) in 2030 in the reference case.

The estimates of India's emissions by 2030 are based on the growth in demand that the country is likely to witness in key sectors such as power, industry and transportation with a GDP growth of 6-9 percent. A five fold increase in building floor space will complement a seven fold increase in the number of vehicles on India's roads, the report says. "In terms of energy alone by 2030, India is likely to need between 760 GW and 790 GW of installed power capacity. Overall coal demand is likely to cross 2.4 billion per annum. India may have to import 10 times its own production of oil and up to 40 percent of its coal needs by 2030", the Report said. According to McKinsey & Company, India could emerge the world's third largest energy consumer by 2030. However, 80 percent of what India could be in 2030 is yet to be built, providing the country an opportunity to effectively manage the economic and environmental costs of growing energy requirements.

The IEA, an OECD agency, advocates greenhouse gases peaking at 450 parts per million, beyond which there will be chaotic changes. Without such restrictions, emissions will rise to 1,000 pm, leading to a 6 degree temperature rise. The IEA scenario envisages an "energy revolution" with decreased use in electricity generations and transport. Two third of polluting gases emanate from the energy sector and the new mix should include renewable and nuclear. Together, these two, which now constitute 18 percent of world energy, should rise to one third by 2030.

Table 4.1 shows energy intensity (per unit of GDP) of different countries.

Table 4.1: Energy Intensity=Total Primary Energy Consumption (Btu) per unit of GDP (2000 Prices)

Country	2003	2004	2005	2006
USA	9,534	9,400	9,146	8,841
EU	6,956	6,877	6,748	6,536
Russia	21,769	20,901	19,950	18,777
India	7,840	7,875	7,582	7,477
China	12,820	13,799	13,919	13,780
Japan	6,767	6,762	6,636	6,492
Brazil	6,979	6,855	6,906	6,844

Source: Energy Information Administration's, International Energy Annual.

Climate Refugees

Climate change, by displacing settled populations, is creating a new kind of refugee. Approximate 24 million people are estimated to have been displaced so far by climate change. Some estimates envisage that by 2010 around 50 million people will be dislocated by global climate change and by 2050 this figure could exceed 150 million. As fears over the potentially devastating impact of global warming becomes apparent, there is also the growing concern over the dramatic increase in this new class of displaced persons. One estimate by the Red Cross places population displacement caused by climate change disasters as larger than that brought about by war and persecution.

Unfortunately, not being officially recognized as refugees, they slip into a bureaucratic grey zone, suffering from definitional heterogeneity. The less developed countries are the least responsible for climate change as having modest industry and lifestyles they produce relatively small amounts of pollution, but their populations are most vulnerable to environmental disasters, caused in particular by climate change. Being poor, large sections of the people in these countries tend to occupy unsafe locations, living along coast lines, flood plains and steep slopes. The existing institutions and organizations-international and national—are not sufficiently equipped to deal with this challenge. The global community needs to extend support to climate refugees and assist them in obtaining refugee status under international law.

One school of thought is that as the homes of this new category of refugees are destroyed as a result of non environmental friendly policies followed by industrialized nations, it amounts to "environmental persecution", and this qualifies them, as legitimate refugees, for legal protection. Although rising sea levels are responsible for dislocation problems of unimaginable proportions, there are also several million environmental refugees who have been forced out of their lands because of numerous other factors like drought, soil erosion, deforestation, forest fires, earthquakes, nuclear accidents and toxic spills. Victims of sudden and highly publicized calamities like the 2004 Asian tsynami benefit from humanitarian relief, but millions of those who are uprooted by "slow motion disasters" receive comparatively little support to cope and adopt.

World Green Index

The World Green Index, released on May 14, 2009, placed India at the top rank among all the nations of the World. The Index is the result of an annual survey conducted by America's National Geographic Society and the international polling firm GlobeScan. It showed that Indian consumers have overtaken Brazilians to take the top spot with a Greendex score of 59.5. The Chinese retained the third spot. At the bottom end of the ladder were the over consumptive Americans Canadians and the Japanese. India's excellent performance in the index was driven by above average performance on all four sub-indices, including ranking first for foods and goods. The survey revealed that Indians are the most frequent consumers of self grown food, with 35 percent Indians eating this type of food several times a week or daily.

They are also the least frequent consumers of beef, which requires greater energy to grow. Only 22 percent of Indians consumes beef weekly, compared with an average of 63 percent by the others. In the same context, the report also mentioned the cold water bath many Indians take in winter because there is no electricity: the earthen pot water storer they use because they can not afford a fridge; and walking to work and back because private transport is expensive and public transport shoddy, etc, among other factors. The Indian consumers also topped the goods sub-index score. Their top placement status is due in part to having lower than average rates in part to having lower than average rates of ownership of large appliances and electronics. It is also due to having the highest rates for buying used goods, avoiding environmentally unfriendly products and excessive packaging.

Economic Crisis, Global Warming and Global Poverty

The economic crisis has quickly relegated global warming and global poverty–once reliable headline generators–down the list of priorities. But it is a mistake to think that government should triage, that is, deal with poverty and the environment only after they have put the financial crisis behind us. The reason is that we actually face a three–fold global crisis: the economic downturn, rise in poverty and climate change. We can not escape one without addressing the others. In the absence of a return to high growth, it is hard to see how poverty will be lessened or environmental actions will be financed. Equally, unless carbon emissions are cut and poverty reduced while reviving the economy, further growth prospects will be doomed.

The truth is that poverty and climate change are no longer distant threats to progress. Carbon dioxide concentration in the air has already exceeded 385 parts per million-perilously close to the 400-450 level that would put us on an irreversible path to an ice free world where sea levels would have risen several meters. The consequences of this scenario for natural disasters alone will dwarf the sub prime meltdown. Similarly, allowing poverty to balloon runs the risk that political stability will be undermined and continuation of growth itself hampered, increasing the prevalence of failed states and making the world less safe for investment and trade. Some 150 million more people slipped into poverty worldwide during 2007-08 and a further 50 million this year.

This threefold conundrum presents especially significant challenges for the large nations, be they emerging economies such as China and India or Organisation for Economic Cooperation and Development countries such as the US and Japan. Their response will crucially affect the prospects for their own population as well as the direction for global development. Yet for anyone of these countries, it is unquestionably tough to attack the three heads of the hydra simultaneously. But remarkably, the current crisis offers some unique opportunities that can be seized. There are policies, investments and deals that can help these nations-separately and collectively–to confront two if not all three of these dangers with a single swipe.

1. First, this is the time for nations to reverse policies that sacrifice the climate in the name of immediate growth. The most egregious example is energy subsidies, which cost almost a third of a trillion dollars in 2007 worldwide. These are frequently justified as protecting the vulnerable but the bulk of subsidies does not reach the poor. They also encourage energy waste and drain fiscal resources. Another dual purpose policy is to set up robust social safety nets, providing a boost to consumption while lifting millions out of poverty. Conditional cash transfers in Brazil and Mexico are examples of efforts to both reduce poverty today and, by trying them to children's education and health, also boost future growth. Outlays amounting to

just about 1 percent of GDP can make the difference.

2. Second, this is the chance for countries to invest a sizeable share of the stimulus packages in energy efficiency. This was a core feature of Barack Obama's election pitch. Government funding for green and carbon saving technologies, as in the US or China could not be better timed. Taking advantage of declining capital costs of hydro, wind, geothermal and solar, it would pay to invest in these technologies now, anticipating the resurgence of fossil fuel prices. Such investments would help sever a link that has long been the bane of anti poverty campaigners. No country has managed to lift living standards without increasing its carbon footprint. But under the vastly changed global environment today, it is essential that they do so. Global warming hurts the poor the most. Climate change is causing a spike in natural disasters as well as gobbling up arable land and reducing water availability in critical areas.
3. Third, this is the moment to make deals leading to a surge in financing for development and its effective use. You only have to look at global projections to see that the boost to growth from the fiscal stimulus is envisaged to be greater in developing countries. That is because infrastructural investments or policy improvements can deliver sharper increases in growth in these economies compared to the more affluent ones.

When the world is increasingly dependent on developing economies to re-energies the failing global economic system, support for such financial flows would be an important aspects of the global stimulus. Policies aimed at immediate growth at the expense of social safety nets or greener investments will be suicidal. Economic, social and environmental dimensions of the recovery are no longer distinct goals with phased solutions. They are part of the same package of needed actions. The Bonn climate change talks are drawing to a close but the real action is yet to begin. Countries are still squabbling over squaring up the bill for climate change mitigation, with insufficient funds and no consensus on where the big bucks will come from. The road from Bonn to Copenhagen where a new protocol is expected at the end of the year looks very long.

As of now, several countries like Japan and Russia are yet to even declare their emission targets and according to present estimation set out by Climate Action Network, at least US$ 140 billion is required for developing countries to use climate control programmes till 2010. The UN sets out an even more ambitious figure of up to US$ 250 billion a year.

But what is available is less than small change. Executive Secretary of the United Nations Framework Convention on Climate Change (UNFCCC) Yvo de Boer points out that even the clean development market would not be able to generate sufficient funds. The least developed country funds have been merely US$ 172 million. Billions more are required for the adaptation funds, he said.

Eco Terrorism

Eco terrorism, as a sub-strand of terrorism, is the possible area of conflict as a sequel of climate change. Eco-terrorism is defined as "the use or threatened use of violence of a criminal nature against innocent victims or property by an environmentally oriented, sub national group for environmental political reasons." In 2005, the United States had identified eco-terrorism as one of the top domestic terror threats. On the other hand, interstate warfare over sharing of resources can be a product of climate change. It is noteworthy that natural resources are not evenly distributed and they defy internal or external boundaries as well. As such resource based conflict can occur between states as well as within states. Over 60 percent of proven oil and gas reserves are located in the Middle East and apart from the developed countries, new burgeoning economies like India China are heavily dependent on middle east oil for their respective requirements.

Dependence on Middle East oil by a large number of countries calls for uninterrupted supplies of oil and any disruption can lead to exacerbation of tension and thereby threatening regional security.

Apart from oil and natural gas , 'water wars' are set to increase in the wake of increasing pressure on water supplies as a sequel to decline in water levels and burgeoning growth in populations. The potential for conflict over water is huge, with over 200 river basins touching multiple nations. Water prone conflicts are present in central Asia, South Asia, Africa and some other parts of the globe. Sharing a water source does not always lead to conflict however, water access between two countries can cause conflict.

In Latin America, interdependence among states who share the Lempa Basin has encouraged the development of regional mechanisms to manage supplies. Indira Gandhi said that poverty was the biggest pollutant. Mrs. Gandhi got it wrong. It is not poverty but progress that's the biggest pollutants. And our successive governments have realized the truth of that axion and acted on it. To make sure that India remains as pollution free as it is progress free. Look at countries like USA and Europe and others, all so hell-bent on this environmentally dangerous thing called progress that they have ended up jeopardizing the entire planet.

Global Slowdown and Carbon Credit Prices

Carbon credits, which are basically offsets of international emission trading schemes implemented to mitigate global warming, touched a peak of Euro 20 in October 2008. Thereafter, prices had started to dwindle. It first dropped to euro 16 at the end of October 2008, and then further declined to euro 13.14 in December. The crash was brought about by a contraction in demand due to lower emissions in the backdrop of a global slowdown which resulted in production cuts or closures. When prices bottomed out at euro 8.9 per unit early this year, a few companies sold large chunks of their issued carbon credits, fearing a further fall in the price. According to an industry expert, the price is expected to rise further to around euro 12-15, where it is likely to stabilize for the next few months. However, prices are unlikely to go back to the euro 20 levels.

"CER prices could go as high as euro 11.5 tonne in the short term, building on present enthusiasm prevalent in all financial markets. However, prices were unlikely to remain at these levels," according to a report by Emergent Venture India. The spurt may prompt companies to sell their issued credits to buyers in the developed nations. Considering that the price has improved after a gap of six months, there may be pent up demand. India has a large quantum of unsold carbon credits-to the tune of over 40 million units. One carbon credit is equivalent to emission reduction of one tonne of carbon dioxide or corresponding greenhouse gases. It is impossible for India to stabilize its climate changing greenhouse gas (GHG) emissions by 2030 without continuing to keep its people in poverty, the World Bank has concluded after modelling a low carbon growth pathway for the country. Optimism seems to have returned to the carbon credits market, with spot prices of certified emission reduction (CERs) or carbon credits testing the euro 13-levels. The December 2009 contracts for CERs on the European Exchange are trading at around euro 12-12.5 over last month (July 2009). The gap between forward contracts and spot prices has shrunk, which means spot prices are also ruling around the same level.

Climate Change, Agriculture and Sea Food

Emerging patterns of decline in water supplies for drinking and irrigation, a decline in agricultural productivity as a result of changes in rainfall, temperature and pest patterns, and large economic and human losses attributable to extreme weather events entail the potential of take their toll on the global system as a whole. Many international experts as well as some Western governments have expressed apprehensions that such fragile climate conditions are prone to create an unstable world that could further spur terrorist activity. Apart from this, the possibility of potential rise in conflict in the most environmentally and politically vulnerable countries can not be ruled out. It is noteworthy that 61 countries have been identifies by International Alert, a peace building NGOs, as being at risk from the 'double headed' risk of climate change and conflict. Scientists recommend that an 80 percent cut in emissions by the developed countries by 2050 is vital to avert the tipping point in climate change. The long term goal post might be un-achieve able under current circumstances but it provides a benchmark to work with. Mean while, improved technology might one day make the target achievable.

In a study that may have vital implications for efforts to combat future climate change, researcher have suggested that global warming could speed up as the world starts becoming free of pollution , after they found that plants absorb more greenhouse gases when the air is polluted.

According to lead author Lina Marcado from the centre for Ecology and Hydrology, "Surprising, the effects of atmospheric pollution seem to have enhanced global plant productivity by as much as a quarter from 1960 to 1999." This resulted in a net 10 percent increase in the account of carbon stored by the land once other effects were taken into account." Mercado added. An increase in microscopic particles released into the atmosphere, by human activities and changes in cloud cover, caused a decline in the amount of sunlight reaching the earth's surface from the 1950s up to the 1980s (a phenomenon known as 'global dimming').

A recently published study has warned that global warming may create 'dead zones' in the ocean that would be bereft of fish and seafood and endure up to two millennia. At the heart of the study model are two well used scenarios which use atmospheric levels of carbon dioxide (CO2), the main greenhouse gas, as an indicator of rise in temperature. Under the worst scenario, CO2 concentrations would raise to 1,168 parts per million (ppm) by 2100, or about triple today's level. Under the more optimistic model, CO2 would reach 549 ppm by 2010, or roughly 50 percent more than today.

We might be stripping 'mother earth' of the ability to feed millions, say scientists while reporting that fertile topsoil could vanish in about 60 years if drastic action was not taken soon. Fertile soil is being lost faster than it can be replenished and will eventually lead to the "top soil bank" becoming empty. Farming soil could run out within 60 years, leading to a catastrophic food crisis and drastically higher prices for consumers, report the telegraph on the basis of researchers. Chronic soil mismanagement and over farming causing erosion, climate change and increasing populations were to blame for the dramatic global decline in suitable farming soil, the scientists said. An estimated 75 billion tones and soil is lost annually with more than 80 percent of the world's farming land "moderately or severely eroded".

A University of Sydney study, presented to the conference, found soil is being lost in China 57 times faster than it can be replaced through natural processes. In Europe that figure is 17 times, in America 10 times while five times as much soil is being lost in Australia. Soil is also a valuable store of carbon and can release the green house gas if it is ploughed or dug up. World soil, including European and British soils, could vanish within about 60 years if drastic action was not taken. This will lead to a global food crisis, chronic food shortages and higher prices.

Despite better than average farming practices, European soil might last for 100 years if no further damage occurs worldwide, scientists said. In reality, however, increased land pressures aimed at compensating global production losses would likely mean it will run out faster, they added. John Crawford, professor of sustainable agriculture at the University of Sydney who presented the study, said it was unknown how long soil will lost. It could be as little as 60 years and that is a scary figure because it is not obvious that we have time to reverse decline and still meet future demands for food. Latest forecast predict the world's population will grow from 6.8 billion to more than 9 billion by 2050, placing even further pressure on food production and farming.

Climate Change and Migration

Climate change, by displacing settled populations, is creating a new kind of refugee. Approximate 24 million people are estimated to have been displaced so far by climate change. Some estimates envisage that by 2010 around 50 million people will be dislocated by global climate change and by 2050 this figure could exceed 150 million.

As fears over the potentially devastating impact of global warming becomes apparent, there is also the growing concern over the dramatic increase in this new class of displaced persons. One estimate by the Red Cross places population displacement caused by climate change disasters as larger than that brought about by war and persecution. Unfortunately, not being officially recognized as refugees, they slip into a bureaucratic grey zone, suffering from definitional heterogeneity. The less developed countries are the least responsible for climate change as having modest industry and lifestyles they produce relatively small amounts of pollution, but their populations are most vulnerable to environmental disasters, caused in particular by climate change. Being poor, large sections of the people in these countries tend to occupy unsafe locations, living along coast lines, flood plains and steep slopes. The existing institutions and organizations-international and national-are not sufficiently equipped to deal with this challenge. The global community needs to extend support to climate refugees and assist them in obtaining refugee status under international law.

Western Countries and USA on Climate Deal

US has instead asked large developing countries like India and China to undertake emission reductions though keeping the language oblique enough not to cause any diplomatic heartburn. While the US has been suggesting that developing countries open their markets to green technologies from the West in order to reduce their emissions, the South has been unequivocal in demanding that the full costs of clean tech should be borne by the countries primarily responsible for the crisis–the industrialized nations. Observers pointed out that the US document reiterated India's piquant position as wedged between EU and the Scandinavian countries demanding emission reductions from it at all cost and the US hiding its own reluctance to take steps behind India and China's economic necessities. Sources said that US officials had been in touch with the Indian counterparts and dropped broad enough hints about what was not acceptable in the US though only faintly outlining what could possibly be in the deal.

The bottomline is that the global slowdown has seen western nations lose their zeal for climate change mitigation. There is now a convoluted effort to pass the buck, UN has demanded countries put forth their Nationally Appropriate Mitigation Action (NAMA) plans but without funding these is not very useful. India, which has its own national agenda on climate change, has its reservations. Putting forth plans without knowing the commitment of others is not a bright idea. India and most of their G-77 countries are holding on to their foremost demand of the polluter pays those there could cracks in their ranks too. India needs to have a clear-cut domestic green policy, in place, without further delay.

India's National Action Plan on Climate Change

India's National Action Plan on Climate Changes talks about intervention to improve the quality of urban services to reduce emissions and energy use. TERI's recommendations have to be taken seriously and put into practice, including the suggestions to strengthen and empower local bodies to improve governance and to encourage public-private partnership to provide urban services. As a first step, the government is introducing a system of indicators to monitor sustainability in the provision of urban services. Data collection and analysis are integral to any master plan. However, that needs to be followed up with actual delivery of services that can put us on a new, sustainable urban growth trajectory. The future of the Indian dream depends on whether we can build better cities today.

India is the world's fifth largest GHG emitter, accounting for 5 percent of global emissions. But per capita emissions are 70 percent below the world average and 93 percent below that of the US. Though India's National Action Plan on Climate Change released in 2008 by the UPA government does not specify vehicle emission cuts, India's vehicle emission standards (Bharat Stage III equivalent to Euro III) are followed in 11 cities, monitored by the Pollution Under Control Scheme. The goal is to follow Bharat Stage III standards nation wide by the year 2010 before progressing to Bharat Stage IV, post-2010. In the mean time, serious efforts need to be directed towards making available hybrid fuels like bio-ethanol and bio-diesel, as well as work out what is more feasible in the Indian context to go for ethanol or electricity from biomass. The US has taken an important step forward. It is in our interest to go for self regulation to reduce pollution and oil dependency.

Effect of Financial Crisis on Climate Change

The current financial crisis has provided "a unique window of opportunity" in dealing with climate change, the Paris-based International Energy Agency (IEA), said during the UN climate negotiations in Bangkok. This year, Energy consumption globally has dropped by three percent as against a historical increase of three percent per year. Many investments have been postponed and several of these were unsustainable, this has helped the environment.

The Asian Development Bank may secure more than US$ 100 million in financing for a fund to buy carbon credits after the expiry of the Kyoto Protocol in 2012. The future carbon fund, which started operations in January with commitments from countries including Finland, Belgium and Sweden, may raise more than US$ 100 million in the first half. The 1997 Kyoto Protocol, an agreement among nations to curb global warming, assigned emission reduction targets to developed countries "for the five years through 2012. Private funds are not investing in projects that issues credits after 2012 because of uncertainty over climate protection plans when the Kyoto protocol expires. ADB is still in the process of screening projects so the fund's first carbon contract, first investment, is not expected until the end of 2010. The Asian Development Bank plans to reduce emissions in Asia by sponsoring energy-reduction projects in Indonesia, the Philippines and India and finance emission reduction ventures through dedicated carbon funds.

The banks has committed more than US$ 50 million in the United Nations sponsored emission reduction projects in the Asia-Pacific under the Clean Development Mechanism as part of the US$ 151.8 million Asia-Pacific Carbon Fund. The APCF expects to commit the entire fund in projects by the end of the 2010. Five European public funding institutions including the European Investment Bank have started a 125 million euros fund to invest in post-Kyoto credits.

The US is 'very interested' in an Indian proposal to create a global network of climate technology centres and thinks it deserves to make it to a UN climate change agreement scheduled for later this year. Developing countries want to see wealthy industrialized nations pledge much deeper cuts in the emissions of their greenhouse gases such as carbon dioxide. But industrialized countries argue that major developing countries such as India and China must also commit to cuts and open up their climate change programmes to international scrutiny. Developing countries say their emissions are tiny compared to those of the developed world when calculated on a per capita basis.

They also point out the entire UN climate change negotiating process is based on the fundamental principle that industrialized countries who are mainly responsible for causing climate change must move before developing countries. Jonathan Pershing, the US President's Deputy Special Envoy for Climate Change said that US negotiations plan to hold a series of bilateral meetings with Indian business leaders to explore how they can be involved in proposals seeking to foster technological solutions to the problem of climate change which is caused by green house gases emitted in the process of industrial production. He specifically welcomed an Indian proposal submitted to the UNFCCC seeking to establish a series of climate Innovation Centres, each focusing on developing a key technological product that would help countries mitigate the emission of greenhouse gases or adapt to the impact of climate change. The US is very interested in that deal. There may be ways to facilitate that in the agreement.

The Indian delegation to the talks, led by the Prime Minister's Special envoy Shyam Saran, highlighted technology transfer as a key Indian demand, arguing in the proposal that 'technology is the only way to achieve the high impact changes required. Significantly, the Indian proposal also calls for a more lenient global patents regime–or-Intellectual Property Rights (IPRs)–on grounds that negotiators privately said resembles those cited some years ago to help loosen patents over life saving drugs in the fight against HIV/AIDS. In order to enable the widest diffusion and transfer of cutting edge climate technologies, it is important that we review the international IPR regime to balance rewards for innovators with the greater good of humankind.

Copenhagen Summit (COP 15) Target

COP 15 is named COP 15 as it is the 15th conference since 1995 (each in a different place; next one in Mexico). Apart from these main summits, there are pre summit meetings (for example, 183 delegates met in Bonn this year, then in Bangkok, then in Barcelona and so on so forth. UN draft says world must cut CO2 by at least 50 percent by 2050.Nations around the world must reduce greenhouse gas emissions at least 50 percent by mid century under a draft proposal being debated by 192 countries at Copenhagen.

The Copenhagen Summit was expected to be a significant milestone in the global Endeavour to stem climate change. There were many reasons behind the importance assigned to the summit, the most crucial reason being the fact that it was the last significant change to reach at a consensus before the expiry of the Kyoto Protocol. However, after the meet concluded, many expressed the view the most of the expectations remained unfulfilled.

The main drawback of the Copenhagen Accord, as perceived by various quarters, is the absence of specific figures, commitments or time lines in the global fight against climate change. Besides, the Accord was not adopted by consensus due to strong objections by some countries. Although the Accord promised mobilization of substantial amounts of fund to tackle climate change, it again fell short of expectations, as mere fund mobilization can not be the most crucial tool for this end. The Accord sets a limit to temperature increases in the globe, however, it fails to specify the green house gas emission cuts that the nations need to commit themselves to in order to meet that goal. One of the main shortcomings of the deal is that there are no deadlines for global emissions to peak. Such serious lacunae have left scientists, climate activists and vulnerable countries disappointed. Table 4.2 and Table 4.3 depict the per capita tonnes of CO2 equivalent and extra annual emission of CO2 of different countries.

Basic Group of Countries Ministerial Meeting

The second Environment ministerial level meeting of the Basic Group of countries was held in New Delhi on January

24, 2010. In the meeting , the group of four major emerging economies–Brazil, South Africa, India and China-expressed their intention to communicate information on their voluntary mitigation actions to the United Nations Framework Convention on Climate Change (UNFCCC).

Table 4.2: Per Capita Tonne of Carbon Dioxide Equivalent: One Measure of Comparison

(Percent)

USA and Canada	19.4
Japan	5.2
EIT Annex I	9.7
Europe Anncx I	11.4
Other non-Annex I	2.0
Latin America and Caribbean	10.3
No-Annex I East Asia	17.3
Africa	7.8
South Asia	13.1

Table 4.3: Extra annual emission of CO2 (Millions of tonnes per year)

Countries	Minimum Scenario	Likely Scenario
US	844	1,926
India	179	486
China	209	275
Kyoto Emission Savings	-483	

At the Basic Ministerial meeting, the group reemphasized its commitment to working with other countries–particularly the G77-to ensure a consensus at the Conference of Parties at Mexico later in 2010. They underscored the centrality of the UNFCCC process and the decision of the parties to carry forward the negotiations on two tracks–Ad Hoc Working Group on Long Term Cooperative Action under the UNFCCC, and the Ad Hoc Working Group on further emission reduction commitments for Annexure I parties under the Kyoto Protocol in 2010 leading up to COP-6 at Mexico.

The member countries also decided to create a fund to help the small island countries, the least developed countries and the vulnerable nations apart from helping them technologically. The Ministers said that the amount of contribution would be decided at the next group meeting to be held in South Africa. In a statement, it was said that the resources would surpass the US$ 10 billion assistance committed by the developed nations at the Copenhagen Conference held in Denmark in December 2009.

Binding Goal to Reduce Emission by Developed Countries

USA vows to reduce emission by 83 percent by 2050. It means 2050 US emission will be at 1910 level when the US population was 92 million. However, with 420 million Americans in 2050, it simply means that US per capita emissions in 2050 would be the same as in 1875. South America's histrionics mired in anti US propaganda continue especially with massive oil and gas discoveries in recent times which Latin American nation's plans to sell to the entire world in coming decades.

China, the biggest emitter of Green House Gases (GHGs) recently declared that it has set a binding goal to reduce emissions per unit of GDP by 40-45 percent below 2005. At the same time, China is adding nearly two coal fired plants per week and its coal powered industry is expanding at the rate of 50 percent for the last few years. India, suddenly realizing that its old position of equal yet differentiated responsibilities was being tossed around as a deal breakers' whim, suddenly took big 'brother' China's direction and declared to reduce its per capita emissions too-voluntarily, brother, voluntarily. Amazingly, amongst the trio (of US, India and China), China continues to have the worst energy intensity with amount of GHGs emitted per US$ 1 m of GDP at 1152 metric tones (MT). The figures for US and India stand at 441 MT and 655 MT respectively.

EU did take the lead and declare to cut its carbon

emissions by 20 percent from 1990 levels by 2020 and is the only region on the planet running a Comprehensive Emission Trading Scheme (ETS). However, it refused to commit to any further cuts unless other rich nations reciprocate its earlier gestures. But, in the midst of this heat that has suddenly raised COP 15 temperature by many degrees, Dr. R.K. Pachauri, Chairman of the Nobel Prize winning IPCC, said at the inaugural speech of the summit that "To limit average temperature increase at 2.0 and 2.4 degree C, the cost of mitigation by 2030 would not exceed 3 percent of the global GDP. In other words, the so called prosperity expected in 2030 would be postponed by just a few months.

Firstly, as Prime Minister Dr. Manmohan Singh has reiterated on many platforms, funding and technology transfer from developed countries to developing nations to curb, mitigate and adopt to damaging effects of climate change must be made a certainty within the confines of any international treaty. However, the rhetoric by the world's largest oil and gas companies, coal power plant owners and timber companies largely sidelined India's stance when the clause about peak oil was introduced some time back by some EU representatives. It was followed by the Chinese per capita reduction commitment and suddenly, India seeing itself as the isolated warrior capitulated immediately.

Under the giant garb of standing its ground, it slowly slithered out and positioned itself behind China in curbing its per capita emissions at 2005 levels by 20-25 percent by the year 2020. With the Indian announcement, at present 105 leaders from all over the world will participate. Together, these 105 leaders represent 82 percent of globe's population, 89 percent of the world GDP and 80 percent of the world's current emissions. If an agreement can be reached within this group, it could change the future of the globe, thus making Copenhagen the global warming turnaround, we all wish for". But such sweeping statements about universal wishes from the West almost never mention anything about technology transfer and a funding mechanism to aid developing nations.

Secondly, the soot from the carbon jargon has been so thick that the greatest sink for carbon dioxide, the largest GHG, the global forest cover, has been but forgotten. Brazil, the largest Latin American economy recently declared post negotiations with other Amazon economies that it would only accept and support a climate agreement if it made mandatory for developed nations to use only 10 percent of their emissions reduction targets to invest in a forestation projects. However, Brazil might have just forgotten that China single-handedly emits nearly 50 percent of the carbon emissions combined by EU and US and it is still a developing economy.

Cleaning Up

The United States emits one quarter of all global carbon dioxide. And within the US, vehicles account for one quarter of all greenhouse gas (GHG) emissions. Considering that has predecessor, George Bush, failed to take air pollution seriously. US president Barack Obama's decision to take tough measures to tackle vehicular emissions is more than welcome. The goal is to move away from dependence on oil and significantly reduce polluting emissions from vehicles by one third by the year 2006. Manufacturers would also be required to improve fuel efficiency in both cars and trucks by 5 percent a year from 2012. By the end of the target period, it is estimated that oil consumption would fall by 1.8 billion barrels. The 34 percent emission reductions envisaged by 2016 would be equivalent of removing 177 million cars from US roads.

The new federal policy will now replace all overlapping rules on emissions and efficiency set by different official agencies and state governments, including California and New York. The American auto industry and green activists are being supportive. Though improving fuel efficiency would push up cost of every new vehicle by approximately US$ 1,300, this would be offset by lower fuel prices within a three year period. For the first time, the US has come up with a national plan to deal with spiralling emissions that contribute to climate change. This might set the pace for constructive dialogue at the upcoming climate change conference in Copenhagen this December, where an international protocol on emission standards and other aspects of environmental importance is to be thrashed out.

While the US has been suggesting that developing countries open their markets to green technologies from the west in order to reduce their emissions, the south has been unequivocal in demanding that the full costs of clean tech should be born by the countries primarily responsible for the crisis–the industrialized nations. Observers pointed out that the US document reiterated India's piquant position as wedged between EU and the Scandinavian countries demanding emission reductions from it at all cost and the US hiding its own reluctance to take steps behind India and China's economic necessities. Sources said that US officials had been in touch with the Indian counterparts and dropped broad enough hints about what was not acceptable to the US though only faintly outlining what could possibly be in the deal.

Environmental Performance Index of 2010

The 2010 Environmental Performance Index (EPI) was released of the World Economic Forum in Washington, USA on January 27, 2010. The index this year was produced by a team of environmental experts at the Yale University and the Columbia University. This is the third edition of the EPI, which has been revisited bi-annually since 2006. India and China ranked 123rd and 121st respectively, in pollution control, reflecting the strain rapid economic growth imposes on the environment.

However, among the other newly industrialized nations, Brazil and Russia ranked 62nd and 69th, respectively, which suggested that the level of development is just one of the many factors affecting pollution control. Iceland leads the world in addressing pollution control and natural resource management challenges. Iceland's top notch performance derives from its high scores on environmental public health, controlling greenhouse gas emissions and reforestation. Apart from Iceland, other high performers include Switzerland, Costa Rica, Sweden and Norway. It is worth mentioning in this regard that the Environmental Performance Index ranks 163 countries on their performance across 25 metrics aggregated into ten categories. These categories include environmental health, air quality, water resource management, biodiversity and habitat, forestry, fisheries, agriculture and climate change.

Copenhagen Accord Not Legally Binding

In a significant development, the United Nations Framework Convention on Climate Change (UNFCCC) said on January 26, 2010 that the Copenhagen Accord ,finalized at the Copenhagen Conference in December 2009, was not a legally binding document but merely a political one. The statement was aimed at putting at rest doubts over the status of the Accord, cobbled together at the 15th meeting of the Copenhagen, Denmark on December 18, 2009.

In a notification addressed to the Parties, Mr. Yvo de Boer, Executive Secretary of the UNFCCC, said that the COP neither adopted nor endorsed the Accord, but merely took note of it. Hence, its provisions do not have any legal standing with the UNFCCC process even if some Parties decide to associate themselves with it. Secondly, since the Accord is a political agreement, rather than a treaty instrument subject to signature, a verbal note to the secretariat from an appropriate authority in the government concerned is sufficient to communicate the intention of a Party to associate itself with the Accord.

The Clarification was issued following numerous enquires received by the UNFCCC secretariat over the wordings of the notification issued to the Parties to convey their intention on whether or not to associate themselves with the Accord. The secretariat also received queries regarding whether the Parties could physically sign the Accord in order to signify their association and support.

Use of Plastic Can Cut Emission Levels

Increased use of plastic in industries such as packaging and automobiles among others can actually help reduce global carbon emission levels that is required to prevent climate change, claimed a study conducted by consultancy firm McKinsey and Oko Institute of Germany. The study that goes against conventional thinking that use of plastic adds to global warming, said that reduction in carbon emission due to usage of plastics in these industries far exceeds the amount of green house gas emitted during production of plastics. The findings are based on an analysis that sought to compare carbon emission through use of chemicals (including products made out of chemicals such as plastics) and non chemical products. For instance, the study said that use of plastics reduced the weight of automobiles and enables lower emissions by making the vehicles more fuel efficient.

This could probably also explain increasing use of plastics in automobile sector over the years. Similarly, in packaging despite a higher production footprint per kilogram of material, due to lower weight, use of plastics results in a lower overall carbon footprint. This means even as carbon emission for producing plastics for packaging allows lower carbon emission compared to glass. This is because plastics is lighter than glass. The study comes at a crucial juncture as various global agencies and representative of different countries are negotiating at Copenhagen to strike an agreement on reducing carbon emission. According to the Intergovernmental Panel on Climate change (IPCC), the current global greenhouse gas emissions are 3-4 times the planet's natural absorption rate of carbon dioxide. The chemical industry that employs more than 3.6 million people globally and generates annual sales of well over US$ 3 trillion is one of the big sources of greenhouse gas. However, the study claims that out of all the industrial innovations to reduce carbon emissions, use of plastic products is one of the most efficient.

The biggest application of chemical products in saving emissions, according to the study, is insulation materials in construction industry as it reduced heat loss by buildings and therefore the need for lower energy. Other top applications where use of chemicals helps cut carbon emission are fertilizer and crop protection, lighting and packaging.

Role of TERI in Green Development of India

TERI should be described as an NGRI (Non-Governmental Research Institute) and not an NGO, Says Mr. Pachauri. TERI was established as the Tata Energy Research Institute in Delhi in 1974, to find solutions to serious environmental and developmental problems. The scope of its activities is vast and its innovative solutions cover among others, rural energy, forest conservation, urban transportation, energy efficiency and global climate change. Founded as a not–for–profit, independent research organization, its focus has widened, as has its size and activities.

TERI was evolved as a unique institution which incorporates the ability to provide policy analysis at the global level to multilateral organizations, governments in many countries of the world, the government of India as well as state governments in India. The institute today is evolved in the development and large scale dissemination of technologies which ensure the efficient use of natural resources. TERI and Mr. Pachauri have undertaken significant work, sensitizing people to not only the dangers posed by green house gas emissions and global warming , but also to the economic opportunities that lie in energy efficiency and climate change prevention and mitigation. However, climate change is just one of the many societal challenges on which TERI carries out research.

In 35 years, TERI has established itself as a leading global think tank on all issues related to sustainable development and acquired a new name along the way, The Energy and Resources Institute (TERI). R.K. Pachauri, its director-general, is also the head of the Intergovernmental Panel on Climate Change, which shared the 2007 Nobel Peace Prize with farmer US vice president Al Gore.

Conclusion

India is the world's fifth largest GHG emitter, accounting for 5 percent of global emissions. But per capita emissions are 70 percent below the world average and 93 percent below that of the US.

India has demonstrated that it takes the climate change issue seriously: the national action plan on climate change has spelt out the details of implementation of eight missions and is to soon establish a climate change mitigation authority that will set targets to reduce emissions by 2020. India has a ministry dedicated to promotion of alternative energy and several projects are underway to promote adaptation measures. Far more could be achieved if developed countries deliver the promised financial and technological assistance. The ministry for environment and forests might appear to be grandstanding by declaring that India is willing to specify the amount of emissions it could cut to demonstrate its green credentials.

Yet, the political rhetoric does indeed reveal a milestone achievement in the way India has evolved from a diffident bystander at international climate change meets to a more vocal and confident frontline participant. This is a good sign, since India badly needed a makeover of its negotiating profile in order to be heard at international climate change meetings, particularly since there is mounting pressures from developed countries to include emerging economies like India and China in an emission reduction protocol that would be time bound and mandatory.

All along, the focus in India has been more on adaptation to the effects of climate change-for instance on how to face the challenges of environmental degradation, changing crop patterns and vanishing habits. The official approach to climate change is now beginning to seriously consider effective mitigation measures that would result not only in reducing dependencies on conventional fossil fuel and oil imports but also expanding and intensifying investment in alternative clean energy solutions. We should simultaneously decide how much burden each country should bear (to cut emission) on the basis of historic responsibility and equity as well as how much total effort to make.

This is the first time that India has accepted a reference to 2 degree C as a possible threshold guiding global action, but this is entirely in line with our stated position on global warming. The rich world has already made a political pledge on green house gas reduction. But some say it is too little, too late-with a drop of just 7-14 percent below 1990 levels by 2030, India has demanded a 40 percent reduction. Some experts believe that the Indian pledge to hold the 2 degree C line, combined with the rich nations' reluctance to vacate carbon space, could lock India into unsustainably low emission levels for good. "The industrialized countries have attempted to corner us," explains one climate observer. "They have already said they shall not empty the space but they have also made us agree that the room is bound to get smaller, which simply means that the poor Indians, already cramped for space, will have to now recede further into the corner." The rich nations are also not ready to share green technology for free or nearly free and not do they want to compensate the developing world for the disproportionate share of carbon space they hold. Clean technology and/or compensation could have helped poorer nations search for alternatives to fossil fuels.

Though India's National Action Plan on Climate Change released in 2008 by the UPA government does not specify vehicle emission cuts, India's vehicle emission standards (Bharat Stage III equivalent to Euro III) are followed in 11 cities, monitored by the Pollution Under Control Scheme. The goal is to follow Bharat Stage III standards nation wide by the year 2010 before progressing to Bharat Stage IV, post-2010. In the meantime, serious efforts need to be directed towards making available hybrid fuels like bio-ethanol and bio-diesel, as well as work out what is more feasible in the Indian context to go for ethanol or electricity from biomass. The US has taken an important step forward. It is in our interest to go for self regulation to reduce pollution and oil dependency.

A combination of both emissions cutbacks as well as employment of new technologies to remove at least some of the stock of carbon that's warming the planet could help reduce somewhat the risks that have multiplied since industrialization began. The 2007 fourth assessment report of the UN international panel on climate change warned that if the global average temperature exceeds the two degree Celsius figure over the pre industrial period, the effects would be disastrous, especially for developing countries like India. But if we manage to act in time, before the 190 giga ton carbon emission tripping point projected to happen in 2050, we have a 75 percent chance of averting planetary catastrophe. There is an urgent need to look at tackling the root causes of climate change and conflict, instead of responding to the symptoms.

Equal emphasis should also be placed on reducing reliance on fossil fuels. While reduce competition over resources, there is a need to address the growing socio economic divisions which are set to fuel environmental conflicts.

References

Aggrawal, P.K. (2008): "Global Climate Change and Indian Agriculture" The Indian Journal of Agricultural Sciences, November, pp-911-19

Business and Economy, December 11-24 2009, pp. 30-31.

Economic and Political Weekly, June 27, 2009, p. 53.

Economic Times, April 11, 2009, p. 12.

Economic Times, April 11, 2009, p. 12.

Economic Times, Dec 2009, p.1.

Economic Times, May 21, 2009, p. 14.

Hindustan Times, February 4, p. 6.

Hindustan Times, February 5, 2010.

Hindustan Times, October 7, 2009, p. 12.
Times of India, April 9, 2009, p. 12.
Times of India, December 9, 2009, p. 1.
Times of India, February 7, 2010, p. 16.
UNDP (2007): Human Development Report 2007-08: Fighting Climate Change, New York, Palgrave Macmillan, p. 69.

5

Power Sector Reforms in India

Ramakrishnan Ramaiah

Introduction

Power Sector in India: Electricity is the most necessary and critical infrastructural input in the development and growth of economy of any country. Consumption of energy, and more particularly of electricity, is recognized world over, as the most important index of the extent of industrial and economic advancement of the country and living standards of people (Shahi, 2005). The development of other sectors of economy depends on the development of power sector. Though power sector in India achieved significant growth in the past fifty years, the sector has been suffering from inadequate generation capacity to meet the demands of all consumers, operational and functional inefficiencies with high transmission and distribution losses, theft of energy, poor metering etc.

After independence, the enactment of Electricity (Supply) Act, 1948 recognized the need for integrated power development at the state level and State Electricity Boards (SEBs) were formed in all states to rationalize the production and supply of electricity. The Central Electricity Authority (CEA) was created in 1948 as a statutory authority for planning, coordinating and regulating the power sector nationwide. During 1970s, the central government joined in generation and transmission areas to supplement the efforts of state governments by setting up the National Thermal Power Corporation (NTPC), and National Hydro electric Power Corporation (NHPC). In 1989, the National Power Transmission Corporation was set up to take care of interstate transmission systems and later renamed as Power Grid Corporation in 1992.

The power sector had a substantial growth during the last 50 years. The installed capacity in the Indian power sector, which was only 1564 MW in 1950-51 increased to 1,41,080 MW in January 2008; the electricity generation increased from 5100 Million Units (MU) in 1950-51 to 704.469 Billion Units (BU) in 2007-08. The per capita consumption of electricity which was less than 15 units in 1950 also rose to 704 units in 2007-08. Table 5.1 provides data pertaining to the growth of power sector in India.

Table 5.1: Growth of Indian Power Sector

Description	1950-51	2007-08
Installed Capacity (in MW)	1564	141080
Electricity Generation (in units)	5100 MU	704.469 BU
Per Capita Consumption (in units)	15	704

MU=Million Units; BU=Billion Units

Source: www.powermin.nic.in, www.cea.nic.in.

Problems Faced by the Sector: Though the achievements in Indian power sector were quite significant, it was found inadequate to meet the ever increasing demand for electricity due to expansion of industries and urbanization. The peak demand gap has been consistently increasing in the order of 10 to 15 percent. The slow growth in capacity addition in power generation could not match with the demand for electricity in the country. Most of thermal power stations, though they run to their total capacity, unable to meet the peak demand. The sector has been suffering from high technical loss, theft of power, poor metering, etc. In most of the SEBs, the technical and commercial losses put together are about 40 percent (Shahi, 2005).

Need for Power Sector Reforms: The Government of India took several initiatives to reform the power sector from 1990-91. In 1991, the central government amended the Indian

Electricity Act, 1910 and Indian Electricity (Supply) Act, 1948 in order to attract private investment in power generation. 'This facilitated tapping of domestic and foreign capital markets, provided assured returns on investment and reduced legal hassles to allow the private investors to setup generation capabilities or operate as licensee in distribution segments, which were hitherto a monopoly of the SEBs' (Singh, 2006). During 1995, Mega Power Policy was announced, which provided incentives like ten year tax holiday, exemption of customs duty for imports, removal of bottlenecks for easy clearance of projects for power plants above 1000 MW. The Electricity Regulatory Commission Act, 1998 enabled constitution of Electricity Regulatory Commissions (ERCs) at central and state levels.

Electricity Act, 2003: The reform processes initiated in 1991 helped the power sector in bringing in new investments and introduction of competition in generation and distribution areas in a few states. Orissa handed over power distribution to private sector and Maharashtra had private sector participation in generation. However, the capacity addition from the private sector was not up to the expectation. The slow growth in the power sector which was about three percent could not match with the fast growing economy of the country, which was progressing at the rate of about 8 to 9 percent. Realising that self sustaining growth of the power sector and its financial viability is essential for the speedy and sustained economic growth and development of the country, the Government of India enacted a comprehensive act, the Electricity Act, 2003, which paved for radical reforms in the sector, open access in transmission and distribution, creation of regulatory commissions to encourage competition in the sector and tariff rationalization.

Objectives of the Reforms: Policy changes are initiated to match or in comparison with the global trends in the power sector and economic and social indicators in human development. The per capita power consumption of India was very low with 543 kWh during the year 2007, while some developed countries had higher per capita consumption over 10000 kWh. [1]

From the IEA's data, India is far behind the world average of 2752 kWh. China is ahead of India with 2346 kWh. As per Central Electricity Authority's website, per capita consumption of India during 2007 was 671.90 kWh. India, still, needed to accelerate the rate of growth in the power sector to catch up with the world average of 2752kWh. Hence, the objective of the reform process initiated in the country was to bring in more investment in the sector, attract private participation, introduce competition, reduce AT&C losses, increase system efficiency, and provide quality and reliable power supply to all.

Policy Making Field and Research Priorities: In order to address the problems faced by the States, reform measures were initiated to encourage private participation in the sector. 'Persistent power shortages, inadequate public investment and the economic crisis faced by India in the early 1990s led investment and major policy initiatives were undertaken to encourage private and foreign investment. The investment climate was further strengthened through gradual restructuring of the state electricity boards and initiation of regulatory reforms at the federal and state level' (Singh, 2007). Economic liberalization in the 1990s has required the industry to be competitive. Reforms of different kinds were followed by different countries in improving the power sector. corporatization, leasing regulatory bodies and involvement control are some of the reform models followed past few decades. Indian power initiatives introduced in sector.

Relevance: Subsequent to the enactment of Electricity Act, 2003, power sector reform process has been accelerated in included unbundling of SEBs and corporatization of unbundled entities privatization of distribution units. Some states utilised the opportunity and made considerable progress in implementing the sector, whereas some states lagged behind. This research paper is an attempt to study the measures initiated by the selected states, relative effectiveness of the strategies adopted by them and the achievement in meeting the objectives of the reform process as envisaged in the Electricity Act, 2003.

Research Methodology

Research Objectives: The main purpose of the research is to find out the performance of the selected state utilities in realising the objectives of the reform initiatives after the enactment of Electricity Act, 2003 such as reducing transmission and distribution losses, bringing in competition, more investments, improving system efficiency, meeting the demand gap and rationalization of tariff structure in order to provide quality and reliable power at affordable prices to all.

Research Questions:

Main Research Question: Power Sector Reforms in India, the Road Ahead for Indian States: A Comparative Study of Selected Indian States.

Sub Research Questions:

1. What are the strategies adopted by different States in meeting the objectives of reform initiatives?
2. How effective are these strategies?
3. What is the role and initiatives of different State Governments towards meeting the objectives?
4. What is the role of Central Government in meeting the objectives?
5. How has the participation of private sector helped in realizing the objectives?
6. What are the politics of providing free power to agriculture, and how does it hinder in meeting the objectives?

Methodology: There are number of articles and books written on power sector reforms in India. Details of some Government websites are given in the reference. The research study mainly used the secondary data available in the websites of Ministry of Power, Government of India, Central Electricity Authority, Power Finance Corporation, State Electricity Utilities, Regulatory Commissions, and Energy Research Institutions like TERI, India, ISS library and articles from energy and power sector journals available in the websites. The meetings with government officials and executives in private/ corporate agencies helped to collect updated information and certain primary data required for the study.

Scope: The research is focused on few selected Indian states to analyze the performance of the power sector after the reform processes initiated in India. The field visits helped to have a personal interaction with officials working in the state electricity sector, and executives in the private corporate sector to know in detail the achievements made in this sector, understand the problems and difficulties faced in achieving the objectives and the new initiatives undertaken by the state utilities.

Data Sources: The websites of Ministry of Power, Central Electricity Authority, Power Finance Corporation and state utilities are of enormous help in collecting most of the secondary data. The Annual Reports, Balance Sheets of the State Power Utilities collected during field visits provided detailed information. The report on the performance of the State Power Utilities for the years 2005-06 to 2007-08 prepared by Power Finance Corporation Ltd provided valuable insights into financial and operational performance of the State Utilities. It also helped in comparing the state's performance on various parameters.

Personal Interviews: During the visit to states and Ministry of Power, Government of India, New Delhi, the researcher could meet the Members and officers of State Electricity Boards, Managing Directors and Executive Directors of the corporatized companies of unbundled SEBs in the states of Karnataka and Maharashtra, Corporate executives who are associated with the power sector, like TATA Power in Mumbai, Chairman, Members and Secretary of State

Electricity Regulatory Commissions and officials in the Power Ministry, Government of India & Power Finance Corporation.

Limitations: Within a limited time period available, it was a challenging task in getting prior appointments for meeting and to have a detailed interaction with the officials of the government departments, State Electricity Boards, corporations/companies, executives from the corporate sector, officials in the State Regulatory Commission and representatives from consumer federations/NGO organizations in the selected states for field visit. Moreover, at the time of field visit, the Board/corporation's officials were pre occupied with board meetings, tariff revision meetings with State Regulatory Commission, public hearing in regulatory commission offices and connected preparatory works. The Chairman and Members of Regulatory Commission in the states were also busy in conducting public hearings and tariff revision meetings. Due to time constraint, the views of consumer forums, ombudsman, and farmers associations on power sector reforms could not be ascertained.

The study is based on four selected states out of 28 states in India. It would be difficult to come to a conclusion on the status and achievements of power sector reform in India, just with a sample study of four states. So, the findings, policy issues and suggestions may not be relevant or suitable for some states, where the local conditions and priorities will be different from others.

Analytical Framework: State Electricity Boards (SEBs) were created in the states in India under the Electricity (Supply) Act, 1948 and made responsible for generation, transmission and distribution of electricity within the state. The Board is headed by a Chairman who is generally a senior bureaucrat or Minister in charge of Energy in some states. The chairman is assisted by members, who are specialised in the fields of generation, transmission, distribution and accounting areas.

After the reforms initiated in power sector from the year

1991 and enactment of Electricity Act, 2003, the SEBs of Orissa, Haryana, Andhra Pradesh, Karnataka, Maharashtra, Gujarat and Uttar Pradesh have already been unbundled/corporatized. Orissa State Electricity Regulatory Commission was the first of its kind in the country, designed as an independent Regulatory Commission to regulate powers sector in the state. Most of the states have either constituted or notified the constitution of SERC. In Maharashtra and Delhi, private companies are involved in power generation and distribution. However, Tamil Nadu, Kerala and Punjab are yet to unbundle their SEBs.

The PFC report on the performance of the state power utilities for the years 2004-05 to 2006-07 has shown that Karnataka, Orissa and Maharashtra made profits during the year 2006-07, whereas states like Uttar Pradesh, Tamil Nadu, and Punjab made losses during the same period. Recently, the states, which made significant progress in implementing reforms like Karnataka and Andhra Pradesh, have started offering free/subsidized power to framers after the Assembly elections in the state.

While discussing about privatisation in the Brazilian Power industry, Tankha (2008) mentions about populist political resistance to price rationalisation as one of the key barriers to implementing Chairman Members (Generation, Transmission, Distribution, Finance) Technical staff, Accounting staff, Secretary, General staff orthodox reform. The populist measure of providing free electricity to farmers, a strategy to appease the farming community in states like Tamil Nadu and Punjab is seen in this perspective for not implementing radical reforms in power sector, when compared to the initiatives taken by states like Orissa, Gujarat and Maharashtra etc. A detailed study on the politics behind power sector reforms, policy credibility, institutional framework, will help to comprehend the reasons behind states like Tamil Nadu attracting more private investment in power generation even though it is lagging behind many states in implementing radical power sector reforms.

Selection of States: CRISIL, a credit rating company was asked by Government of India to analyse the performance of states in implementing the reforms in power sector.

The agency submitted its report in 2006. They analyzed the performance of the state utilities on various parameters and ranked states, which is reproduced in Table 5.2. The agency assigned weights to various parameters like the role and cooperation of State Government, Regulatory Process, Business Risk Analyses, Financial Risk Analysis, and Progress in attaining commercial viability etc.

Table 5.2: Top Ten State Utilities (from 2003 to 2006)
Rank: 2003, 2004, 2005 and 2006

Rank	2003	2004	2005	2006
1	A.P	Delhi	A.P	A.P
2	Karnataka	A.P	Gujarat	Gujarat
3	Haryana	Goa	Delhi	Delhi
4	Rajasthan	Karnatakaa	Karnataka	Karnataka
5	Maharashtra	Gujarat	Tamil Nadu	West Bengal
6	Delhi	Haryana	Goa	Goa
7	Gujarat	Punjab	H.P	H.P
8	H.P	H.P	West Bengal	-
9	Tamil Nadu	U.P	U.P	Maharashtra
10	Punjab	Rajasthan	Chhattisgarh	Kerala

A.P- Andhra Pradesh, H.P-Himachal Pradesh, U.P-Uttar Pradesh
Source: CRISIL/ICRA (2006, 2005, 2004, 2003).

CRISIL study covered the reform period up to the year 2006. Since, to answer the research question; the performance of the states in achieving the objectives power sector reforms after the enactment of Electricity Act, 2003, four states were chosen based on a comparative analysis of following five parameters.

- Installed capacity-SEBs.
- AT&C losses (Aggregate Technical and Commercial

losses).

- Meeting the peak demand.
- Private Sector participation.
- Financial performance of the State Boards/Corporations.

Table 5.3: Comparison of State's Performance

States	Installed Capacity (increase + Decrease - in percent)	AT&C Losses (Increase + Decrease - in percent)	Meeting the Peak demand (surplus + Deficit - in percent)	Financial Performance (Increase + Decrease – in percent)	Private Participation in Generation (decrease - increase + in percent)
A.P	8.28	-12.34	-9.80	33.03	48.81
Karnataka	24.24	-4.48	-4.99	139.56	121.92
Gujarat	14.13	-22.59	-24.33	1780.00	67.07
Maharashtra	8.72	40.64	-23.73	135.03	29.02
Kerala	3.66	-22.10	-13.71	190.79	-6.73
Tamil Nadu	5.50	3.61	-6.00	-61.00	87.44
Haryana	22.50	-27.42	-13.06	24.01	15.01
Punjab	13.74	3.67	-15.89	34.22	53.72
Rajasthan	12.94	-15.90	-3.20	38.22	162.66
UP	1.26	-0.96	-22.09	48.47	342.12
MP	53.24	-10.43	-9.97	177.98	445.42
Delhi	-7.54	-20.18	-0.05	147.29	0
Bihar	9.26	-48.32	-27.63	0.35	0
Orissa	10.19	-7.93	-2.45	13.21	0
West Bengal	83.36	+29.23	-0.15	1254.55	-10.

(The sources used for deriving the table are the website of Central Electricity Authority and Report on the Performance of State Power Utilities published by Power Finance Corporation. The year 2004-05 was chosen as base year for the analysis for the reason that the new electricity act was enacted in the year 2003).

From the Table 5.3, AP and Karnataka are found to be the best performing states. The state of Karnataka was preferred, because the state performed comparatively better than AP in reducing the AT&C losses and meeting the peak demand. When comparing the states which are doing better, Maharashtra and Gujarat, Maharashtra was selected for the reason that despite having private participation in distribution, the AT&C losses have increased over the years and the demand gap also increased.

The study tries to find out the reasons for increase in AT&C losses and increase in demand gap in Maharashtra, though it has increased private participation in power generation and the state being the number one in installed capacity in the country.

When comparing the states like Punjab, Tamil Nadu, West Bengal and Uttar Pradesh which are incurring huge losses annually, Tamil Nadu was preferred as the state could attract more private investments in generation in the country, though the state has not implemented much of reform activities.

Punjab was selected to find out the reasons for less private investment in Generation in the state and politics behind free power supply to farmers. For the research study, the selected states are 1.Karnataka, 2.Maharashtra, 3.Punjab and 4.Tamil Nadu.

Profile of the States: Before analysing the performance of state power utilities of Karnataka, Maharashtra, Punjab and Tamil Nadu, a general profile of the states describing predominant economy activities in the state, demographic details, Per capita Income, Per capita Power Consumption. Contribution of Agriculture and Industry for the economic growth of the state is given in Table 5.4.

Karnataka: Karnataka is situated in the western coast of Indian peninsula between the states Kerala and Maharashtra. The capital of the state, Bangalore is hub of software and biotech industries in India.

Karnataka recorded software exports of ₹ 48700 crore [2] during 2006-07. The state has 66 percent rural population 55.50 percent workers are agricultural labourers.

The state has 60 percent cultivable land and 72 percent of the cultivable area is rain fed and only 28 percent is under irrigation.

Maharashtra: Maharashtra is located in the western coast of India, between Karnataka and Gujarat. About 65 percent of the total workers in the state depend on agriculture and allied activities. The state has been identified as the country's power house and Mumbai, its capital as the centre point of India's financial and commercial markets. Industrial sector occupies prominent position in the economy of Maharashtra. The State ranks first amongst major states in terms of state domestic product and accounts for 15 percent of national income. The state contributes 22 percent India's net value added in organized industrial sector. 40 percent of India's internet users are in Maharashtra and the state accounts for around 30 percent software exports.

Table 5.4: Profile of the States

	Karnataka	Maharashtra	Punjab	Tamil Nadu
Total Population	52850562	96878627	24358999	62405679
Rural Population	34889033	55777647	16096488	34921681
Urban Population	17961529	41100980	8262511	27483998
Literacy rate in percent	66.64	76.88	69.65	73.45
Per capita Income (Rs.)	27291	37081	36759	29958
Gross Per Capita Power Consumption (in Units)	660.04	879.09	1245.23	918.08

(Population figures as per 2001 Census, Per capita power consumption during the year 2004-05

Sources: The Economic Survey, 2007-08, www.cea.nic.in, www.censusindia.gov.in, www.pbplanning.gov.in.

Punjab: The state with only 1.5 percent geographical area of the country produces 22 percent of wheat and 12 percent rice and 12 percent cotton in the country. The cropping intensity of Punjab state is more than 186 percent which has earned a name of food basket of the country and granary of India. It has been pooling 40 to 50 percent of rice and 50-70 percent of wheat for the last two decades. In Punjab, per hectare consumption of fertilizer is 177 kg. as compared to 90 kg at national level. Also Punjab has been awarded national productivity award for agricultural extension services for consecutively ten years from 1991-92 to 2003-04, except in 1999-2000. On the irrigation front about 60 percent of the total irrigated land is served by private and government tube wells and remaining 40 percent is irrigated through canals.

Tamil Nadu: Agriculture continues to be the most predominant sector of the state economy, as 70 percent of the population is engaged in agriculture and allied activities for their livelihood. The total cultivable area in the state was 56.10 million hectares in 2007-08. The major industries in the state are cotton, heavy commercial vehicles, auto components, railway coaches, and power pumps, leather tanning industries, cement, sugar, paper automobiles and safety matches. Knowledge based industries like Information technology and biotechnology have become the thrust area in the industrial scene in Tamil Nadu. In 2006-07, the export from software industry of the state was ₹ 20700 crore and in 2007-08, it was expected to be around ₹ 25000 crore.

(Source: The information about the states are collected from the websites of respective state governments)

Comparison of Net State Domestic Product at Current Prices for the Year 2007-08: Table 5.5 gives the comparative figures Net State Domestic Product and contribution of agriculture and industrial sectors for the state NSDP.

Table 5.5: Comparison of Net State Domestic Product

State	Net State Domestic Product (in crore)	Contribution of Agriculture (in crore)	Percent of NSDP (Agri.)	Contribution of Industries (in crore)	Percent of NSDP (Ind.)
Karnataka	133878.5	37024.4	27.66	32800	24.50
Maharashtra	285773.8	62362.1	21.22	86919	30.42
Punjab	63137.1	43153.1	68.35	17167	27.19
Tamil Nadu	182135.6	38740.0	21.27	47790	26.24

Source: www.rbi.org.in.

Conceptual Framework

New Public Management (NPM): There was a paradigm service delivery over the last few decades. The old public administration, which emphasized direct government delivery, hierarchical control, politics and management, was criticised for slow and inflexible in public service delivery. Public choice theory says that the rent seeking public official with little scope for incentives are unlikely to NPM proponents argued adopted in public sector, it would give the public officials rewards and motivation.

The New Public Entrepreneurialism (NPM): The NPM provided the scope for efficiently by adopting market methods and private sector It propagates public services departments in the government to adopt the values and practices followed in the private sector like efficiency, effectiveness, flexibility, responsiveness, result oriented management, more explicit and measurable performance indicators to improve performance and achieve higher results. The State Electricity Boards were making losses, meet the demand gap which has been increasing need to revamp the functioning the clutch of traditional hierarchical control Consumers Bureaucrats shift in understanding of the role of the states in public sized and separation improve performance of public sector.

That if market type management approach is the right Management primarily focuses on competition and managing the public sector management principles operates standards, more active control based on preset output unable to bring in new investments and every year. There was an urgent of the State Electricity Boards and free they control.

The techniques well developed in the management of private enterprises contracting out, performance based contracts, the creation of autonomous agencies, separation of policy making from implementation, user fees, citizen charters and technology driven sector to various degrees have different interests and expectations from the power sector. They wanted the sector to be efficient and competitive to fulfil power sector before reforms failed to fulfil the needs of all stakeholders due to its rigidity in operation.

Since the quality and reliable of power supply is an

important factor for industrial growth and for the welfare of all citizens, the state governments realized the need to undertake urgent reform measures to speed up the growth of power sector to ensure sustained socio economic development of the state. Policy makers in the government felt that the customer oriented principles as propagated in NPM would help to deliver services better than before. Many state governments, by adopting the concepts of New Public Management, unbundled the State Electricity Boards (SEBs) and corporatized the functioning of the unbundled entities.

Effectiveness: Effectiveness means the (degree of) achievement of higher level objective: outputs, purpose, or goal (Gasper, 2002). Gasper calls it as economic efficiency. In management studies, it is defined as getting the right things done. Government programmes and policies are now designed to focus on effectiveness while implementing schemes for achieving higher level goals. Incentives are provided for effectively implementing the schemes. For example, the Accelerated Power Development and Reforms Programme (APDRP) provides incentive to state governments in the form of grants if the states achieve the targets set for them in reducing the AT&C losses annually.

The success of the reform programmes depends on how effectively the state governments implement the policies. The research paper tries to analyse the effectiveness of different the reform strategies adopted by the Karnataka, Maharashtra, Punjab, and Tamil Nadu in meeting the requirement and improving the service delivery in the states. The effectiveness of the reform programmes are analysed through substantial reduction in AT&C losses, improvement in plant load factor, increase in the installed capacity, meeting the demand gap, collection efficiency, attracting more private investments etc.

Policy Credibility: Orissa, Karnataka and Maharashtra took initiatives in power sector reforms in the country. However, these states could not attract much private investment in power sector, though they had a favourable investment climate in the states. The reason attributed was inconsistency of their policies. 'Decision-makers and implementers inevitably face opposition in attempting to pursue reform initiatives; in consequence, it is important to consider feasibility in terms of support and opposition to change, what stakes they and the governments they serve have in the pursuit of reform, and the political and bureaucratic resources need to sustain such initiatives' (Grindle and Thomas, 1991). Investors should have faith in government's policy announcements and implementation process.

A weak policy environment will drive away potential investors. 'A business environment characterized by incredible rules such as unclear property rights, constant policy surprises and reversals, uncertain contract enforcement, and high corruption most likely translates into lower investment and growth' (Brunetti,1998). 'After the Dhabol fiasco involving the now-defunct Enron corporation and the withdrawal of AES from power distribution in Orissa, it became clear to both domestic and foreign investors that the Indian power sector was not ready for large scale private sector participation' (Tankha and Misal, 2009). Many argue that the Enron debacle in Maharashtra, misadventure in power distribution by AES Corporation in Orissa and Cogentrix withdrawal from Karnataka had not only slowed down private investment in these states, but it also decelerated the reform process in power sector in the country as a whole.

Role of Regulation: The important role of regulation is tariff setting. Tariff setting is a primary instrument of economic regulation. The fundamental objective of tariff determination is to ensure that prices lead to optimum level of investment, operation and consumption in the sector (Garg et al., 2008). After the enactment of Electricity Regulatory Commission act, 1998, regulatory bodies were created both at central and state level in the country. The main function of central regulatory commission is to regulate the tariff of generating companies owned by central government and the state regulatory commissions are to determine the tariff for state utilities, involved in generation, transmission and distribution. Regulatory authorities for public utilities like gas and electricity have been in place in the United States of America for nearly a hundred years. With the privatization of these sectors worldwide, regulatory bodies now exist in almost a hundred countries. 'The assessment of regulatory governance is based on the principles of good regulation. Internationally, different organizations set different indicators of good regulation. It is widely accepted that credibility, legitimacy, and transparency are essential for the success of any regulatory system' (Garg et al., 2008).

Regulation contributes to fill up the gap in public investment. Singh (2007) says that favourable policy environment and regulatory framework are essential for attracting investment in the power sector. Powers sector reforms have been initiated in many countries with a view to create a favourable climate for attracting private investment, which helps to bridge the gap in public investment. The role of regulatory institution is also aimed at mitigating risks associated with long-term investment in the power sector while protecting consumer's interest. With the replacement of public monopolies by private monopolies, the role of independent regulation is ensuring justifiable rates of return to investors while protecting consumers' interest (Singh, 2006).

Regulatory Institutions are required not only for tariff setting, but also to regulate investments in the sector, to mitigate risks associated with new investments and to protect consumer's interest.

Electricity Act, 2003

Background: Table 5.6 gives the annual financial losses of electricity boards during the Huge T& D losses associated with substantial gaps between cost of supply and tariff resulted in heavy losses of State Electricity Boards. The T&D losses were high in the range of 40 to 50 percent. As a result, the biggest sufferers are the consumers in terms of reliability and quality of supply of power. Voltage profile, range of frequency of operations, disruptions of power supply, its restoration promptness to respond to consumer complaints, establishment of new connections–have all suffered in view of the totally non commercial work culture among most of the electricity utilities (Shahi, 2005).

Table 5.6: Financial Losses of SEBs

Year	Annual Losses (₹ in crore)	RoR with subsidy (in percent)	RoR Without Subsidy (in percent)
1991-92	3083	-7.6	-12.7
1997-98	13962	-11.8	-22.9
2000-01	26103	-27.6	-35.1

After the economic reforms initiated in the country during 1991, the economy started growing at the rate of 8-9 percent, whereas power sector was growing at the rate of about only 3 to 5 percent. The sector could not attract investments as the state power utilities were incurring losses.

Enactment of the Act: To sustain growth in the economy, it was felt necessary by the policy makers to accelerate the reform process in the power sector and to help the sector to come out from the problems like high transmission losses, power cuts, power thefts, perennial loss making of the SEBs and to help the economy to sustain its growth. The Government of India came up with a new act, the Electricity Act, 2003, which paved way for radical reforms in the sector, opening up the sector for private investment, open access in transmission and distribution, creation of regulatory commissions to encourage competition. The act has repealed three acts namely (i) The Indian Electricity Act, 1910 (ii) The Electricity (Supply) Act, 1948 and (iii) The Electricity Regulatory Commission Act, 1998.

Important Aspects of Electricity Act, 2003

1. No license is required for generation and captive generation has been freely permitted. Hydro projects exceeding the capital cost notified by the central government however, need concurrence of central electricity authority.
2. No license required for generation and distribution in notified rural areas.
3. Transmission utility at the centre as well as state level, to be a government company-with responsibility for planned and coordinated development of transmission network. Provision for private licenses in transmission.
4. Trading, a distinct activity recognized with thc safcguard of the regulatory commissions being authorized to fix ceilings on trading margins, if necessary.
5. Open access in distribution with provision for surcharge for taking care of current level of cross subsidy with the surcharge being gradually phased out.
6. Distribution licensees would bc frcc to undertake generation and trading.
7. The state governments are required to reorganize the SEBs. However they may continue the SEB as state transmission utilities and licensees for such time the state and central government agree.
8. Setting up of the state electricity regulatory commission made mandatory.
9. An Appellate tribunal to hear the appeals against the decision of the CERC and SERCs.
10. Metering of all electricity supplied made mandatory.
11. Provisions relating to theft of electricity made more stringent.
12. For rural and remote areas stand alone systems for generation and distribution permitted.
13. Thrust to complete rural electrification and provide for management of rural distribution by panchayats, cooperative societies, non-governmental organizations,

franchises, etc. [3]

Open access and multiple distributions are important provisions of this Act which encourages competition in the power sector. In open access, a consumer can get electricity from any generating company or licensee of his/her choice. This facility of providing choices to consumers in accessing electricity generates competition in the sector, ultimately it would lead to supply of quality power at affordable prices. The act provides for framing National electrical policy. Ministry of Power notified National Electricity Policy in the year 2005.

National Electricity Policy: The salient features of national electricity policy are:

1. Access to electricity: available for all household in next five years.
2. Availability of power: demand to be fully met by 2012. Energy and peaking shortages to be overcome and spinning reserve to be available.
3. Supply of reliable and quality power of specified standards in an efficient manner and at reasonable rates.
4. Per capita availability of electricity to be increased to over 1000 units by 2012.
5. Minimum lifeline consumption of 1 unit/household/day as a merit good by year 2012.
6. Financial turnaround and commercial viability of electricity sector.
7. Protection of consumer's interest.

Tariff Policy: The Tariff Policy was notified by the Government of India during 2006. The objectives of the tariff Policy are:

1. Ensure availability of electricity at reasonable and competitive rates.
2. Ensure financial viability of the sector.
3. Promote transparency, consistency, and predictability in regulatory approaches across jurisdictions and minimize perceptions of regulatory risks.
4. Promote competition, efficiency in operations

improvements in the quality of supply.

Strategies, Objectives and Performance of SEBs

Unbundling of SEBs and Corporatization: There was an immediate need to address the problems faced by the State electricity boards (SEBs) and make them viable and sustainable with restructuring. The NPM propagated for bringing in market principles to address the problems faced by the public sector and run the government companies as corporate entities with set goals and time limit in meeting the objectives. The central government enacted the Electricity Act, 2003 which requires states to unbundle SEBs within prescribed time limit.

Karnataka: Orissa was the first state to adopt power sector reforms in the country. With the enactment of Orissa Electricity Reforms Act, 1996, the State Electricity Board was unbundled into three separate entities for generation, transmission and distribution. A number of states followed Orissa model. However, Karnataka claims that they are first state in the country to conceive and setup a professionally managed corporation to plan, construct, and maintain power generation projects in the country. The Karnataka Power Corporation Limited (KPCL) was created in 1970. When KPCL was created in 1970, the installed capacity was 746MW. As on 30.04.2009, the state is having an installed capacity of 6068.52 MW in the state sector, 2314.64 MW in the private sector and 1263.57 MW in the central sector.

Karnataka started the reforms process with the enactment Karnataka Electricity Reforms Act in 1999 and subsequently unbundled State Electricity Board and created Karnataka Power Transmission Corporation Ltd (KPTCL) and Visveshwaraya Vidhyuth Nigama limited. In June 2002, KPTCL was further unbundled into the following four distribution companies.

- Bangalore Electricity Supply Company limited (BESCOM).

- Mangalore Electricity Supply Company limited (MESCOM).
- Hubli Electricity Supply Company limited (HESCOM).
- Gulbarga Electricity Supply Company limited (GESCOM).

Mangalore Electricity Supply Company limited was bifurcated during 2005 and Chamundeswari Electricity Supply Corporation Ltd (CESC) was created. Presently, Karnataka got five distribution companies.

Maharashtra: The Maharashtra State Electricity Board (MSEB) was created in the year 1960 with initial generation capacity of 760 MW. As on 30.04.2009, the state is having an installed capacity of 10563.54 MW in the state sector, 4466.50 MW in the private sector and 5385.43 MW in the central sector. MSEB was unbundled in 2005 and the following companies were established under the holding company of Maharashtra State Electricity Board Holding Co. Ltd.

- Maharashtra State Electricity Generation Company limited (MAHAGENCO).
- Maharashtra State Electricity Transmission Company limited (MAHATRANSCO).
- Maharashtra State Electricity Distribution Company limited (MAHAVITARAN).

Tamil Nadu: The state is having a total installed capacity of 14088.75 MW as on 30.04.2009, with 5697.70 MW from state sector, 5433.85 MW from private sector and 2957.20 MW from central share. The state is yet to un-bundle the SEB. However, the state government has accorded approval in principle for the reorganization of TNEB by the establishment of a holding company by the name TNEB ltd and two subsidiary companies namely Tamil Nadu Transmission Corporation Ltd (TANTRANSCO) and Tamil Nadu Generation and Distribution Corporation Ltd (TANGEDCO). The state has already hired the services of a consultancy firm namely M/s Feedback ventures private ltd for providing 'Consultancy services for restructuring of TNEB' on

02.04.2009 and the reports to be submitted within three months. [4]

The state has been providing free power supply to farmers from the year 2003, the same year the new electricity act was enacted in the country which proposed radical reforms in the sector including phasing out subsidies. The state had to face stiff resistance from employee's organizations as well as pressure groups for unbundling the board. Now with almost all the states unbundled the board, including the communist ruled state of west Bengal, the state is left with less options. The state has obtained extension for unbundling till December 2009. Employee organizations of TNEB made visits to neighbouring states to study the present status of the companies after unbundling and to clear doubts and misconceptions on the functioning of the companies, working conditions and problems faced by the employees during and after transition.

Punjab: Punjab electricity Board was formed in the year 1959 under the Electricity Supply Act 1948. Subsequently with the reorganization of the erstwhile state of Punjab under the Punjab reorganization Act 1966, the present form came into existence with effect from 1st May 1967. [5] The Board started with modest installed capacity of 62 MW. As on 30.04.2009, it is having a total installed capacity of 6780.01 MW with 5073.72 MW in the state sector, 37.57 MW in the private sector and 1668.72 MW in the Central Sector. The state is yet to unbundle the SEB. The state is facing strong opposition from farmers associations and employees associations of PSEB for unbundling, which they perceive that it would affect their interest in the near future. On 8th September, 2009, one person was killed in police firing in Chandigarh, when police opened fire on agitating farmers against the government's move for unbundling the SEB. Due to vehement opposition of employees union of PSEB and farmers associations, the state government has requested the central government for extension of time for unbundling. The central government has granted time up to December, 2009 for unbundling the SEB.

Private Sector Participation in Generation: Table 5.7 gives the details of private sector participation in the selected States of Karnataka, Maharashtra, Punjab and Tamil Nadu as on 30.4.2009.

Table 5.7: Private Sector Participation in Generation (in MW)

State	Thermal	Hydro	RES	Total
Karnataka	886.50	-	1428.14	2314.64
Maharashtra	2080	444	1942.50	4466.50
Punjab	-	-	37.57	37.57
Tamil Nadu	1164.76	-	4269.09	5433.85

Source: www.cea.nic.in.

Karnataka: In Karnataka, KPCL Karnataka power corporation is looking after the after generation activity in the state from 1970. Many activities took place in the distribution sector, but capacity addition in generation from private sector was quite less. TATA Power Company is having generating capacity of 81.30 MW, RAYALASEEMA CO with 27.80 MW. Major supply comes from Independent power producers from non conventional energy resources projects, mainly wind energy at 1765.27 MW.6 Jindal Power Company has set up a 260 MW thermal power plant at Torangallu in Karnataka.

Maharashtra: Maharashtra has three private companies namely, Tata Power Co., Bombay Suburban Electric Supply, BSES, now it is Reliance Energy, Brihanmumbai Electric Supply and Transport (BEST) are involved in generation as well as distribution in the city of Mumbai. TPC is having an Installed generation capacity 1774 MW, Reliance Energy is having 500, and DPC is having 728 MW.

Tamil Nadu: In Tamil Nadu, about 4379.64 MW is produced in the private sector using renewable energy sources mainly from wind energy. The generation of power from wind mills was introduced in Tamil Nadu during the year 1986 by installing 20 numbers of 55 KW windmills at Mullaikadu in

Tuticorin district as demonstration project under the financial assistance of Ministry of Non Conventional Energy Sources (MNES) now renamed as Ministry of New & Renewable Energy (MNRE). From 1986 to 1993, the Board had installed around 120 windmills to a capacity of 19.355 MW as demonstration projects. On successful performance of these demonstration windmills and various benefits in the forms of subsidies and concessions extended by the Government of India and Government of Tamil Nadu, private developers shown keep interest in this sector and started investing from the year 1990 onwards. Initially the purchase price was fixed at ₹ 1 per unit during 1990 and the same was fixed at ₹ 2.25 per unit from 1.12.1995 with annual escalation of 5 percent for next five years.

During September 2001, it was fixed at ₹ 2.70 per unit without escalation, the Tamil Nadu Electricity Regulatory Commission has issued tariff order No. 3 dated 15.5.2006 on which the wind mills are categorized under two groups, the wind mills commissioned before 15.5.2006, was under Group I, for which purchase price was fixed at ₹ 2.75 per unit. The windmills commissioned dafter 15.5. 2006 came under Group II, for which the purchase price was fixed at ₹ 2.90 per unit. The private developers are permitted to wheel the energy generated by their windmills to their HT industries or their group companies, situated anywhere in Tamil Nadu. They are also permitted to bank the surplus energy for their future use. The wheeling and banking charges are fixed at 5 percent each by the Regulatory Commission during the year 2006. [7]

Punjab: The state is having negligible presence of private investors in Power sector. The state is having 37.57 MW under renewable energy sources.

Private Participation in Distribution: Among the selected states, only in Maharashtra, private sector is involved in distribution. In Maharashtra, there are three service providers in the Mumbai area, Tata Power Company Ltd., BEST Ltd., BSES Ltd. (Reliance Energy), who are involved in power distribution. The remaining part of the state is served by MAHAVITARAN, the state owned distribution company. The state introduced Distribution Franchise; which is considered to be a new experiment in the country, and handed over the responsibility of power distribution in Bhiwandi circle to a private company, Torrent Power, on agreed terms and conditions for a specific period of time. The experiment has paid off well and the textile town of Bhiwandi has been enjoying a better quality of power since 2006. The experiment is considered to be a successful initiative with T&D losses coming down to under 20 percent from 44 percent and the collection efficiency increased to 97 percent from 65 percent. However, when the same model sought to be implemented in Nagpur by Crompton Greaves Company, local groups opposed it and the case is pending in courts. MAHAVITARAN has put on hold its plans to implement the model in Ulhasnagar (Near Mumbai), Aurangabad, and Jalgaon. Other states such as Uttar Pradesh are now implementing the model. Torrent Power has been awarded the franchise for Kanpur while franchise for cities such as Agra is expected to be announced soon (Gadgil, 2009).

Regulatory Commission: As per the Electricity Act 2003, most of the states have formed electricity regulatory commission. The First regulatory commission in the country was formed in Orissa during 1998. The Orissa regulatory commission had set many examples for other states to follow. The state regulatory commissions issued tariff orders, addressed issues like efficiency, competition and reliability of the service in the sector which went unnoticed so far. Punjab SERC issued tariff order for the year 2008-09. The Punjab State Electricity Board has been incurring huge losses, with the free power being provided to farmers. The regulatory commission insisted the government to pay the subsidy amount to SEB before issuance of tariff order. In Karnataka and Maharashtra, hearings are being held to decide the tariff for the current year. In Tamil Nadu, Tariff order was issued in

2003. After that no revision has been effected.

The significant achievement of the regulatory system is giving voice to consumers and transparency to the tariff making process. In public hearings, consumers could raise their concerns and contribute constructively to the regulatory process. Singh (2006) says regulatory system has given a much needed voice to consumer's point of view which has hitherto been missing from the system. The consumer organisations come to the public hearing well prepared and support their arguments with facts and figures, which forces the state power utilities to work hard in convincing the regulatory commission.

Meeting the Objectives/Performance Indicators:

Reduction of Losses: One of the objectives the power sector reform is to reduce T& D and AT&C losses. In Karnataka, during the year 2007-08, the T& D losses were around 25.17 percent and AT&C losses were around 31.33 percent Among the distribution companies, BESCOM, Bangalore is able to reduce T & D losses from 26.44 percent in 2004 to 16.9 percent in 2009 and AT&C losses from 34.26 percent 2006 to 20.58 percent in 2009. MESCOM has done well in reducing TD losses. During the year 2006-07, it was recognized as one of the best distribution companies in India and placed at number 3 by Government of India. [8] The company is proposing to reduce its distribution losses to 12.90 percent in 2009-10 from 12.95 percent in 2008-09. However, Hubli and Gulbarga based distribution companies are having higher AT& C losses. They are also making all efforts in reducing the losses. As on August 2009, HESCOM is having AT&C losses at 25.23 percent. [9] GESCOM brought down distribution losses to 22.61 percent in 2008-09 from 30.84 percent in 2007-08. [10]

In Maharashtra, the losses are varying from 27.98 percent in the year 2005 to 39.35 percent during the year 2007. As per the annual report of MAHAVITARAN 2006-07, the T&D losses were reduced from 31.78 percent in 2005-06 to 29.60 percent in 2006-07. The company is taking efforts to reduce the losses with various measures such as replacing faulty meters, introducing spot billing, conducting antitheft drives, dedicated police stations, and appointment of distribution franchise.

Tamil Nadu and Punjab have been consistently reducing the losses during the reform period. The states are implementing projects in towns under GOI sponsored Accelerated Power Development and Reforms Programme. Once the projects are implemented, the distribution in the urban areas will be reduced substantially in the states.

Meeting the Demand Gap: In almost all the states, there is shortfall of power supply. From official sources, in Tamil Nadu, there is a peak deficit of 2000 MW, in Karnataka, about 1700 MW, and Punjab is having a shortage of 1400 MW. 'Maharashtra is having a demand supply gap of 4500-5500 MW during peak hours' (Gadgil, 2009).

Profitability: The generation and transmission companies in Karnataka and Maharashtra are making profits. The SEBs of Tamil Nadu and Punjab are making losses. Karnataka Power Corporation ltd made a profit of ₹ 206 crore during the year ending March 2008 as against ₹ 322 during the previous year. The Maharashtra Government made a profit of ₹ 269 crore.

The financial losses in Tamil Nadu is due to many factors like, no tariff revision since 2003, free power to agriculture, high purchase price, increase in raw materials and input costs. The reasons are more or less applicable to many SEBs. However, corporatization helped states like Orissa, AP, Maharashtra, Gujarat, and Delhi to perform better.

Installed Capacity: At the time of Independence, the country was having an initial installed capacity of about 1400 MW and in every decade the capacity has been doubled to meet the increase in demand.

The capacity addition has been doubled between 1990 and 2007 due to the spur in the growth of the economy after the reforms initiated in the year 1991. After the reform programmes initiated in the country, in general, there is an increase in installed capacity of power generation. The installed capacity as on 31.04.2009 is 1,48,265.41 MW out of which Hydro-36877.76 MW, Thermal-94025.24 MW, Nuclear-4120 MW, and Renewable-13242.41 MW.

Maharashtra has not added any capacity addition in generation from 1998 to 2008 in the state sector. The state had recently added 500 MW, from Parli and Paras thermal plants with 250 MW each.

To meet its supply demand gap of 4500-5500 MW during peak hours, the MAHAGENCO planning to go for new projects as well as capacity addition in existing plants and by 2012 they are sure to meet the gap. The state is having an ambitious capacity addition programme of 3250 MW from state sector, 1460 from IPPs and 1683 from central share. There is not much increase seen in the state sector in Tamil Nadu.

But the state attracted new private investments, particularly in wind energy generation. Similar is the case with Karnataka. The private participation has come mainly from renewable wind energy sources.

The state has been providing an attractive purchase price for private generators in wind energy. In Karnataka, there is an increase of 24.24 percent from 2004-05. In Maharashtra, it is about 8.2 percent and in Punjab the increase is 13.74 percent.

Private Participation: Spurred by the sustained economic growth, rise in income levels, and increased availability of goods and services, India's incremental energy demand for the next decade is projected to be amongst the highest in the world.

This increasing energy demand also translates into higher demand for electricity. The electricity sector forms the backbone for the economic development of a country. As per Ministry of power, GOI, in order to support a rate of growth of GDP of around 7 percent per annum, the rate of growth of power supply needs to be over 10 percent annually (TERI, 2006). Unless private investments come in the sector, it would be difficult to chive the growth as projected for power sector.

Tamil Nadu and Karnataka have increased private sector participation mainly from wind energy sources with attractive power purchase prices. Maharashtra is having three private companies in power generation in Mumbai. The Enron experience in Maharashtra and Cogentrix pullout from Karnataka did not augur well in the sector to send a positive message to the long term private investors to make new investments in power projects in India. Now, with regulatory commissions taking roots and encouraged with positive leadership in the states, many private companies are participating in power generation in the states. The Initial Public Offerings (IPOs) floated by the power companies recently are oversubscribed.

Improvement in Collection Efficiency: After unbundling, collection efficiency has increased in Maharashtra and Karnataka. Interestingly, Tamil Nadu and Punjab, which are yet to unbundle, are doing well with higher collection efficiently.

Improvement in Plant Operational Performance: There is a visible improvement in operational performance of the state utilities. Tamil Nadu and Punjab have shown improvement in PLF during the period from 2004-05 to 2006 states.

Role and Contribution of Governments

Role of Central Government: Electricity is a subject listed in the concurrent list; both states and centre can make laws. As per the Electricity Supply Act 1948, State Electricity Boards were created and the electricity sector was left to the states to mange. Seeing the growing demand for power and the limited capacity in the states to meet the peak demand, during 1976, the central government entered in the Generation field by starting public sector company, NTPC to supplement state capacities in the generation. Subsequently companies like PFC, Power Grid, and NHPC were created according to the needs of the situation. As on 30.04.2009, the country is having total installed capacity of 148265.41 MW. The Ministry of Power, Government of India is now responsible for the administration of Electricity Act, 2003 and Energy Conservation Act, 2001.

Functions and Responsibilities of Central Government

1. General policy in power sector and issues related to energy policy and coordination thereof.
2. Matters related to hydroelectric power, thermal and transmission system network and distribution system.
3. Rural electrification
4. Power supply development schemes/programmers/ decentralized and distributed generation
5. Matters relating to energy conservation and energy efficiency.

In addition to providing policy guidelines in the sector, the central government, from time to time, comes out with special schemes for development and management of power sector in the country.

With the increase in power generation and consumption, per capita consumption has been increasing over the years. The national electricity policy, which was announced on 12.02 2005, states that per capita consumption should be 1000 units by 2012. Going by the average annual increase of 30 units over the years, it may be difficult to reach 1000 units by 2012. At the maximum, the country could reach between 850 to 900 units by 2012. There will be a shortfall of 100-150 units in the annual per capita consumption. However, the interest shown by many private players in the power sector may help to reach the target, if the new projects envisaged in the sector including the Ultra Mega Power Projects are successfully executed and commissioned in time.

Accelerated Power Development and Reforms Programme (APDRP): The distribution sector could not attract much private investments due to higher T&D losses. 'The poor state of state owned distribution utilities, weak link in the supply chain of electricity, undermines the process of reforms and seems t have hampered private investment in the sector' (Singh, 2007). Realising the need to reduce losses in the distribution sector, APDRP was launched in the year 2002 -03 as additional central assistance to states. This scheme has an investment outlay of about ₹ 50000 crore with a target to bring down AT&C losses to 15 percent. The focus of the programme is on establishment of baseline data and fixation of accountability and reduction of AT&C losses through strengthening and up gradation of sub-transmission and distribution network and adoption of information technology.

The schemes are taken up into stages. Part-A includes project for establishment of baseline data and IT applications for energy accounting/auditing and IT-based consumer service centres. Part-B includes regular distribution strengthening projects including segregation of feeders. Overall the distribution sector has shown a move towards lower AT&C losses in the past there to four years. AT&C losses have been reported below 20 percent in 215 APDRP towns in the country of which 163 towns have brought AT&C losses below 15 percent. [11] The Southern Power Distribution company of Andhra Pradesh reduced its losses to 11.48 percent in 2007-08 from 12.66 percent in 2006-07, which was the lowest distribution loss in the country. [12]

Power Exchanges: Power exchanges are formed for transparent, neutral and efficient electronic form of power trading. Indian Energy Exchange (IEX) and Power Exchange India ltd (PXIL) started in the year 2008. 'An energy exchange could help to bridge nationwide demand supply mismatch in the sector by allowing surplus regions to trade power at optimal price with all buyers'. [13] According to Minster for Power, India, during the year, the total number of members and clients IEX have crossed 130 and over 3600 million units of power worth ₹ 3000 crore has been traded through the power exchange. [14]

Ultra Mega Power Projects (UMPP): The Government

of India has taken an initiative for facilitating the development of a few ultra mega power projects of about 4000 MW capacity using super critical technology, under tariff based competitive bidding route. For meeting the growing needs of the economy, generation capacity is to double itself in every ten years for next three decades at least. As such there is need to develop large capacity projects at the national level to meet the requirements of the states, under the competitive bidding guidelines. Development of UMPP is one step in that direction' (PFC Report, 2009). Out of nine identified projects in various states, three projects, Sasan–Madhya Pradesh, Mundra-Gujarat and Krishnapatnam–Andhra Pradesh were awarded and remaining projects are being pursued (GOI, Ministry of Power).

Achievements at National Level

1. Reduction of AT&C losses from 38.86 percent in 2001-02 to 30.56 percent in 2007-08.
2. Consumer metering from 78 percent to 89 percent Installed capacity-1,49,391 MW in 31.5.2009 from 66,086MW in 1990 (1, 01,708 in 2001).
3. Per capita consumption (kWh) increased from 612.50 in 2004-05 to 704.2 in 2007-08.
4. All India thermal PLF (Plant Load Factor) increased from 74.8 percent in 2004-05 to 82.53 percent in April 2009. [15]

Role of State Governments: The role of state government is very important in taking the lead and accelerating the reform process. The investment climate and political environment are essential for attracting private investments in the states. In 2008, Tata Motors had to shift its NANO-mini car production factory from West Bengal to Gujarat due to violent protests from public supported by political parties.

In recent survey on investment climate in the states, conducted by India Today, a weekly magazine published from New Delhi, Punjab ranked 3, while Himachal Pradesh and Gujarat ranked 1 and 2 based on criteria such as availability of skilled manpower, better labour climate, lower level of sickness, Government capital expenditure on a per capita basis, per capita commercial bank credit, and gross capital formation in the manufacturing sector on a per capita basis. The ranking is given in Table 5.8.

Table 5.8: State Ranking in Investment Climate

State	Score in 2009	Rank in 2009	2008	2007	2006	2005	2004	2003
Punjab	4.47	3	5	8	6	3	1	3
Maharashtra	4.17	4	2	2	4	7	6	5
Tamil Nadu	4.16	5	4	7	8	9	7	7
Karnataka	3.80	6	7	6	7	6	10	6

Source: India Today, September 28, 2009: www.indiatoday.in.

Andhra Pradesh and Gujarat are doing well in due to the presence of strong leadership in the state. In both the states, T&D losses were reduced to a great extent, power subsidy is minimized and collection efficiency has increased. The two utilities are making profit after implementing up the reform measures. The Gujarat model of feeder separation for agriculture is being followed in Karnataka, Maharashtra. In fact, the leadership in Orissa state took all the initiative to undertake the reform process first in the country, which set an example to other states to follow. Strong leadership and the favourable political and business environment are essential for any reform process to succeed in the states.

New Initiatives by State Governments

Distribution Franchise: The Electricity Act 2003 provides for handing over the responsibility to franchisee to distribute on behalf of the distribution company. Maharashtra used this provision for the textile town, Bhiwandi circle and Torrent Power; a private company took over the distribution in the town in 2007. The franchisee brought down AT&C losses from 56.4 percent to 37 percent, reduced transformer failure rate from 44 percent to 9 percent, collection efficiency increased from 66 percent to 89 percent, reduced the proportion of unmetered consumers from almost 50 percent to about 10 percent and increased the proportion of billed consumers from 46 percent to 87 percent. The private company is making profit from the circle, whereas under MSEB the circle was making losses to the tune of Rs. 30 crore annually (Tankha and Misal, 2009).

The MAHAVITARAN wants to emulate the success of the Bhiwandi experiment to Nagpur, Nasik and other towns. Due to local politics, the reform process is delayed from implementing in other towns in Maharashtra. However, Karnataka and UP are taking up Bhiwandi experience in their cities for implementation.

Police Stations: Maharashtra state set up six dedicated police stations at six theft prone towns to deal with investigation of power thefts. These police stations started functioning from 2006. As a positive impact of dedicated police stations, a total of 2133 FIRs have been lodged assessing for ₹ 1667.32 lakh from September 2006 to March 2007. With a result of strict monitoring and vigilance, the company has brought down AT&C losses from 31.78 percent in 2006-06 to 29.60 percent in 2006-07. [16]

Separation of Agriculture Feeders: Maharashtra has completed separation agricultural feeders to the extent of 60 percent. Karnataka has started recently the separation of agricultural feeders. Punjab has completed the process of feeder separation. Tamil Nadu is also following other states. The feeder separation will help agriculture to get reliable and quality power supply. Till now, the supply to all consumers; domestic, industry and agriculture is mixed up. The utilities are finding difficult to run the distribution system effectively as demand is always more in rural areas for agriculture. When power is switched off for agriculture usage, everyone in the supply line, domestic and rural industries suffer in the process. The feeder separation will help to regulate power supply to different consumers effectively and account properly for the usage of power through computerized metering.

Findings and Observations

Status of Reforms in the States: Table 5.9 provides the status of reforms activities undertaken by the states.

Table 5.9: Status of Reforms in the States

Reform	Karnataka	Maharashtra	Punjab	Tamil Nadu
Unbundling of SEBs	√	√	X	X
Corporatization of Companies	√	√	X	X
Private Sector in Generation	√	√	√	√
Private Sector in Distribution	X	√	X	X
Regulatory Commission	√	√	√	√

Remarks:

- Unbundling: Tamil Nadu has taken initiates to unbundle the board.
- Generation: Tamil Nadu got maximum generation from wind energy sources under private sector; Punjab is having very negligible quantity of power generation from private sector (about 37MW), mainly from wind energy.
- Distribution: Maharashtra has handed over distribution of Bhiwandi circle to a private agency under franchise model, in addition to power distribution by private corporate sector in Mumbai urban areas.

Findings:

Unbundling of SEBs: Maharashtra and Karnataka unbundled the SEBs and corporatized generation, transmission and distribution companies. Tamil Nadu and Punjab were given extension time up to December, 2009 for unbundling. Tamil Nadu has taken initiative to unbundle the Board by engaging the services private consultants to advise the Board in this regard. Punjab is facing stiff resistance from employees association and farmers lobby. However, the chairman of PSEB is of the view that unbundling of the board will enhance the efficiency and accountability of the Board. [17] When we do have prerequisite understanding of the business cycle, the implication of out analysis is that policy makers should follow rule rather than have discretion. The reason that they should not have discretion is not that they are stupid or evil but, rather, that discretion implies selecting the decision which is best, given the current situation. Such behaviour either results in consistent but sub-optimal planning or in economic instability' (Kydland and Prescott, 1977). The policy makers in Punjab and Tamil Nadu might think that the postponing the decision of unbundling the SEBs is the best action in the current political situation. But, when comparing the advantages, states like Karnataka and Maharashtra are having in unbundling the boards, the delay in unbundling may prove to be costly in long run.

Meeting the Peak Demand: Among the states visited, all the states are having peak deficit. Maharashtra is topping with 4500 to 5500 MW peak deficit. The state could not attract investments after Enron debacle. Now the peak demand by 2012. Similarly, other states have ongoing projects and investment plans along with participation from private sector, are confident of meeting the peak demand in coming years.

Generation: Since all these years the SEBs were making losses, the Boards could not generate required funds for new projects. With unbundling of the Boards and separate tariff fixation at each level, generation, transmission and distribution, the generation and transmission companies started making profit. Financial institutions like PFC are willing to help the companies in new investments as the companies are making profit. Making use of the opportunities, corporatized companies in Maharashtra and Karnataka have chalked out plans to add capacity addition to meet the peak demand within two or three years.

Distribution: After reforms, the distribution companies

are getting much needed attention. The states are making use of the central programme APDRP and trying to reduce AT&C losses. Interestingly, SEBs in Tamil Nadu and Punjab are performing well when compared to unbundled SEBs, Maharashtra and Karnataka. In urban areas, DISCOMs are doing well by effectively reducing AT&C losses, whereas in rural areas, the losses are still high at about 30 percent. Separation agricultural feeders and more Distribution Franchise in urban areas would help to reduce AT&C losses in future.

To have operational advantage, distribution companies are formed region/zone wise. Some officials in the corporations felt that it affects the work environment and efficiency of the staff. Many staff members are reluctant to work in rural areas leaving metropolitan cities like Bangalore. They also quote that urban based DISCOM company is making higher profits due to more customer base than the rural based distribution companies. If the situation continues, the urban areas will grow faster with more investments and availability of funds and rural areas will continue to suffer with shortage of funds, even to meet routine maintenance.

Private participation: After the initial unpleasant experiences in the power sector, the response of private sector is quite cautious in investing in power sector. Again the fluctuation in import prices for gas, oil and naphtha in the international market, single buyer, power purchase agreements are causes of worry for private investors to enter in to the market. Now, many private companies like Reliance Power, Jindal Power Company, Adani Power Company have shown interest in the development of power sector and entered in to capital markets for mobilising funds.

Tamil Nadu and Karnataka have attracted more private participation in renewable energy sources by paying higher purchase price. Tamil Nadu SEB buys power mainly from privately owned wind mills at a higher cost and supply at lower prices to meet the growing demand thus the board incurring heavy losses. The official sources quoted the same reason for BESCOM, Karnataka incurring losses last year. The political party in power wanted to provide uninterrupted power supply, by purchasing power at higher price, to gain advantage during the election.

The strategy adopted by these states is to attract more private investments, even at higher purchase price. The state power utilities are hopeful that when more players enter the field and regulatory mechanism takes deep root, the prices will get stabilized and tariff will be rationalized. Their strategy to attract private investors by higher purchase price will help the states in meeting the long term demand needs effectively.

Regulatory Commissions: Though, the regulatory commissions in the states are criticised for politicization with the appointment retired bureaucrats as chairman and members, it has been seen that commissions are taking all necessary efforts to protect the interest of consumers. Surprisingly, many of the members of the commission are either retired bureaucrats or one way or other associated with the power sector prior to their joining in the commission .While glancing through the orders passed by the regulatory commission in the states, it was seen that most of the orders passed in favour of consumers. During interaction with officers in the state power utilities, they said that the regulatory authority protects the interest of consumers at the cost of the board/company's interest. They also opined that regulatory authority is quite strict and does not allow any wasteful expenditure, which is seen by the commission as additional burden to consumers. It shows the commission's intricate role in protecting the consumer's interest at the same time not neglecting the problems of the electricity boards/companies. While interacting with private sector executive, he also expressed his satisfaction with the functioning of Maharashtra State Regulatory Commission and with the tariff fixed for his company, which is involved in generation and distribution of power in Mumbai.

Now, with regulatory commissions, taking over the role of government, in granting permission for new investments, projects, tariff fixation, the role of state government is limited to facilitating the growth of the sector by providing required financial and human resources, but the responsibilities of the regulatory commission have become enormous in promoting and regulating the sector.

Policy Issues and Challenges

Autonomy of Boards/Corporations: Most of the SEBs and power companies are managed by the full time directors, mainly serving bureaucrats appointed by government. Rarely private, independent members are appointed to the board. In Karnataka, the chairman of the board is Chief Minister and vice- chairman is the Minster for Energy. In Maharashtra, a retired bureaucrat was appointed as part-time chairman of the generation company. It is argued that the appointment of political bosses in the board invariably affects the independent thinking of the board/corporation. But, it has also got advantages; having chief minister as chairman helps to take major policy decision without much hassles and facilitates in bringing in major investments in the sector. However, while dealing with policy issues such as subsidized/free power to agriculture, poor families, and effecting tariff revision, the political bosses may not be very supportive to a decision which may affect their vote bank politics.

Independence of Regulatory Institutions: Independent regulatory institution is prerequisite for creating a favourable environment to attract potential investors and for rationalisation of tariff. 'Regulatory institutions developed in India continue to live under political influence due to influence over appointment of regulators and financial dependence on governments. This problem is more serious in case of state level regulatory institutions' (Singh, 2005). In Tamil Nadu, Karnataka, Maharashtra and Punjab, the chairman of the commission are retired IAS officers. Most of members are retired government servants, either worked or connected with the sector in their official capacities. It is criticised that since the chairman and members are appointed by the parties in power, they are reluctant to take radical decisions with regard to tariff revision. In Tamil Nadu, the last tariff revision was done in the year 2003. The SEB is making huge losses. The officials opined that if the board is allowed to revise the tariff on par with the neighbouring states, it would recover the losses in two years time. In these kinds of situations, the role of the commission would play an important role in improving the financial conditions of the SEB, if the commission exercises its powers and remain active and independent.

Issue of Power Subsidy: After green revolution started in the country in late 1960s, the use of high yielding crop varieties required more inputs of water and fertilizer in fields. In states like Tamil Nadu and Punjab, green revolution helped to harvest 2-3 crops in a year. Much of the early irrigation projects were large, public funded ones involving surface water sources, but especially in the 1980s, ground water pumping on individual farms using electrical or diesel pump sets became increasingly popular. Irrigation of both forms was widely credited with significant increases in food protection in the country. Power subsidy was first offered by Andhra Pradesh in the late 1970s, followed by Tamil Nadu, Maharashtra, Karnataka, Punjab and many other states (Dubash and Rajan, 2001). Presently, in Tamil Nadu, Punjab and Karnataka, power is being provided to farmers at free of cost. The agricultural lobby is quite strong in these states and the government is forced to listen to the demands of the farmers. Table 5.10 gives the details of power subsidy provided by Punjab and Haryana during the year 2008-09.

Issue of Cross Subsidy: Electricity is provided at subsidised rates to agricultural and domestic consumers in most of the states. The commercial and industrial consumers are charged at higher rates to make up the revenue losses incurred as a result of subsidized power given to domestic consumers and farmers. Table 5.11 gives the details of cross subsidy in the year 2007-08.

Table 5.10: Power Subsidy in Punjab and Haryana

How it was in 2008-2009?			
State	Total food grains (Lakh tones)	Value (₹ in crore)	Power Subsidy (₹ in crore)
Punjab	227.86	21337.12	2600
Haryana	74.25	7425.00	2800

Source: www.tribuneindia.com dated 30.6.2009.

Table 5.11: Cross Subsidy in the Year 2007-08

State	Agriculture (in percent)		Industry (in percent)	
Maharashtra	22	11	45	56
Karnataka	36	9	23	35
Punjab	31	24	34	52
Tamil Nadu	20	-	40	59

Source: PFC Report.

Policy issues and Suggestions for Policy Making: After the reform process initiated in the power sector, visible improvements could be seen in the operational efficiency of the system. SEBs and corporations reduced AT&C losses substantially, PLF increased or sustained between 70-80 percent, collection efficiency of all SEBs/companies increased, some DISCOM even achieved 100 percent collection efficiency. However, the power sector faces issue such as shortage of power, free power, subsidised power, cross subsidy and the problem of tariff rationalisation. To meet the demand of all consumers, more investment is required. Unless the state owned power Utilities generate income on their own, it would be difficult to go for new projects in generation, transmission and distribution. To have a steady growth in the sector, the above said issues are to be addressed in a phased manner. It would be very difficult to implement any reform model without appreciating and understanding the ground realities.

Is Free/Subsidized Power to Agriculture a Problem?: India is a developing country with more than 60 percent of the people involved in agriculture, which contributes about 20 percent of GDP and ensures food security of the country, which has more than 1 billion population. The agriculture provides maximum employment in the rural areas. The growth agriculture from 1950-51 to 2007-08 is given in the Table 5.12. It is felt that the rate of growth about 2 to 4 percent per annum is not sufficient to accelerate growth in all sectors of a developing economy like India.

Table 5.12: Growth of Food Grain Production

Year	Food Grain Production (Million Tonnes)	Percent Increase
1950	50.83	-
1960	82.02	61.36
1970	108.42	32.19
1980	129.59	19.53
1990	176.39	36.11
2000	196.81	11.58
2007	230.78	17.26

Source: www.rbi.org.in.

In order to increase agricultural productivity and to have a steady growth in agriculture, free/subsidised power supply is being given to agriculture by many state governments. The power supply provided to pump sets in the states is given in Table 5.13.

In a recent survey on agriculture in the states, conducted by India Today, a weekly magazine published from New Delhi, the states, Punjab and Haryana topped the list with ranks 1 and 2 respectively. Tamil Nadu ranked 3 while Maharashtra and Karnataka ranked 7 and Karnataka at 5. The criteria are yield of food grain production, net irrigated area, electricity consumption on a per capita basis for agriculture, usage of new technologies and credit availability to farmers. The ranking is given in Table 5.14.

Table 5.13: Duration of Power Supply to Agriculture

State	Three Phase Supply (in hours)	Single Phase Supply (in hours)
Maharashtra	13 to 15	18
Karnataka	6	6
Punjab	7.79	-
Tamil Nadu	10	14

Table 5.14: States' Ranking in Agriculture

State	Score in 2009	Rank in 2009	2008	2007	2006	2005	2004	2003
Punjab	8.75	1	1	1	1	1	1	1
Tamil Nadu	5.42	3	3	2	3	3	3	3
Karnataka	2.96	5	5	6	6	6	7	6
Maharashtra	1.92	7	7	7	10	11	15	9

Source: India Today September 28, 2009: www.indiatoday.in.

The survey is as an indication that the states, Punjab, Haryana and Tamil Nadu, which are extending free/subsidised power to the farmers, are topping in the agriculture sector performance in the country. From the Table 5.11, power subsidy in Punjab and Haryana, it can be seen that the states Punjab, Haryana contributed food grains worth about ₹ 21,000 crore and ₹ 7400 crore respectively for the common pool of the country. While interacting with officials working in the powers sector in the selected states, some of them are of the opinion that free or subsidized power to agriculture is the main obstacle for accelerating the power sector reform processes in the states. For all the ills faced by the power sector, it may not be very appropriate to blame everything on free power to agriculture, which remains the back bone of the country's economic development. So, a careful analysis is required before coming to a conclusion that subsidized or free power to farming community is a stumbling block in the progress of the sector.

How Rational is the Tariff Structure in India?: Power sector reforms helped the states moving in the right direction of improving the overall system efficiency and reducing AT&C losses and rationalization tariff structure. With regard to rationalization of tariff structure, the question arises, what is a rational tariff structure? Everyone think of the uniform or average sale price at distribution points and fails to recognize the difference in generation costs for various modes. While hydro power can be generated at 50 paise per unit, the price of thermal power, produced from naphtha or gas goes up to 12 rupees per unit. Whether it is rational if the power generated from a hydro power plant and power purchased from a high cost gas/naphtha plant could be clubbed together in a common pool and selling at a same average price for a poor farmer in the village and a shopping mall in the urban metropolitan.

Reserving Hydro Power for Agriculture: Power generation in India started with constructing hydro power stations across the country. Now, power is produced from various modes using variety of raw materials as inputs. Still, the power produced from the Hydro is comparatively cheaper. It will be more appropriate and rational if the tariff structure is based on ability to buy or the purchasing power of the consumers. Everyone in the society cannot be treated on the same pedestal while deciding the issue of power tariffs. The cheapest power produced from hydro which is around 25 percent of the country's total generation, which is more or less equivalent to the agriculture's consumption of 25 to 30 percent. It would be more appropriate if the power generated from hydro sector is invariably reserved for the use of farming sector. The selling price may be the cost of generation plus (ROR) the rate of return on investment, 14 to 16 percent, as allowed by the Electricity Act.

It is generally agreed that the hydro power is cheaper power and pollution free. However, the initial investments costs are quite high when comparing with other modes of power generation. The NHPC charges about ₹ 2.50 per unit for the hydro power. Private investors in small hydro power generation sector are selling power at about ₹ 3.50 per unit. In India, most of the hydro power plants were constructed during 1950s and 1960s. The capital cost might have been recovered long back. World Bank [18] in its assessment report on power sector in India mentioned that the operation's cost of old hydro plant, Bhakra Nangal plant is only ₹ 0.10 per unit. The initial cost might be higher in hydro power generation. But once established, the operational cost is very less in the hydro sector, which can effectively meet the demand of agricultural power consumption.

Power Tariff and Ability to Pay: Once the cheapest mode of power is reserved for agriculture, the next cheaper power, from thermal or other resources, shall be reserved for rural consumers. The next level of power should be sold to industries in the rural areas and sub urban consumers. The urban industries should pay more than the urban domestic consumers. If shopping malls and big industrial units in the urban areas need more power during the peak hours, they should buy the power available from private producers or from the government companies at a higher price and the price may be the cost of generation plus rate of return on investments. Here the question of cross subsidy will not arise. The power supply is rationalized or regulated to meet the demands of consumers in proportion to the ability to pay or the purchasing power of the consumers living in different locations and involved in different economic activities.

Partial or Full Reimbursement of Power Subsidy by Central Government: It will be appropriate to mention here that the Finance Ministry, Government of India made a budget allocation of ₹ 39,100 Crore during the year 2009-10 for NREGA [19], flagship programme of Government of India, which aims to provide minimum 100 days of guaranteed employment to unemployed people in rural areas. In addition to that, the government had waived off agricultural loans to farmers to the tune of ₹ 71,000 cores during the year 2008-2009. [20] The central government spends every year a substantial amount for fertilizer subsidy.

The provision for fertilizer subsidy for the year 2008-09 is kept at ₹ 20,139 crore. [21] The State governments have multiple number of schemes and programmes on their own for the growth and development of agriculture sector and rural farmers. Considering the magnitude of the amount, the governments are spending for the betterment of agriculture sector and rural farmers, the cost of power subsidy may not be difficult to deal with. However, it is appropriate to mention that, the revenuc base of the states may not be sufficient to bear the full cost of power subsidy being given to agriculture. The state governments are not able to release the subsidy as their revenue mobilisation is less when compared to central government. The demand for reimbursement of cost of power subsidy, either partly or fully, by the state governments is justifiable in view of the state's small revenue base when compared to centre and the contribution to country's food security.

Importance of Agricultural Metering: It is essential that the power supplied to all consumers, whether it is provided free of cost or with different subsidized rates, should be accounted properly with accurate meter reading at every point. Now with the utilities taking all necessary steps to reduce losses and thefts by strict monitoring and control and creating separate feeder for agriculture, it would be easy to identify the exact quantity of power supplied to agriculture. Once the supply points are metered, the data will be available for the policy makers to take an appropriate decision whether the power should be supplied free of cost or at different subsidized rates according to the level of consumption by different category of farmers, such as small, marginal and large. To avoid wastages and excess use of water and power by the farmers, it is advisable to charge the actual generation cost plus ROI and to encourage the farmers to pay for the service they are getting. It will also improve the quality of power at all stages, supply and consumption.

Various studies conducted on farming practices in Punjab show that the excess use of ground water and fertilizer has caused salinity of the top soil. In order to prevent excess use of ground water, which causes salinity and the degradation of the soil quality, it is advisable to charge according to the quantity consumed by the farmers depending on their farming needs. In a study about power sector in Karnataka, Bose et al. (2006) found that farmers were willing to pay at least ₹ 1.99/kWh for getting reliable power supply based on estimated cost of running a pump set, though the average revenue realization in the state from agricultural sector was a mere ₹ 0.25 to ₹ 0.35/ kWh. They argue that metered consumption for agriculture purposes induces change in behaviour of consumer to pay for the quality power supply received, and finally helps in improving the supply of power.

Again in a developing country like India, it is a fact that we cannot do away politics in any sector. In fact, it is not only developing countries, even developed countries like USA do play politics by providing higher subsidy to their farmers, which is against WTO norms and regulations and asking the developing countries to stop giving subsidies to their farmers. Similar to Right to employment, Right to electricity is also important for all citizens, especially, the rural population as their livelihood depends on the supply of power; cheaper and reliable power.

Hydro Power Generation, only to be with Public Sector: It is not prudent in a country like India to hand over or entering into partnership with private sector for the power generation in hydro sector. Considering the economy in producing cheaper power from hydro plants, the exclusive right of owning hydro power should be with public sector. The hydro generation may be affected by seasonal rainfalls and climate changes, but not by the market push and pull factors.

The power generated from thermal and other sources using gas and other fuels depends on import prices from international market and accordingly the tariff may vary. Since, it is suggested to reserve hydro power invariably for use of agricultural purposes and the hydro power generation should be left with government agencies only. The market forces and import policy changes should not be allowed to affect the selling prices to farmers. If hydro power is reserved for agriculture, it is in a way to assure farmers in getting cheaper power and ensures food stability in the country and to keep inflation under control.

Moreover, in India there are many long pending, unresolved disputes between riparian states for sharing of water for irrigation and drinking purposes and quite a number of cases are pending in the higher courts for delivery of justice. A day may come, the entire water source in the country will be nationalized and the hydropower stations owned by different agencies may be declared as national property. It is appropriate to mention here that the power ministry is also proposing for a National Grid to regulate the power sector. A National Grid will take care of power needs of all category of consumers across the country at competitive and affordable process. Under these circumstances, entrusting private sector for establishing of hydro power plants, using a national resource, paying almost negligible input cost and collecting exorbitant money as tariff from consumers and thereafter making enormous profit, is not advisable for a developing country like India, where it is required to supply power at a cheaper and affordable price to vast majority of the people. The poor and neglected section of the society mainly depend on the cheaper power supplied by the public sector. Keeping this in mind, it is suggested that the hydro sector should be with public sector only.

Role of Public Sector Power Utilities in Future: Policy makers expect that the urban population will be around 50 percent by the year 2020.With open access, which may materialize in the near future, like in telecom industry, consumers will have a choice in choosing the service provider, mainly in the urban areas. There would be many service providers in the urban areas, which increases competition and regulators will be ensuring reasonable price for the consumers. Whereas in the rural areas public sector is needed to serve the farming community and marginalized section of society who cannot afford to buy power at higher price or on par with the price level set for urban consumers. However, the presence of public sector is also a must in the urban areas to keep up the competition. The presence of public sector will definitely make the prices cheaper and competitive. It is seen in telecom sector in India. The presence of BSNL (Bharat Sanchar Nigam Ltd., a Central Government undertaking in India) made the telephone tariff cheaper every year. Even in a competitive environment, BSNL is making profits year after year and increasing its customer base. India is having more than a billion population and there is no dearth of market. The rural tele density is 7.9 percent which is very low when compared global average in telephone connectivity. Similarly, the per capita power consumption in India is very low when compared with global average. There is sufficient unexploited market for both private and public companies to compete and invest in the sector. The public sector needs to be competitive in the urban areas with efficient functioning and more investments in generation, transmission and distribution.

Conclusion

The enactment of Electricity Act, 2003 provided the needed momentum for the power sector to grow. Maharashtra and Karnataka followed the Orissa model and unbundled the electricity board, created separate companies for generation, transmission and distribution and constituted regulatory commission. Among the left over states, Tamil Nadu has already taken initiative to unbundle the SEB. Punjab is yet to unbundle the board.

While discussing New Public management, Warner (2008) argues that though NPM helped to increase efficiency and citizen choice, it fails to recognise the subtle and important ways, where markets and government differs.

After reform processes are initiated, the performance of state utilities in reducing losses, improving plant load factor, increasing collection efficiency is a commendable one. However, the NPM methods could not to provide a readymade market solution in dealing with politically sensitive issues like power subsidy and cross subsidy in power sector.

Though the SEBs in Tamil Nadu, Punjab are making losses, they are not far behind the unbundled states in operational performance of power plants and improvement of system efficiency. In fact, they are ahead of many reformed states in reducing losses, PLF improvement and collection efficiency.

What they lack is corporate culture and management. Moreover, it is practically impossible for one chairman of the board to go into technical nitty-gritty of all three activities of generation, transmission and distribution. In the unbundled states with separate Management/Board for each company looking after generation, transmission, distribution activities in the state or region, each sector is getting priority attention. After unbundling, all companies involved in generation, transmission and distribution could attract investments from financial institutions, which was considered to be very difficult earlier.

With unbundling, the work environment and culture changed for better. The Managing Directors of corporations agreed that they enjoy autonomy in most of the operational matters. But again, in a political environment like in India, political interference in administrative and transfer matters of employees, cannot avoided in total. The officers working in the sector agreed that this could not be a reason for poor performance of the sector.

With the implementation of APDRP programme, many

utilities will benefit and overall AT&C losses in the country will go down further. Reduction in AT&C losses will also help to reduce the demand gap. In Maharashtra, the demand gap is around 4000 MW. The present AT&C losses are around 30 percent. A 10 percent reduction will be equivalent to 2000 MW which can comfortably reduce the demand gap by 50 percent. Realizing the importance of AT&C reduction, the state DISCOMs and SEBs are trying to minimize the losses by strengthening transmission and distribution system, computerized meter readings, detecting power thefts by establishing special police stations, activating vigilance mechanism, innovative approaches in payment system. The new initiatives by the states such as distribution franchise, feeder separation for agriculture and anti power theft drives though dedicated police stations would also help the states in reducing AT&C losses. Now, with private investors showing interest in power sector and many new projects are on the anvil, the officials in power sector are hopeful of meeting demand gap within a few years of time.

With the states showing improvement in operational performance, the power utilities in the states would be in a position to manage better, if government considers the issue of cross subsidy and power subsidy and take an appropriate decision to save the boards from incurring further losses. A study conducted on agricultural power consumption in Karnataka shows that farmers are willing to pay for electricity if reliable and quality supply is ensured to them. To control excess water consumption and to prevent degradation of agricultural lands due to salinity, the farmers should be impressed upon to pay minimum user fee for the power consumed. However, if the government thinks that power should be given free charge to the farmers for various reasons, the subsidy amount should be released to the utilities to enable them to function effectively.

The tariff structure should be made according to the paying capacity of the consumers. The utilities should not indulge in buying power at higher cost and provide to consumers at a cheaper average price. The tariff policies should be linked to the purchase price.

With the reform process initiated in the sector, some states are in the right track and they set examples to others to follow. The sector reforms create competition among the utilities in achieving higher level performance. The innovations and new initiatives are being followed in other state utilities to increase overall system efficiency, which is seen as a positive trend for the power sector to grow. The reform process is going on. It will go on, till the objective is met; supplying quality, reliable power to all at affordable prices.

Notes

1. kWh-kilo Watt hour- Unit of power.
2. 10 lakh = 1 million, 100 lakh = 1 crore =10 million.
3. Source: Ministry of Power, GOI, www.powermin.nic.in.
4. www.tneb.in.
5. www.pscbindia.org.
6. www.kptcl.com–Karnataka Power Transmission Corporation Ltd. 31.
7. TNEB- Annual Administration Report 2006-07.
8. www.mesco.in (website of Mangalore Electric Supply company Ltd., Karnataka).
9. www.hescom.co.in (website of Hubli Electric Supply company Ltd., Karnataka).
10. www.gescom.in (website of Gulbarga Electric Supply company Ltd., Karnataka).
11. www.powermin.nic.in (website of Ministry of Power, Government of India).
12. AES (Advanced Energy Software Solutions Pvt. Ltd.). http://www.aes-solutions.com.
13. News report of The Times of India, (http://timesofindia.indiatimes.com/articleshow/2523481.cms).
14. AES (Advanced Energy Software Solutions Pvt. Ltd)-News letter, July 2009 (http://www.aes-solutions.com).
15. www.powermin.nic.in.
16. Annual report of MAHAVITARAN, 2006-07.
17. Tribune News Report dated 11 Jan 2009, www.

tribuneindia.com.
18. www.worldbank.org.in.
19. National Rural Employment Guarantee Act (www.nrega.nic.in).
20. Budget speech of Honourable Finance Minister, GOI, for the year 2009-10 (www. indiabudget.nic.in) 21 www.finmin.nic.in.
21. www.finmin.nic.in.

References

Arun, T.G. and Nixson, F.I. (1998) 'The Reform of the Power Sector in India: 1991-1997'. Journal of International Development, 10, 417-426.

Bose, R.K., Shukla, M., Srivatsava, L. & Yaron, G (2006) 'Cost of unserved powerin Karnataka, India'. Energy Policy, 34(2006)1434-1447.

Brunetti, A. Kisunko. G. & Weder. B (1998) 'Credibility of Rules and Economic Growth: Evidence from a Worldwide survey of the Private Sector' The World Bank Economic Review, Vol. 12, No. 3:353-84.

Dubash, N.K and Rajan, S.C. (2001) 'Power politics, process of power sector reforms in India'. Journal of economic and political weekly, September 1, 2001.

Gadgil, M. (2009) 'MAHA POWER Struggle', Special report 2008/09 (www. energy business. in).

Garg, A., Gaba, V., & Bajaj, J.L. (2008) 'Regulation in Practice, Impact of tariff orders on the Indian Electricity Sector'. New Delhi: TERI Press.

Gasper, D. (2002) 'Efficiency and Effectiveness-mainstream development evaluation in theory and practice'

Grindle, M.S and Thomas, J.W (1991) 'Implementing Reform: Arenas, Stakes and Resources. Public choices and policy change: The Political Economy of reform in Developing Countries'. Baltimore: Johns Hopkins University Press.

Grindle, M.S and Thomas, J.W (1990) 'After the Decision: Implementing policy reforms in developing countries' .Massachusetts: Harvard Institute for International Development.

Hood, C. (1991) 'A Public Management for all seasons? 'Public Administration, 69, spring, 3-19.

Joshi, A. (2008). 'Producing Social Accountability? The Impact of Service Delivery Reforms'. Institute of Development Studies, IDS Bulletin Volume 38 Number 6 January 2008.

Kannan, K.P. and Vijayamohanan Pillai, N. (2002). 'Plight of the Power Sector in India' Thiruvananthapuram: Centre for Development Studies.

Kukde, P.K. and Kulkarni, S.V. (2008). 'Accelerated Power Development and Reform Programme in India'. Mumbai: Indian Institute of Technology.

Kydland, F.E. and Prescott, E.C. (1977) 'Rules Rather than Discretion: The Inconsistency of Optimal Plans'. The Journal of Political economy, Vol. 85, No. 3 (June 1977) pp. 473-492.

Mishra, R.K. 'Looming crisis of Indian Power sector'. Austin: University of Texas.

Mooij, Jos. (2005). 'The Politics of Economic reforms in India' .New Delhi: SAGE Publications.

Osborne, D.E. and Gaebler, T. (1992) 'Reinventing government: How the entrepreneurial spirit is transforming the public sector' Reading , MA: Addison-Wesley. 61

Parker, D. and Kirkpatrick, C. (2005) 'Privatization in Developing Countries: A Review of the Evidence and Policy Lessons'. Journal of development Studies, 41:4, 513-541.

Pillai, N.V (2008) 'Power Sector Reforms: Some Lessons for Kerala' MRPA paper No. 12334, posted 23, December, 2008/8.35 (http://mpra.ub.unimuenchen. de/12334).

Prayas. 'India Power reforms update' Issue XI – December 2005.

Savas, E.S. (1987) 'Privatization: the key to better government'. Chatham, NJ: Chatham House Publishers.

Shahi, R.V (2005) 'Indian Powers Sector: Challenge and Response'. New Delhi: Excel Books.

Singh, A. (2006) 'Power sector reform in India: current issues and prospects '. Journal of Energy Policy, 34(2006), 2480-2490.

Singh, A. (2007) 'Policy Environment and Regulatory Reforms for Private and Foreign Investment in Developing Countries-A Case of the Indian Power Sector' ADB Institute Discussion paper No.64.

Sioshansi, F.P. (2005) 'Electricity Market Reform: What has the experience taught us thus far? '. Journal of Utilities Policy, 14 (2006), 63-75.

Subramaniam, Kandula. (2004) 'Thirteen years of Power Sector Reform in India: Are we still groping in the dark?'. Pennsylvania: Centre for the Advanced Study of India.

Tankha, Sunil. (2008) 'Lost in translation: Interpreting the failure of

Privatization in the Brazilian Electric Power Industry'. Cambridge University Press.

Tankha, Sunil and Misal, A. (2009) 'Transmitting Reforms through Weakly Conducive Environments: A case from the Indian Power Distribution Sector'. Working Paper No. XXX, The Hague: The Institute of Social Studies.

TERI (2006). 'Alternative Development Paths, scope for mobilizing international resources for funding the power sector in India'. New Delhi: TERI press.

Warner, M.E. (2008). 'Reversing privatization, rebalancing government reform: Markets, Deliberation and Planning'. Journal of policy and society, 27(2008), 163-174.

Website of Ministry of Power: www.powermin.nic.in.

Website of Central Electricity Regulatory Commission: www.cercind.org.

Website of Central Electricity Authority: www.cea.nic.in.

Website of Power Finance Corporation Ltd: www. Pfcindia.com.

Website of Rural electrification Corporation Ltd: www.recindia.nic.in.

Website of Punjab State Electricity Board: www.psebindia.org.

Website of Tamil Nadu State Electricity Board: www.tneb.in.

Website of Maharashtra State Electricity Board: www.msebindia.com.

Website of Gujarat State Electricity Board: www.gseb.com.

Website of Delhi Vidyut (Electricity) Board: www.delhigovt.nic.in.

Website of Karnataka Power Corporation ltd: www.kpcl.com.

Website of Karnataka Power Transmission Corporation Ltd.: www.kptcl.com.

Website of Kerala State Electricity Board: www.kseboard.com.

Website of Orissa Electricity Board: www.orissa.gov.in/energy.

Website of AP Power Generation Corporation: www.apgenco.gov.in.

Website of AP Transmission Corporation: www.aptransco.gov.in.

Website of AP Electricity Regulatory Commission: www.ercap.org.

Website of Maharashtra Electricity Regulatory Commission: www.mercindia.org.in.

Website of Karnataka Electricity Regulatory Commission: www.kerc.org.

Web site of Tamil Nadu Electricity Regulatory Commission: www.tnerc.tn.nic.in.

Website of Punjab State Electricity Regulatory Commission:

www.pserc.nic.in.
Website of UP Electricity Regulatory Commission: www.uperc.org.
Website of Orissa Electricity Regulatory Commission: www.orierc.org.
Website of Tata Power Company: www.tatapower.com.
Website of Reliance Power Company: www.reliancepower.co.in.
Website of BEST: www.bestundertaking.com.
India Power Sector Reforms Update, Prayas, Pune.

6

Right to Information in India

M.R. Biju

Transparency seems to be the only means for sustaining democratic governance. That is why the right to information has been legislated in about 70 countries of the world, and another 30 countries are in the process of legislation.

It was in this context that the RTI was enacted in India in 2005. The experience of 5 years shows that the response to this Act has been very positive and optimistic. It has also been widely welcomed by the people at all levels. They have been seeking various types of Information from different authorities. The RTI Act confers on all citizens the right to seek information and makes it the duty of the public authorities to disseminate the same for better governance and accountability. It covers the central, state and local governments and recipients of Government Grants but does not apply to the intelligence and security organisations except if the information released to the allegations of corruption.

Against this back drop, an attempt has been made here to discuss the various dimensions of the RTI along with its features, experiences and gray areas. The debate would also focus on the major impediments in its implementation and also few suggestions for its effective functioning in the days to come.

Comparative Position of RTI in Various Countries

In most of the countries where large scale administrative reforms have been carried out, emphasis has been laid on liberalizing the extent to which information is made available *to* the general public. In the U.K. Citizen's Charter in the

Official Secrets Act, 1911 to narrow the scope of official information falling within the ambit of the Act. Besides, a White Paper guaranteeing a statutory right of access to personal records held by the government has also been implemented in April, 1994. Canada has an access to Information Act which gives all Canadian Citizens, as well as people and corporations present in Canada, the right to have access to federal government records that are not of a personal nature. The government has taken steps to ensure that information about its activities are broadly available to the people with exceptions being limited and narrowly defined, and provisions for resolving any disputes over the application of such exceptions independently of the government. An Information Commissioner has been appointed to investigate complaints from members of the public arising from the above-mentioned Act. Government of Malaysia has also taken various steps to provide an open and transparent government in terms of decision-making. These include publication of reports on public complaints, progress of administrative efforts undertaken by the government etc.

As would be clear from the above, there is a trend worldwide to have increasing openness in the system of governance. Various factors like changing socio-economic milieu, increased awareness of the public about their rights, the need to have a fully accountable and responsive administration and growing public opinion which views efforts at secrecy as enhancing the chances of abuse of authority by government functionaries, have led to a demand for a greater transparency in governmental functioning. However, complete openness is neither feasible nor desirable. Accordingly, a balanced approach to openness in government functioning has to be devised.

Openness to the Public and Administrators

All governments in the world practise studied concealment of information from the people though the nature, degree and extent thereof varies. While capitalist and democratic countries have a higher degree of openness *vis-à-vis* authoritarian regimes, nowhere in the world in government functioning totally open. The effort is to satisfy public demands as far as is reasonable and practicable. Transparency also has to be fully compatible with the constitutional and parliamentary system of the country and the cost of sharing information should be commensurate with the benefit to the public. It may also not be practicable to give information about any proposal under consideration while it is yet to be finalized, as this is likely to bring into play several pressure groups with attendant increase in corruption. Thus, what we need in the country today is a limited openness in government functioning, which would make available ex post facto information about various, but not all, government decisions to the citizens of this country. While anything that is detrimental to the interests of the nation, the security of the state or its commercial, economic and other strategic interests, may not be made public, nothing should be held back just to subserve the interests of individual bureaucrats and politicians.

Experience of other countries shows that *we* will have to initiate the process by passing a Right to Information Act, somewhat on the lines of Canada and the United Kingdom. Adequate safeguards will have to be built into the legislation to ensure the primacy of the national interests as also the privacy of the individual citizen. At the same time, an independent authority will have to be constituted to decide whether a document can be made public or not.

Public relations wings, which already exist in most of the government departments, should be converted into Public Relation-cum-Information Wings. Their functions should include dissemination of information to citizens on payment of a prescribed fee. People should be able to inspect Government papers and, if necessary, take photocopies of desired documents. No extra staff should be employed for this work, as the existing staff of PR. Wing can take on these duties additionally. Departments should also publish information of general interest and keep copies of these in their libraries for general consumption. They should put information on computers with linkage to Internet and other global networks.

Every important government decision involving a shift in policy should invariably be accompanied by a White Paper in the nature of an explanatory memorandum.

A new kind of office structure, with a counter system, as in the case of banks, should be adopted in all field offices involving public contact. This has already been used with success in the Ahmednagar Experiment wherein the district office was restructured, demystified and made more open so as to facilitate the work of the general public. We have to move towards a government office which gives a clear-cut time-limit for disposing of any request of a member of the general public. An individual, if he so wishes, should be made aware about the exact stage of his case at any point of time. In such a system, an applicant is given a fixed time-limit, at the time of submission of his application giving the date on which the final decision on his request would be conveyed. The Passport Officer has already initiated a system, where the status of an application can be ascertained at any point of time.

Openness also implies that the reasons for Government decisions are placed on record in black and white. For this purpose, formulation of criteria that would be used for decision making is a must. Accordingly specific rules, criteria and norms have to be laid down for every activity of the Government.

Genesis and Evolution

The Evolution of the Act may be traced to the following developments and factors.

1. **Effectiveness of the Good Governance:** The access to information is cardinal to good governance and the whole mechanism of governance in the country has been vitiated owing to lack of it. According to a paper prepared by the

Human Rights Initiative, good governance has eight major facets. It is participatory, consensus oriented, accountable, transparent, responsive, effective and efficient, equitable and inclusive and follows the rule of law. It is an ideal which is difficult to be achieved in its totality. However, to ensure sustainable human development, action must be taken to work towards this ideal. Access to information is a vital factor for achieving the goals of good governance. It promotes transparency and public accountability in the working of government functionaries.

2. **Emergence of New Forms of Democracies:** Since the 1980s, the emergence of new democracies after the collapse of authoritarian regimes has given rise to new constitutions that include specific guarantees of the Right to Information. At the same time, older democracies such as the United Kingdom too are seeing the wisdom of enacting such legislation. International bodies like United Nations Organisation, the Commonwealth, Council of Europe and the Organisation of American States have drafted guidelines or model legislation to promote freedom of information.
3. **Access to Information and Governance:** Access to information is the basic requirement in democratization of governance. Despite the LPG regime's stress on curtailing the role of the state, the functions and powers of the government have grown many-fold. These are not always for public good and public interest. There are instances of its use for private gains. In such a scenario, there is always a conflict between power and justice. Therefore, some control mechanism needs to be evolved to discipline the arbitrariness of power to promote justice, equity and fair play.
4. **Participation of the People at All Levels of Administration:** Governance in a democracy implies that people should participate in the process of governance. For this, they must have the necessary information to make

informed choices between available options. The RTI is also expected to improve the quality of decision-making by removing unnecessary secrecy in the decision-making process. The citizens would be enabled to participate in the processes of decision-making and policy formulation on issue of their concern and to know the criteria applied by government agencies for making these decisions.

5. **New Models of Administrative Accountability:** The RTI is necessary to promote a culture of accountability. Accessibility of information pertaining to finances, proceedings and decisions of all the social actors whose activities have an impact on the public, is the guarantee that which actors shall make them accountable. It shall check mismanagement, abuse of discretion, bribery, other forms of corruption and malpractices.
6. **Empowerment at the Grassroots:** Right to information has a rights perspective as well since correct information at the right time reduces the chance of misuse of resources and lessens corruption. It also helps governance function better, makes service providers accountable for their actions, creates participatory and transparent environment for people to contribute in policy formulation and establishing rule of law. It also gives people a legal right to demand entitlements and monitor the use or misuse of funds meant for them. Right to Information regime is also a means for government to empower the poor and inform them about pro-poor policies and safety-net programmes.
7. **Put an End to the Corrupt Practices:** The most effective systemic check on corruption is to enable the citizens to take the initiative to seek information from the state, and thereby to enforce transparency and accountability. The RTI is, therefore, likely to reduce corruption and increase administrative efficiency. This is because it provides every citizen the enforceable right to question, 'examine, audit, review and assess government acts and decisions, to ensure that these are consistent with the principles of

public interest, probity and justice.

8. **Discretionary Powers should be Minimized:** Officers are given discretionary powers for carrying out their duties effectively, and they don't have to depend on seniors for approval. Officials can abuse their discretion to suit various political or vested interests or to misappropriate funds. In absence of legislation on Right to information they tend to be hidden from disclosure. Although it is possible to seek courts intervention to compel disclosure of the information in practice it is not possible for the poor, villagers, due to cost, distance and delays involved.
9. **Efficiency in Administration should be Assured:** As far as administrative efficiency in government is concerned, it comprises of conducting the administration without unnecessary delays. It should not have ulterior or corrupt motives while passing orders.
10. **New and Vibrant Society:** There can be no democratic participation in decision making without transparency and sharing of information. Secretive government is nearly always inefficient. The free flow of information is essential if problems are to be identified and resolved. Furthermore, a secretive governing culture fosters suspicion and encourages rumours and conspiracy theories.
11. **Preserving Liberties:** The Right to information is also essential for protecting liberties of citizens by making it easier for civil society groups to monitor wrong doings like custodial deaths and abuse of preventive detention legislation.
12. **To Achieve Development Goals:** Legislation on right to information is fundamental to furthering the effective development of society and eradicating poverty. Effective anti-poverty programmes require accurate information on problems hindering development to be in the public domain. Meaningful debates also need to take place around the policies designed to tackle the problems of

poverty.

13. **On Government Schemes:** In rural areas, numerous schemes for providing food, housing, employment and education are run by the Central and State Government. These schemes meant for the poorest of the poor in the rural areas are routed through the network of government agencies. There is widespread criticism of these funds being routinely misappropriated or misused on Right to Information and Good Governance a large scale. In most cases, people do not know about the existence of these schemes. Even if they know, they fail to derive the benefits of these schemes. Furthermore, records are often tampered because no one outside the administration has access to them. By providing entire information on these schemes to the public would make the administration more accountable.

14. **Right to Information as a Fundamental Right:** That the RTI is a Fundamental Right flowing from Art. 19 (1) (a) of the Constitution is now well-settled. Over the years, the Supreme Court has consistently ruled in favour of the citizen's Right to Know in a number of cases .like: Bennett Coleman vis-à-vis Union of India, 1973; Raj Narain vis-à-vis Government, of Uttar Pradesh, 1975; S.P. Gupta vis-à-vis Union of India 1982 and People's Union for Civil Liberties (PUCL) vis-à-vis Union of India, 2004. In all these cases, Supreme Court pronounced that the citizens of this country have the Right to Freedom and Speech under Article 19(1) (a) of the Constitution and this Right is not complete unless and until the citizens have the Right to Know. The Right to Information was further elevated to the status of a Human Right by the Schedule Caste in 2004 case of 'People's Union for Civil Liberties vis-à-vis Union of India' judgment.

15. **Media's Effectiveness:** The citizens resort to the media like newspaper, radio, television etc. for day to day information about government activities. The media serves

as a link between the citizens and government. So, it is essential that media have access to information. The media's right to information is not a special privilege, rather an extension of the public's right to know. The lack of a right to access official information causes many problems for the media. Balanced reporting becomes difficult when denied the primary sources of information. In absence of exact information they provide biased news, suppress or distort information. Right to Information and Good Governance and citizens would together make the government more accountable.

16. **Movement for Transparency:** The Right to information has not come on a platter and there have been many activists and citizens' groups whose continuous struggle and efforts and movements have brought about this change. A mass based organization, called the Mazdoor Kissan Shakti Sangthan (MKSS), movement led by Aruna Roy, in May 1990 took an initiative to organize people, in a very backward region of Rajasthan: Bhim Tehsil, to assert their Right to Information by asking for copies of bills and vouchers and names of persons who have been paid wages mentioned in muster-rolls on the construction of school, dispensaries, small dams and community centres. It spread quickly to other areas of Rajasthan and to other States. The attempts of Harsh Mandar the then Divisional Commissioner of Bilaspur, Madhya Pradesh in 1996 to throw open the registers of Employment Exchanges and the records of Public Distribution System to the citizens or the agitation led by Anna Hazare in Maharashtra in 2001 are some the examples.

Right to Information: The International Perspective

At present, the RTI exists in about 70 countries either in the Constitution or through specific laws. Another 30 countries are in process of enacting such legislation. However, there are still many states, including democracies, where people are still denied access to information. UNDP's conditional laws have compelled many countries to enact the relevant Right to Information: Genesis and Evolution legislations. It has been of the view that people's awareness on RTI directly impacts the life of the people.

United Nations: Freedom of information was recognised as a Fundamental Human Right by the UN at the first session of the UN General Assembly in 1946. It adopted Resolution 59(1) which states: "Freedom of information is a fundamental human right and the touchstone of all the freedoms to which the UN is consecrated."

In ensuing international instruments on Human Rights, freedom of information was made a part of the Fundamental Right of Freedom of Expression, which included the right to seek, receive and impart information. In 1948, the UN General Assembly adopted the Universal Declaration of Human Rights (UDHR) which guarantees Freedom of Opinion and Expression: "Everyone has the right to freedom of opinion and expression; this right includes freedom to hold opinions without interference and to seek, receive and impart information and ideas through any media and regardless of frontiers." This declaration recognizes freedom of expression' including Freedom of Information and free press as Fundamental Human Right.

Article 19(2) of the International Covenant on Civil and Political Rights adopted by General Assembly in 1966 states: "Everyone shall have the right to freedom of expression; this right shall include freedom to seek, receive and impart information and ideas of all kinds, regardless of frontiers, either orally, in writing or in print, in the form of art, or through any other media of his choice". Article I of the UNESCO Declaration of 1978 on 'Fundamental Principles Concerning the Contribution of Mass Media to Strengthening Peace and International Understanding, to the promotion of Human Rights and to Countering Racialism, Apartheid and Incitement to war demand a free flow and a wider and better balanced dissemination of Information.

Legislating the Right to Information in India

Objections to the Official Secrets Act have been raised ever since 1948, when the Press Laws Enquiry Committee recommended certain amendments. In fact, the Act has been used time and again to suit the purposes of the government.

In 1977, a Working Group was formed by the Janata Party government to look into the possibilities of amending the Official Secrets Act. Unfortunately, the Working Group did not recommend changes, as it felt the that Act related to the protection of national safety and did not prevent the release of information in the public interest; despite overwhelming evidence to the contrary, Official Secret act remained unaltered.

In early 1989, V.P. Singh's National Front Government came to power and declared its decision to make Right to Information a fundamental right.

Later a Committee set up in 1989 by the National Front Government recommended limiting the areas where government information could be hidden and opening up of all other spheres of information. As most of the members of the Committee were bureaucrats, something different was not expected, so no legislation followed from these recommendations.

Finally, the focus of citizens' groups shifted from demanding merely an amendment to the Official Secrets Act, to its replacement by a comprehensive legislation towards the Right to Information. The initiative for the Right to Information was taken by a mass based organization, the Mazdoor Kisan Shakti Sangathan (MKSS) in early nineties in a very back ward region of Rajasthan—Bhim Tehsil. This agitation for transparency was started by asking for copies of bills and vouchers and names of persons who have been paid wages mentioned in the muster rolls for the construction of school, dispensaries, small dams and community centres in the

Block Development and Panchayat Officer. After years of knocking at officials' doors and despite the usual apathy of the State Government, MKSS succeeded in getting photocopies of certain relevant documents. Misappropriation of funds was clearly obvious. MKSS organized several Jan Sunwai (People's hearing), between December 1994 and April 1995, in Rajasthan. This grassroots movement spread very fast to other areas of Rajasthan and to other States establishing firmly that information is power and people should have the right to official information.

Subsequently, the National Campaign for People's Right to Information (NCPRI) formed in the late-1990s became a broad-based platform for action. As the campaign gathered momentum, it became clear that the right to information had to be legally enforceable. It was demanded that information that cannot be denied to Parliament or state legislatures cannot be denied to a citizen either.

In 1996, Justice P. B. Sawant, the Chairman of the Press Council of India, drafted the bill keeping in view the dire need of the day and the observations made by eminent persons that in a democracy, it is the people who are the masters and those utilizing public resources and exercising public power are their agents.

Press Council of India and the 1998 Resolution

The Press Council of India, the Press Institute of India, the National Campaign for People's Right to Information and the Forum for Right to Information unanimously submitted the Resolution on February 20, 1998 to Government of India for amending the proposed bill.

Main Points of the 1998 Resolution are as follows:

- The Right to Information should also be extended respect of companies, NGOs and international agencies whose activities are of a public nature and have a direct bearing on public interest; (ii) The law must contain strong, penal provisions against wilful and wanton withholding or delay in supplying information or deliberately supplying misleading or inaccurate information.

- The law must contain an appeal mechanism of an independent nature to provide reliable redress to any citizen dissatisfied with any decision of a public authority under this law.
- The categories of information, which can be restricted or - withheld by the Government, are too wide in the draft Bill. In particular, the restriction on disclosing internal nothings and official correspondence between public officials and offices has no justification whatsoever.
- Similarly the restriction on confidential communications between the State and Centre and their agencies have no justification, unless they harm public interest.
- The restriction on disclosure of the record of discussions of Secretaries and other public servants also needs to be removed. However, this draft also went into cold storage due to the fall of two United Front Governments.

Freedom of Information Bill, 2000

The BJP led National Democratic Alliance reworked on the Shourie's draft to finalise the Freedom of Information Bill, 2000. It was introduced in the Lok Sabha on July 25, 2000. However, after the president's signature this Act could not be notified in the Government Gazette.

This Freedom of Information Bill included some provisions that were not in the Shourie draft, such as the requirement that urgent requests in cases involving life and liberty should get a response within 48 hours. Various provisions of the Act were similar to that of the RTI Act except on the points on which it has been criticized.

The Act has been criticised on the followings main points: It reinforces the controlling role of the government official, who retains wide discretionary powers to withhold information. For example, requests for information involving "disproportionate diversion of the resources of a public authority" can be shot down by the public information officer. This leaves open the danger that government officials might be transformed from gatekeepers of the Official Secrets Act to gatekeepers of the Freedom of Information Act.

The most scathing indictment of the Act has come from the critics who focus on the sweeping exemptions it permits viz. restrictions on information relating to security, foreign policy, defence, law enforcement and public safety. The Act also excludes Cabinet papers, including records of the Council of Ministers, secretaries and other officials. Information shared between the Centre and States were not subject to disclosure. These exemptions effectively shielded the whole process of decision-making from mandatory disclosure.

RTI Act, 2005

The Parliament of India passed legislation on Right to Information in 2005. It is a landmark legislation in Indian context. It is in consonance with provisions of International Covenants on the issue and has brought India in line with other development democracies of the world. Right to Information Act, 2005 was passed by both the Houses in the Summer Session of the Parliament and received assent of President on June 15, 2005. Around 150 amendments were introduced in the original draft. The Act replaces relatively weak and ineffective legislation, the Freedom of Information Act, 2002.

Salient Features:

- The Act provides all citizens the right to information, subject to the provisions of the Act.
- It covers all the three tiers i.e. central, state and local government and also the three branches i.e. legislative, executive and judiciary of the government.
- It applies to "Public Authorities" established or constituted by or under the Constitution; by any law made by the appropriate Government or, any other body owncd, controlled or substantially financed directly or indirectly by' the appropriate Government and includes non-

government organizations substantially financed by the government.

- The ambit, covers even the private bodies and their information can be accessed through the controlling public authority.
- The Act provides that information of the third party can be accessed after giving ten days notice to the third party.
- It casts an obligation on Public Authorities to grant access to information and to publish certain categories of information. Public Authorities are also supposed to maintain their record in the indexed and catalogued manner. The responsibilities about suo-moto disclosure/publication 'by public authorities have been considerably enlarged.

The Act lays down the machinery for the grant of access to information. The Public Authorities are required to designate Public Information Officers and Assistant: Public Information Officers for dealing with requests for information and also to assist persons' seeking: information.

1. Provision has been made for transfer of a request by a public, authority to another public authority, wherein the subject' matter/information is held by the latter.
2. A time limit has been prescribed for compliance with requests for information under the Act, viz. 30 days for normal information; 40 days for third party information; life and liberty information in 48th hours and information relating to human rights violation in 45 days.
3. The Act provides that in case PIO rejects the application, he/she is bound to give reasons of such rejection; the period within which can appeal against such rejection may be referred as well as the particulars of the appellate authority.
4. The Act excludes the time taken for calculation and intimation of fees from the time frame.
5. The Act prescribes for reasonable fee for providing information. Also, no fee to be charged from persons who

are below poverty line. Further, information to be provided free of charge where the response time limit is not adhered to.

6. Certain categories of information have been exempted from disclosure. The categories, by way of illustration, include, information likely to affect security of the State, strategic, scientific or economic interests of the State, detection and investigation of offences, public order, conduct of international relations and Cabinet papers. Trade or commercial secrets, information the disclosure of which would cause breach of privilege of Parliament of State Legislature and personnel information which has no relationship with public activity and could cause unwarranted invasion of the privacy of any person are also exempted from disclosure. However, exemptions provided are not absolute and -withholding of information must be balanced against disclosure in the public interest. Information is to be released even if harm is shown to the public authority if the public benefit in knowing the information outweighs the harm that may be caused by disclosure.
7. The Act contains a provision for reveal of certain information, which is otherwise, exempted from disclosure on completion of 20 Years after the incident.
8. The Act also incorporates the principle of severability.
9. Envisages creation of an independent non-judicial machinery, viz., Central Information Commission and State Information Commissions comprising a Chief Information Commissioner and Information Commissioners to decide 2nd stage appeals. At the same time, there is no hierarchy of Commissions.
10. Legal framework for exercise of powers by the Commission defined in the Act.
11. The Commission while inquiring into any matter has the same powers as are vested in a civil court while trying a suit under the Code of Civil Procedure.

12. The Act provides a two-tier Appellate Forum. First appeal to departmental officer senior to the Public Information Officer. The second appeal to be made to the Commission.
13. On a request for information being refused, the applicant can prefer an appeal to the prescribed authority within 30 days of the decision; the time limit for disposal of appeal being also 30 days extendable to 45 days. The second appeal can be made within 90 days of the decision of the first appellate authority.
14. In case of a grievance at PIO level, there is a provision for making a complaint directly to the Commission.
15. Intelligence and security agencies specified in Schedule II to the Act have been exempted from being covered within the ambit of the Act. However, the exemption is not absolute; agencies shall have the obligation to provide information in matters relating to corruption and human rights violations.
16. The decisions of the Commission are binding.
17. The jurisdiction of subordinate courts has been barred.
18. The provisions of the proposed Act have been made overriding in character, so that the scheme is not subverted through the operation of other minor Acts.
19. Under the provision of the Act CIC/SIC can impose a penalty of ₹ 250 per day on PIO. This penalty can go up to a maximum of ₹ 25000.
20. There is a provision of disciplinary action against PIO for any contravention of the Act. A disciplinary action can be recommended as per the service rules applicable to the PIO.
21. The Act provides that there is no criminal liability of the PIO and the PIO is immune from the actions done in good faith.
22. Central Information Commission and State Information Commissions to monitor the implementation of the Act and prepare an Annual Report to be laid before Parliament/State Legislature.

23. Rule making power for effective operationalisation of the Act is with the competent authority i.e. Central/State Government subject to the approval of Parliament and Assembly respectively.
24. The Act repeals the Freedom of Information Act, 2002.

Deficiencies in the RTI Act

In spite of being very exhaustive and with all its positive features, the RTI Act suffers from some weaknesses which has impeded its uniform and effective implementation during the last three years. These deficiencies are discussed below:

1. **Substantial Financing:** The Act does not define the word "substantially financed". Though some Information Commissioners both at the Centre and the State level are of the view that since the word control is there in the definition of public authority so why the need of the definition of substantial financing has not aroused as one can have the information of public authority even if it has not been financed because it is controlled by some agency or department under certain existing Act. However, the substantial financing has created a lot of confusion for the user and providers of information under the Act. Therefore, it should have been amplified by way of an explanation. This omission will result in different interpretations of the term by different states and public authorities.
2. **NGOs:** There is another dimension to this issue. The expression Non-Governmental Organisations as used in the Act is ambiguous. The NGOs, are a class and category apart from the other private sector organisations. The use of the phrase 'Non-Governmental Organisations' creates an illusion that the Act is applicable only to NGOs because they receive funds under various projects and schemes of the Government as partners in implementation. There are many other private institutions specially the Government aided private schools and colleges who believe that they

should not be designated as .public authority on the spurious argument that they belong to the private sector.

3. **Lack of Clarity on Public Authorities:** The Act also imposes certain obligations on public authorities in Section 4. Primarily, these relate to (a) proper maintenance and upkeep of records, and (b) suo moto dissemination of information through publication of information directories about the functions and functioning of each public authority. But, the public authorities have generally been treating this provision as optional rather than compulsory. The dictionary meaning of obligation is binding power, written bond, duty, some thing that obligates one to a course of action, etc. But it appears that in the absence of any penalty clause, the task is not viewed as an obligation, this gives rise to the question: What option the Information Commission has if the Public Authority does not comply with this provision? Unless enforced, these obligations wall remain only on paper.
4. **On Life and Liberty:** The Act does not define the information falling under life and liberty. Sikkim has defined life and liberty in its RTI rule as if the information requested relates to a person's confinement, internment, arbitrary detention, imminent death at the hands of the State or another individual, torture or violation of due process rights. Moreover, there is no provision for relatively speedier disposal of appeals/complaints regarding information pertaining to 'Life and Liberty' unlike 48 hours time stipulated for providing such information. The Act should be amended to include such provisions.
5. **On First Appellate Authority:** The Section 19(1) provides for the designation of an appellate authority at the Public Authority level who is an officer senior in rank to the Public Information Officer (PIO). However, the Act is silent about the powers and functions of the first appellate authority. As a result, there is confusion about the role and

responsibility of the first appellate authorities. Moreover, the Act does not in a way, make the first appeal mandatory when it says that any person aggrieved by the decision of the PIO may prefer an appeal to such officer who is senior in rank to her/him. In general perception, an applicant is supposed to appeal with the Information Commission only after she/he has exhausted all options. The Act does not support this perception. It is not clear whether the information commission can entertain an appeal when the first appeal has not been preferred by the appellant.

6. **On Appeals and Complaints:** The grounds of a complaint under Section (u/s) 18 and for an appeal u/s 19 are over lapping. Separate grounds should be there for appeals and complaints. Three clauses of Section 18 (1) i.e. Clause (b) relating to refusal of access to information; (c) relating to no response to the request for information within the stipulated time; and (e) relating to giving incomplete, misleading or false information may be deleted as these ground's are basically for exercising appellate powers u/s 19.
7. **Contempt Provisions:** Section 19(7) of the Act states that the decision of the Information Commission shall be binding. But it is not supported by 'Contempt of Court' provision to enforce compliance of its decision by the public authority. Due to the absence of such a provision there are instances of non-compliance of orders passed by the Commission.
8. **On the Powers of Civil Courts:** Information Commissions have been conferred powers of a civil court u/s 18(3) under the Civil Procedure Code, 1908. The powers of civil court u/s 18(3) have been given only for limited purposes. These do not cover powers concerning execution of decrees and recovery of fine etc. The ICs powers of civil courts may be incorporated into a separate section within the same Chapter V so that it becomes applicable to all proceedings (including enquiry, appeal

and penalty proceedings). Similarly, the provisions under Section 19 (7) and 19(8) may be incorporated in separate sections in Chapter V so that these powers can be applied in case of all proceedings before the Commission. Similarly, there is no uniformity of procedure of enquiry, the procedure for hearing under Section 19 and for conducting enquiry u/s 18 which points should be clearly outlined.

9. **Time Frame for the Information Commissioners:** Unlike the time limit for the First Appellate Authority for giving decisions on appeals, the Act does not provide for any time limit to decide the appeal. Due to the absence of this provision, ICs are very often not giving the decisions on appeals on time and not only this, the disposal rate is also not very good. To avoid any delay in disposal of appeals, there should be a provision regarding the time limit in the Act.

Concluding Observations

Every citizen has the right to know how the government is functioning. Right to information empowers every citizen to obtain information from the government. It is duty of public authorities to maintain records for the easy access and to publish within 120 days the name of the particular officers who should give information and in regard to the framing of the rules and regulations. All information shall be disseminated widely and in such form and manner which is easily accessible to the public. It has been provided that it is required that the request to be disposed of within 30 days provided that where information sought for concerns life or liberty of a person, the same shall be provided within 48 hours. If a request is rejected it shall be communicated giving reasons and specifying the procedure for appeal and the designation of the appellate authority. The Act also exempts granting information where it would disproportionately divert the resources of the public authority or would be detrimental to the safety and preservation of the record in question.

Knowledge and information is the prerequisite for the enjoyment of this right because the lack of authentic information on matters of public interest leads to the wild rumours. Freedom of speech and expression includes the right to receive and collect information. Since the democracy is the government of the people who are the sovereign masters. There can be no government by the people if they are ignorant of the issues to be resolved, the argument for and against different solutions and the facts underlying those arguments. The taxes collected by the government belong to the people. They have the right to know in what manner they are being governed and how their money is being spent. The business of the government should be a participatory process. The fact should be made public. Only a fully informed citizenry can be better equipped for the performance of these duties.

The Right to Information Act enables the citizens to get the required information for the redressal of the grievances within a specified time from the date of filing application. Any citizen can ask for information under this law by applying in writing or through electronic means to the Public Information Officer (PIO), specifying the particulars of the information sought for. The right to information has been judicially recognized as a part of the fundamental right to speech and expression. Information is sine qua non for the efficient functioning of democracy. It keeps the people informed about the socio-political and economic affairs and issues. In a developing country like India, the availability of the information is required to be assured to the people in a simple and speedy manner because the development process depends on it.

Over the past few years, RTI has gained increasing importance in the human rights discourse as well as the larger democratic discourse. Since a democratic government must be sensitive to the public opinion for which information must be made available by it to the people. Effective accountability rests on the peoples' acquaintance with the information. A system that operates in secrecy tends to loose the faith of the people as much as its own legitimacy and credibility. Openness and full access to the information are the two pillars of the democratic state. It will equip the citizens to participate meaningfully in the democratic and political process. Governance is undoubtedly strengthened by the RTI. That is why the RTI has been recognized as an essential requirements of the good governance. The enactment of the RTI Act, 2005 is a bold step. The Act covers not only the public sector but also the NGOs and the private sector to some extent. In addition to this, it has various other positive features like provision of First and Second Appellate Authorities. It is also one of the toughest legislations in the world, as it is the only RTI Act imposing penalty for any contravention of the provisions of the Act.

However, mere conferment of the right is not enough. Its successful implementation in the true spirit is needed. The revision and review of legislations contrary to this right is required. Suitable amendments in the conduct rules for public servants, attitudinal change in the behaviour of the bureaucracy, creation of efficient information management system, more frequent use of this right by press and will of the citizens are also required. Many loopholes need to be plucked. However, despite the weaknesses, it is a Magna Carta for introducing reforms in the governance in the country and will go a long way in strengthening the roots of democracy by introducing transparency and accountability in governance.

References

B.L. Fadia and K. Fadia, Public Administration, Sahitya Bhavan, 2004.

Harinderjit Kaur, Right to Information, South Asia Politics, Vol. 8, No: 12, April 2010.

J.G. Roy, Right to Information Initiatives and Impact, IIPA, New Delhi, March 2006.

M.M. Semwal and Sunil. K, Right to information and Judiciary,

IJPS, Volume LXIX, No. 4, December 2008.

M.R. Biju, Democracy in the Modern World: The Indian Experience-Two Volumes Kanishka, New Delhi, 2009.

M.R. Biju, Democratic Political Process. (ed.) Mittal, New Delhi, 2008.

M.R. Biju, Development Issues in Contemporary India, Concept, New Delhi, 2010.

M.R. Biju, Strategic Management, Social Security and Banking Sector Reforms: Issues and Concerns, Authors Press, New Delhi, 2010.

R.S. Dhaka, Right to Information and Good Governance, Concept, New Delhi, 2010.

S. Pande and S. Singh, Right to Information Act 2005, NBT, New Delhi 2008.

Sapna Chadah, Right to Information Regime in India, IJPA, March 2006.

7

Social Entrepreneurship in India: Experience of SEWA

Sudha Menon

Introduction

Social Entrepreneurship is a relatively new concept in development and social science literature. It implies applying business skill in social issues. In other words, social enterprise is an initiative which identifies a social problem and finding out a solution using the entrepreneurial skills and principles. It is self sustaining on one side and maximizes social return on the other. Social entrepreneurs try to solve a social problem through inventing new approaches, harnessing managerial skill and applying business models which are replicable, scalable and sustainable.

Though the theory of social entrepreneurship is in its nascent stage, the practice of social entrepreneurship is well ahead of theories and definitions. There are many grass root initiatives which effectively utilized entrepreneurial capabilities to solve a social problem. These initiatives have combined passion of a social mission with an image of business to transform the lives of marginalized people. Self Employed Women's Association [SEWA]—the largest independent trade union in India—is a classic example of this trend. SEWA has indeed heralded a new milestone in the history of social entrepreneurship through building poor women's own sustainable enterprises, managed and owned by the actual producers who belong to hitherto marginalized and excluded sections of the society.

Against this context, the present paper attempts to analyze the factors associated with social entrepreneurship in SEWA.

First part of the paper briefly introduces the concept and examines various approaches towards social entrepreneurship. In the second part, we attempt to analyze the social entrepreneurship initiatives of SEWA and its content and spirit. The concluding part critically examines lessons learnt and future challenges ahead.

Social Entrepreneurship: The Concept and Meaning

An entrepreneur is a person who organizes and manages a business undertaking, assuming the risk for the sake of profit. (Webster 1982). A social entrepreneur is someone who recognizes a social problem and uses entrepreneurial principles to organize, create, and manage a venture to make social change.

There exists a variety of approaches towards conceptualizing social entrepreneurship. Emerson and Twisty views social entrepreneurship as an initiative combining commercial enterprises with social impacts [Emerson and Tweesky, 1996]. According to them resources generated through successful commercial activities are used for advancing and up scaling their social activities further so that social impact can be reached more people.

Social entrepreneurship is also viewed as innovating for social impact. Creation of any innovative initiative to address social problems through mobilizing resources is social entrepreneurship [Dees, 1998].

Another approach towards social entrepreneurship perceives it as a way to catalyze social transformation. According to this perspective, social entrepreneurship produces small changes in the short term that reverberate through existing systems to catalyze large changes in the long run [Ashoka Foundation, 2000].According to this school of thought social entrepreneurs are not only concerned with short term impact of their project but also the long term result it can produce on the system of injustice or disharmony prevail in the society. Naturally, social entrepreneurship will result in changing the social structure within which the original problem is embedded in.

However, the most popular definition of social entrepreneurship is given by Professor Gregory Dees who has combined diverse ideas and approaches on entrepreneurship. According to him, social entrepreneurs play the role of change agents in the social sector, by:

- Adopting a mission to create and sustain social value (not just private value),
- Recognizing and relentlessly pursuing new opportunities to serve that mission,
- Engaging in a process of continuous innovation, adaptation, and learning,
- Acting boldly without being limited by resources currently in hand, and
- Exhibiting heightened accountability to the constituencies served and for the outcomes created.

This is an idealized definition. The closer a person gets to satisfying all these conditions, the more that the person fits the model of a social entrepreneur [Dees, 1998].

What Makes it Social and Enterprise?

There are certain inherent features which constitute a social enterprise. The uniqueness of social enterprise lies in the nature and structure of supply chain, products and services, production process and above all the use of profit.

In social enterprise raw materials are provided by co-operatives or farmers or producers groups directly without an intermediary or middlemen. The value added through the production process will largely remain with the producers and role of brokers and middlemen will be minimum or irrelevant in a social enterprise. In other words, throughout the supply chain the producer will get maximum benefit and lead role in decision making process than any other factors or process.

Second aspect is the inherent social value attached to products and services. Social enterprises generally focus on products which address a social issue or problem that affects the society. It may be providing low cost education to marginalized people or extending solar cookers to rural community having no access to electricity or micro credit services to poor marginalized farmers without any access to institutional sources of credit. Thus the inherent social value is important which differentiate a social entrepreneur from business entrepreneur. While a business entrepreneur thrives on competition and profit, social entrepreneur has different motivation—a commitment to society and dedication to changing the existing system and pattern.

Social enterprises follow affirmative and progressive HR policies and practices. As the main objective of these entities are not maximizing profit and monopolizing market; social enterprises can recruit and sustain a team of skilled and committed people including women and disadvantaged sections. Thus, social enterprises follow inclusiveness both in structure and function.

Another aspect which makes social enterprises unique is the nature of production process. They follow environmental friendly production process and are committed to reduce the health hazards and ecological impact to minimum extent possible. Apart from that, social enterprise always tries to cater to the needs of under privileged sections of society. Their clients are often the sections of people who are underserved by market or existing institutions or rural consumers or people living in remote areas.

Lastly, the use of profit is another important aspect which makes this distinct. In social enterprises profits are used for the benefit of beneficiaries or reinvested in the same entity for growth and scalability. It is distributed for the benefit of the same group for whom the entity is functioning.

Social enterprises also focus on income generation and systems and standards to measure the social impact of the venture. Thus it indeed is a paradigm shift in both business and social literature. In this concept, the entrepreneurial energies of producer groups, socially sensitive management teams and other stakeholders will be harnessed for a new paradigm in social entrepreneurship.

Social enterprises should be profit oriented. Otherwise it can't be sustainable for long run. There are certain attributes which make a social enterprise profitable and sustainable. Some of them include the following:

- Clarity in focus and objective.
- Good information system, measurement system and process.
- Leveraging technology to drive scale and bring in efficiency.
- Professional team committed to the cause.
- Innovative business plan, design, quality etc.

There are two schools of thought regarding the basic strategies of social enterprises. First school focuses on figuring out the best business model and scaling up gradually to reach maximum people. Second stream of thought focuses on the needs of the community or people and attempts to design a product which addresses that particular problem or need. In this process emphasis is more on social problem than business model. Naturally level of profitability will be lower.

The legal structure of social enterprises can be for profit, non-profit or hybrid structure. Each model has its own problems and prospects. So we should identify which structure is the best alternative to suit our vision and accomplishment and design it accordingly. It depends on the nature of the clients, vision, goals and the specific context in which we operates.

Traditional non profit	Non-profit income generating	Non-profit social enterprises		Business with social perspectives	Business with CSR	Business for profit

In social entrepreneurship, stake holder's interests are important where as in business firms' shareholders interests prevail over everything. Apart from that in social enterprises profit is reinvested for social progress whereas in business entities it is decided by directors of the company. In short, to make a social enterprise, we should emphasize on the following aspects.

1. Develop a business model that meets a need not currently served by the market or there is a perceived lack of demand or perceived risks or cultural resistance.
2. To create a market where one doesn't exist.
3. To reach the full market realm, mix of for-profit and non-profit distribution channel needs to be designed. There should be a combination of market rate and subsidized rate for different group of clients.
4. To view clients as decision-makers and not merely as consumers.
5. It should combine the advantages of both non profit and business firms without compromising on the goals and mission.

On the basis of this analysis, we would like to examine the forms and patterns of social enterprises practiced in SEWA. For specific study five social enterprises with SEWA are selected including SEWA Trade Facilitation Centre, RUDI Multi Trading Company, SEWA Nirmaan, SEWA Salt-making Cooperatives, Vermicomposting Initiatives.

Social Entrepreneurship in SEWA

SEWA: A Brief Introduction: Self Employed Women's Association (SEWA) is an organization of poor, self-employed women workers. These are women who earn a living through their own labour or small businesses. SEWA's main goals are to organize women workers for full employment and self reliance. Full employment means employment whereby workers obtain work security, income security, food security and social security (at least health care, child care and shelter). SEWA organizes women to ensure that every family obtains full employment. Self-reliance means that women should be autonomous and self-reliant, individually and collectively, both economically and in terms of their decision-making ability. This is SEWA's core and fundamental mission. As one of the major objectives of SEWA is that the members of SEWA do not remain just workers but develop themselves as owners and managers of their own enterprises, SEWA has facilitated in developing social enterprises.

SEWA's Approach

SEWA considers freedom from poverty as 'second freedom'. SEWA believes that poverty is the worst kind of a violence—a condition which deprives the affected of resources, abilities and choices necessary to enjoy certain basic human rights. A world living in peace and free of violent practices is not possible unless extreme economic disparities among the communities are done away with. The poor need care and justice the same way as the victims of violence need them. Hence, the emphasis is on inclusive and pro poor interventions. Members of SEWA possess traditional skills but lack in access to finance, market information and technical knowledge. For over 3 decades, SEWA has been working with its rural members to help them improve their livelihood through various initiatives in technical trainings, microfinance, market linkages and natural resource management, across a number of trades. SEWA, through its livelihood finance support, provides its members with access to credit, access to market and access to technology. SEWA focuses on the inclusive growth of these poor workers through women's leadership and enterprise building. In order to eliminate the middle men and provide direct technical, financial and marketing facilities to the rural poor.

SEWA functions on a democratic basis and is a strong believer in Gandhian philosophy. The leaders are groomed from within the grassroots. Eighty percent of its organizers come from the grass-root members and twenty percent are recruited from outside. *Agewans,* the village level leaders are selected from our members. Every village has an *agewan,* who is provided with a series of capacity building trainings and their leadership skills are built. The activity wise experts are chosen from amongst the *Agewans* and their capacities are further nurtured to develop them as spearhead team members. The spearhead member then becomes a link between the community and the district level federation. The leaders are specifically taught to be selfless and do service for others keeping the needs and requirements of others as a priority rather than their own needs. Also, the major quality of SEWA's leader is one who brings others forward. In the capacity building trainings to the leaders, they are provided with the following knowledge and skills.

The participatory approach ensures that SEWA's enterprises work for members' needs and issues. Any new program or an initiative is taken up only after consulting the members. This brings up the ownership feeling amongst our members and also makes them accountable.

SEWA's growth has been through word of mouth. The members themselves bring up more members to join SEWA. The progress made by the existing member attracts the future members. The chain continues and thereby the membership continues to grow, strengthening the base.

Social Enterprises within SEWA

SEWA has built members own sustainable economic organisations—the social enterprises in the areas of agriculture, salt, craft and eco-friendly construction. The objective is to link the producers directly with the markets. SEWA attempts to develop the producers as the owners and managers of their enterprises. By developing their own enterprises, the members get good prices as well as they get recognition. They are able to develop their own brand and a name for themselves. They not only get sustained livelihoods but are also proud owners of their own enterprises and develop a strong sense of ownership. Right from the day the worker becomes member of SEWA, SEWA inculcates amongst them to develop themselves as owners and managers of their own enterprises.

Objectives:

1. Members become the owners and managers of their own enterprises.
2. Ensure sustainable livelihoods for members throughout the year.

SEWA Trade Facilitation Centre (STFC)

SEWA's experience of working with the artisans after the earthquake clearly showed that craft proved to be a good source of income for members. The SEWA Trade Facilitation Centre (STFC) was established in May 2003 as the commercial arm of SEWA by more than 15,000 women artisans in the textiles and handicrafts sector. The vision of STFC is to ensure that craftswomen in the informal sector have socio-economic security and full employment, by building a grassroots' business enterprise of the artisans. STFC achieves this by sustained, profitable, and efficient coordination of the design, production, and marketing of their products and services in mainstream national and global markets. STFC has transformed the grassroots craft activity into a full fledge commercial enterprise. Erstwhile the artisan women though skilled in hand embroidery had to forcibly migrate in search of work, or undertake earth-digging work.

Lack of market information hindered artisans from building a strong relationship with the buyers. With the inception of STFC, integrated supply chain mechanism was created and the production became organized. Now STFC is a growing producer company, producing ethno-modern apparel and accessories, blending contemporary designs with traditional embellishment techniques (such as embroidery). STFC markets its products under the brand name *Hansiba* to the upper middle and upper class, and has outlets in Delhi, Mumbai and Ahmedabad. STFC's turnover in the year 2008-09 was 2.5 crore with an active artisan/textile worker base of about 3,000 and an overall worker base of about 15000.

As a capacity builder, STFC has been very energetic, and more importantly, alive to the changing trends of the fashion sector. Till date, STFC has trained over 20,000 women in various disciplines, with trainees hailing from different states of India and from different South Asian countries. In the year 2008-09 alone, STFC has upgraded the skills of 3000 of its women artisans, trained 500 women from Afghanistan and 100 from the countries Bangladesh, Pakistan, Sri Lanka and Nepal. STFC has a cadre of dedicated trainers who build and deliver training modules in line with contemporary requirements.

STFC has designed the training modules in collaboration with National technical agencies such as National Institute of Design (NID) and National Institute of Fashion Technology (NIFT).

RUDI Multi Trading Company

SEWA Gram Mahila Haat (SGMH), a state-level Apex marketing organization of SEWA was founded with the help of Commissionerate of Rural Development, Government of Gujarat and SEWA in 1999 to eliminate middlemen and provide direct technical, financial and marketing facilities to the Rural Poor Producer Groups of Gujarat. SEWA Gram Mahila Haat now reaches out to markets all over the country for its agricultural products.

SGMH aims at providing integrated marketing services to the rural producers through exploring, developing and establishing first the internal (local market) and then the national market for rurally produced products. Gram Haat has focused on four sectors: agriculture, salt, forest produces and handloom/handicrafts, as members in these sectors constitute a large proportion of SEWA's membership.

SGMH has set up a RUDI Multi Trading Company with an objective to internally generate funds for the rural producer groups so as to enhance the quality, capacity and efficiency of production through the use of better technology for the farming, warehousing and post-harvest processing of the agro commodities. This helps in scaling up the profit margins by way of bulk procurement and a well organized sales and distribution network. The profits are shared by the members of the rural self-help groups, which brings a positive change in the economic condition of marginal farmers and workers who are struggling to survive and are below the poverty line. The company enables to provide direct market to the agro commodities through the rural retail network that it has set up across all the villages in 9 districts of Gujarat. RUDI Company has also enabled multiple employment opportunities, reduced incidental expenses, availability of good quality agricultural & non-agricultural products to the rural consumers at affordable prices and required quantity, elimination of middlemen, better earning for the producers and thereby socio economic development of the underprivileged rural people.

RUDI's annual turnover for the year 2008-09 was 1.5 crore. RUDI boasts of supplying products of the highest quality at affordable prices to families that normally pay for adulterated products in their local village stores.

Most important, RUDI procures produce at market prices by paying cash at the time of procurement. The RUDI team also educates the marginal farmer in standard grading practices which empowers her with information on quality of her produce, thereby providing her with greater bargaining power with the buyers.

SEWA Nirmaan

Following the Earthquake, SEWA's approach was not that of just reconstruction of the damaged houses but that of an integrated revival of livelihoods and to turn it into a livelihood opportunity. Thus the construction related trainings like masonry, carpentry, and production of construction items were a part of the rehabilitation efforts. Today, SEWA has a trained workforce of nearly 1400 masons whose lives and livelihoods have become securer on account of SEWA efforts. In order to compete in the markets and take up construction work on a sustainable basis these masons need access to funds, access to new technology and regular refresher trainings for better building practices; they need to organize. As a group they will be in a better position to access schemes programmes, as also high value work opportunities and negotiate terms of trade in their favour. These workers shall be trained for creating and strengthening rural infrastructure and they will be provided market linkages. Towards this end, SEWA and its members have formed a Company for construction and allied workers– SEWA Nirmaan. SEWA Nirmaan members have also been trained by Mahindra GESCO.

SEWA Nirmaan undertakes work related to building and reviving of rural infrastructure in the villages. This include construction of check dams, repairing, revival and construction of wells, water tanks, ponds, toilets and other rural infrastructure in the villages. These workers are then linked with ongoing government schemes in developing rural infrastructure.

Salt-making Cooperatives

Over 30,000 families are involved in salt production activities in the tough conditions of the dry regions of Gujarat. Households involved in salt production lead a gruesome existence, living in makeshift tents near the salt farms, spending hours working on the farms barefoot, surviving on inadequate nutrition, and lacking any facilities whatsoever to educate their children.

Adding to their woes, most of the salt farmers are caught in a vicious cycle of debt with the local traders who exploit them to purchase produce at prices much lower than that in the market, leaving the household with virtually no margin at all. Over the past decade, SGMH has been working with the salt farmers of Surendranagar, simultaneously offering them microfinance, market linkages and training in the production of the high-margin industrial salt.

SEWA has established links with entities such as Gujarat Alkalis Chemicals Limited (GACL) who directly purchase the salt from the farmers, thereby eliminating the middlemen. To provide extensive technical training to the farmers, SEWA has tied up with the Central Salt and Marine Chemicals Research Institute (CSMCRI).

Vermicomposting

SEWA promotes the use of vermicompost and organic cultivation. Almost 18,462 farmers from the State of Gujarat have started to use Vermicompost on their own farms. As the demand for Vermicompost among members became clear, SEWA facilitated the process by setting up a plant at the village level. Training is given to local farmers and presently, 232 members from 14 groups have started the production of Vermicompost on a commercial basis. Current production is around 1 to 1.5 tons of fertilizer per month per member. The groups are also using this on their own fields and are also marketing it for selling others.

Features of Social Enterprises in SEWA

Social entrepreneurship is not new in SEWA. Through various innovative models for income generation and producers own initiatives SEWA have been using the social entrepreneurship principles for the benefit of poor women. Whether it is TFC or RUDI, SEWA is using business model that combines revenue generating business with a social commitment and outcome. Hence, SEWA itself is the classic example of what a social enterprise is.

In SEWA, all income generating or livelihood support projects were initiated on the basis of the demands expressed by the members and the model identified by them. Hence the collective interest always prevailed over individual interest and the benefits were shared by the entire group collectively. In RUDI or STFC, the ultimate benefit is shared by the members of artisan group and farmers who enjoy better pay and better livelihood options with a sustainable income. So SEWA is the embodiment of a successful social enterprise based on collective strength and goals. Another interesting aspect is that SEWA tries to measure the impact of the initiative with its own parameters rather than mere profit. Even though, profit is less or negative, SEWA never fails to pay the producers/artisans on time. Also the shareholders always get payment on time. So a non-compromising strategy towards the interests of both our clients and producers make this unique in its own way.

In SEWA's marketing models, the supply chain also operates in a unique way. SEWA has its own system of internal supply chain in which they directly procure products from farmers without middlemen. For example, the cotton which is directly procured from farmers is woven by members of SEWA's own weaving cooperatives. Then further value will be added by the traditional artisan group who do embroidery work on these clothes. The finished product will be sold under brand name using retail outlets and distribution network. In this whole process focus is mainly on producers' wellbeing and conserving their traditional livelihood through market linkages. Business skill is utilized throughout the process with a view to tap maximum profit for the real producers.

In any social enterprise, learning the demands of the market and then providing tailor made customized products is very important. For example, majority of salt workers were traditionally engaged in making common salt. But the income from common salt making was very less and there was no market demand for this low quality salts. Hence, the workers decided to shift to industrial salt production as it attracts potential customers and there is large market for it. So SEWA started providing training for industrial salt production with the help of experts and now the workers are getting better returns. Income from this new business venture is almost double. Thus, SEWA strongly believes that understanding the market and identifying the nature of the product as per market needs are of most important in social enterprise.

Another notable feature of SEWA concept of social

enterprises is commitment towards social goals rather than profit. Apart from the income, members get benefit of social security as well. SEWA provides micro credit to rural entrepreneurs, assist in market linkages and avoid middle men from the whole process. In SEWA's endeavour, decision making resides with the producers and not with the implementing team of external experts. Demands of members and their priorities always prevail over other considerations.

From SEWA's experience it is evident that social capital which involves the collective strength, trust and sense of harmony among the members played a vital role in forming social enterprises. Whether it is RUDI or STFC, it was build on the collective consciousness of the community members which was later translated into income generating ventures. Hence, social capital is a driving force behind social entrepreneurship and both these concepts reinforces each other. There is a need for building collective strength for making social enterprises more sustainable and result oriented. The membership strength and trade unions always stood as a backbone of the success of SEWA's profit making ventures. The members support wholeheartedly for any effort towards further consolidation and income generating initiatives as they know that ultimately the benefit will be equally shared by the members and ensure livelihood security to them. Hence collective strength, internal consensus and harmony are the soul of SEWA.

Lessons Learnt

SEWA has always given emphasis on forming viable and sustainable enterprises. Right from the beginning, this objective is very clearly brought out. It has been SEWA's experience that the first three to five years the social enterprises establish a base and develop their roots. The next three years, the enterprise strengthens its infrastructure and builds its leadership and managerial skills. In the period of seven years, the social enterprises of SEWA invest in building, human resources, develop systems and processes, finalize their business plan, set up bank linkages and build relations with the banks, penetrate the market and build their brand.

SEWA feels that if an enterprise does not get viable in the period of seven to eight years, the board gives a critical re look at the decision. The strategy is reworked and at times even a painful decision of closing the venture is undertaken.

During the initial years, no rate of return is expected in tangible form. However, intangible returns are there in the form of building human capital and developing the enterprise as a sustainable institution. There is a huge risk involved in the initial stages and losses are also incurred before the turnaround takes place. Once the investment and the risk of the initial years are carefully met by properly designed strategies, there is no looking back for the enterprises. A strong visionary Leadership under the full time CEO and a strong Board with sector Experts gives proper directions to the enterprises of SEWA to expand and develop and prosper.

It is also a big challenge to draw a line to distinguish between the business and non-business issues. The profitability of the enterprise is to be maintained and at the same time the core values and social goals are also not compromised. Attaining the right balance is a task in itself. Significant investment in the form of building alliances in terms of product development, Branding, Brand promotion, marketing is important for future growth. Strengthening managerial effectiveness is most important. Continuous capacity building and skill enhancement of the team and all stakeholders is required to sustain the passion, efficiency and market demands. About Sustainability aspect SEWA realized that there is a need to focus on progressive level of sustainability and it should be realistic based on the business logic of each entity.

Till 2005, SEWA's social entrepreneurship initiatives were donor dependent. After that some business plan reached up to 60 percent or 70 percent sustainability. But 100 percent is still a dream. When both the entrepreneurs and consumers are local, it is easy to sell the products. But when the consumers are outside the locality we find it difficult to sell which ultimately slow down the pace of our growth. In this regard, it is suggested that producing for the outside market will fetch more money and make it more profitable. At the same time producing for export depend on other factors including fluctuating international prices and market forces which are not under own control. Hence, it is risky as well even though margin will be higher. Another option is to create a vibrant local market for our products which is relatively risk free and provide a stable income though not very high.

The Way Ahead

Based on the real life experiences SEWA is always open to refine and reconstruct the strategy towards sustainability. Members of SEWA and the visionary leadership know that the credibility of social enterprises will be ultimately judged by long term sustainability rather than short term goals. For this purpose SEWA constantly invest on the following aspects:

1. Building Local capacity among poor marginalized women members.
2. Searching for new models of innovative packages which will be beneficial for making social transformation. Eg: investing in green skills, solar lantern making etc.
3. Building movement and sense of collectivity among the members which will ultimately develop social capital.
4. Focus on continuous learning and development of local leaders.
5. Long term commitment to the goal and capability to adapt itself to the emerging challenges within and outside organization.
6. Building external linkages wherever possible without compromising on the basis philosophy of Gandhi and self-reliance.

Conclusion

In short, the success of social enterprises in SEWA contributes an important ingredient to social enterprise theory- Community participation, community ownership and collective demands are more important in social enterprise than financial and other assets. Re-integration of business and social goals requires a perfect blending of social value generating structure with revenue generating business models. The unique Model—ownership model in which stakeholders own the enterprise and they take the responsibility of maintenance of the system- is the greatest asset of SEWA. Success of SEWA mainly depends on the two important assets- social capital and human capital. Through the effective leveraging of managerial techniques and skills; SEWA can certainly make any social enterprise sustainable.

References

Dees, J. Gregory.1998. *The Meaning of Social Entrepreneurship.* October 31.Comments and suggestions contributed from the social entrepreneurship Funders' Working Group.

Emerson, Jed and Fay Twerksy. (eds.) September 1996. *New social entrepreneurs: The success, challenge and lessons of non-profit enterprise creation.* San Francisco: The Roberts Foundation, Homeless Economic Development Fund.

www.sewa.org.

www.stfc.org.

8

Democracy, Media and Gender

Dolly Phukon

Democracy is regarded as the best form of governance in the present world. The basic norms of democracy such as liberty, equality, freedom, order, justice, rule of law etc. have gained worldwide respect. The Liberal democratic theory has developed at the time of renaissance and reformation in response to an age characterized by absolutist state, established religion, and a society encrusted with restrictive customs and authoritarian ways. [1] Individual's freedom became the focal point of the liberal democratic tradition in place of the unquestioned authorities of Church, Kings, feudal authorities etc. The classical liberal democratic theory maintained that all the social institutions were for the betterment of man as an individual. It can be traced back to the development of the social contract theory by Thomas Hobbes who put forward the proposition that the state was created by the people through a social contract.

Though Thomas Hobbes contributed significantly to liberal theory, he favoured strong and even unrestrained government opposed to democracy in the form of Leviathan. He opined that the man of the state of nature is characterized by nasty and brutish traits devoid of freedom and reason. He believed that only after surrendering the natural rights to the sovereign or Leviathan by the creation of a political society based on social contract, freedom and reason can become the rule of man. But later on Hobbes's absolute powerful State was criticized by John Locke through his theory of limited and constitutional government arguing that sovereignty resides in the people, and that government gains its authority only from the transfer of individual rights by means of a contract. Locke's aim was to promote a government which would respect individuals' 'natural rights' of life, liberty and property. For that purpose, man enters into the civil society by forming a contract and the people of the civil society form the government for preservation of their natural rights.

Locke assigned to the people the right to rebel, if a government acted tyrannically and fails to protect their property. Locke's views on property lies on his belief that man by mixing his labour with the unowned matters of nature can make property which accepts unquestioningly the capitalist accumulation of wealth. According to him, property owners have the power of command over the labour of the poor as poor men's only property lay in 'the *Labour* of his body and the *Work* of his Hands'. [2] During the 18th century, proponents of rationalism and enlightenment elaborated the classical liberal democratic theory with the values like civic virtue and participation of the citizens for the better functioning of the democratic State.

Rousseau formulated his concept of General Will or the common interest of the community where the citizens contributes without the thought of their personal advantage to political decisions and always aims at the public good. [3] During the 19th century, another trend of the classical liberal democratic theory developed known as the Utilitarian tradition under the aegis of Bentham and John Stuart Mill rejecting the social contract theory. According to them men obey authority not because of any contract but because of self defined utility. Bentham in this regard framed an elaborate pleasure-pain theory and believed that the end of the state was to promote greatest happiness of the greatest number. [4] John Stuart Mill in his book *on liberty* (1859) tried to reform Benthamite Utilitarianism by standing as the savoir of minority rights against the curtailment by the majority as prescribed by Bentham.

In order to protect individual freedom Mill limited the

state's authority by dividing individual's action into self regarding and other regarding actions where the state's interference is limited only to control the other regarding actions. Mill considered freedom as a necessary requirement of a liberal society and was necessary for pursuing individual's own good in their own way as long as they do not hamper similar rights and freedom of others. [5] The classical liberal democratic theory contributed towards the growth and development of capitalism and also indirectly led to the growth and development of socialist ideas. In this connection it may be noted that the liberal democratic theories led to the establishment of capitalist society replacing the feudal estates.

However, the new society slowly developed two contradictory classes i.e. the employers and the bourgeoisie. The worker's opposition to the capitalists showed itself more and more in strikes and even as armed rebellions like, rebellions of the Lyons in France (1831 and 1834), the uprising of weavers in Germany (1844), England (in the 1830s and 1840s) saw the spread of the first revolutionary proletarian movement. The Industrial Revolution, which took place in Great Britain at the end of the 18th century, followed in France in the early 19th century, and then in Germany after 1870, caused an immense increase in the manufactures of each country and a consequent need for foreign markets. The principal field for the European policies of economic expansion was Africa, and on that continent colonial interests frequently clashed.

Several times between 1898 and 1914 the economic rivalry in Africa between France and Great Britain, and between Germany on one side and France and Great Britain on the other, almost precipitated a European war and led to the First World War. [6] The pursuit of `equality' under the liberal democratic tradition, proved to be a vague concept and the situation led to the growth of Socialism. During this period, more and more argument were set forth for the activist state and the ever increasing influence of the Fabians and Marxists moved governments again towards central control of the economy, but this time in a far more pervasive form.

The intellectual influence of the classical liberals waned into insignificance. But the intervening period between the First World War and Second World War experienced the economic difficulties, unemployment and unstable currencies. These conditions seemed to demand much more economic control by government and led to a revival of protectionism and other nationalistic policies. There was the rise of dictatorial or totalitarian regimes in large parts of Europe not only extinguished the weak liberal groups which had remained in the countries immediately affected, but the threat of war which it produced led even in Western Europe to an increasing government dominance over economic affairs and a tendency towards national self-sufficiency.

After the end of the Second World War there occurred once more a temporary revival of liberal ideas, due partly to a new awareness of the oppressive character of all kinds of totalitarian regimes, and partly to the recognition that the obstacles to international trade which had grown up during the inter-war period had been largely responsible for the economic depression. [7] After the Second World War, an important contribution to liberalism was made by F.A. Hayek, I. Berlin, John Rawls and Robert Nozick. [8] An economic traditionalist and advocate of the free market economy, von Hayek won a wide reputation with The Road to Serfdom (1944), in which he argued that governments should not intervene in the control of inflation or other economic matters.

He opined that socialism will not lead to freedom but only to servitude. He identified the fallacies of the ideas like social justice and state planning which would violate individual right to choose their own good. In order to make the liberal democratic theory more convenient, John Rawls in his A Theory of Justice (1971), tried to revive the Social Contract Theory of Hobbes, Locke and Rousseau by interpreting the idea in a hypothetical way to remove the inconsistencies about during the social contract how governments could be just if those agreeing were already poor or exploited, or if people were simply born into a state and had never consented to it explicitly, so that the principles of justice chosen would be fair.

Rawls assumed that in the hypothetical plane i.e. the Original Position, the people will form the Contract under the Veil of Ignorance where the people forming the contract can choose impartially, without regard to their own interests or prejudices. He laid down two principles of Justice where the "first principle" establishes equal liberties for all, subject only to maintaining them for others and he "second principle" or "difference principle" establishes fair equality of opportunity, and restricts social and economic inequalities in the basic structure of society to those benefiting the least advantaged members of society. Thus Rawls's democracy ensured equal freedoms to every person compatible with similar freedoms of others and inequalities were permitted if they are to everyone's advantage.

Thus the government of Rawls was assigned the role of regulating economy to keep market competitive, resources fully employed, property and wealth widely distributed. [9] Robert Nozick in his book Anarchy, State and Utopia (1974) challenged Rawls's theory of Justice and developed his powerful defence towards the minimal state which jurisdiction was limited to the providing protection to the life, property and rights of the individual.

The debates on the implications of the liberal notion of basic rights and freedoms in the liberal democratic tradition manifest themselves in the securing of a social, economic and political space where equal opportunity for all individuals can be achieved. This is accomplished through the creation of liberal institutions, the establishment of a universal state enforced legal framework, increased role of civil society and the prioritization of the means of social regulation through market mechanisms. [10] The western liberal theorist Francis

Fukuyama in his book, The End of History and the Last Man, viewed that there is no alternative to the western liberal democracy because the communism has already failed; the Islamic fundamentalism and the eastern authoritarian seem to be the passing phase of history. According to him, the liberal democracy is the only path for humankind to travel and no other alternative is there.

Thus the liberal democratic theories uphold the values of freedom, reason and toleration, which are said to be necessary to liberate people from the hold of custom, tradition, status, absolutism etc. of the pre-liberal order. The liberal theorist advanced the idea of the free and equal individuals with natural rights which cannot be taken away by the rulers. Within this context it is seen that liberal democratic theory defines and defends a private sphere of the life of the individuals and the civil society which are to be free from state interference. [11] The civil society is seen as the sphere of rights and the rule of law which is guaranteed by the state. It is regarded as the sphere where the rational self determining individual enters voluntarily into social relationships with others on the faith that the relationships are based on the assumption that no human being can achieve his/her goals without the help of others. [12] It is recognized as the site in which the society enters into a relationship with the state. The institutions of the civil society are associational and representative forums, free press and social associations. The inhabitants of this sphere are the right bearing individual who is juridically defined as citizen. [13]

Moreover, from the discourses of the liberal democratic theorists as discussed above, it could be seen that, the sphere of civil society is conceptualized so that the power of the state could be controlled and checked from encroaching into the sphere of right bearing individuals or citizens. But civil society can however carry out this task only when it itself is democratic. In this regards the Marxist interpretation of civil society gives a discriminating view of the civil society, where the liberal democrats remained unconcerned and indifferent to the ability and disability of the inhabitants of the civil society to participate in the sphere of discussion and debate on equal terms. [14] For Marxists, the liberal conceptualization of civil society as a sphere of rights legitimizes the domination of the capitalist classes. According to them civil society is a sphere for buying and selling of labour power based on exploitation and class inequality. [15]

The Marxian tradition provides insight into the oppressions within the civil society domain. Like the Marxist, the feminist argument also gives a negative picture of the civil society as an arena of gender based discrimination based on the liberal democratic idea of public/private division within the domain of civil society. Liberal democratic theory according to Neera Chandoke has relegated the civil society as a private arena as it is a realm of the right to privacy of the individuals where the state is barred from any kind of interference into it (Hegelian argument). Again the sphere of family within the civil society is regarded as private and the rest including every association in the civil society is public. The feminists criticized the relegation of the household to the private sphere as it tended to depoliticize the gender discriminations and disempowerment of women in this sphere which lays a greater implication on women's participation in the so called public sphere of the civil society. [16]

According to them by creating the public/private dichotomy, the liberal democratic state is trying to naturalize women's subordinate status in the society. Thus they termed the liberal democratic set-up as patriarchal in nature. The liberal conceptualization of civil society as a sphere of liberty and equality of the individual irrespective of gender according to feminist is a vague concept. Feminists argue that the liberal conceptualization of the individual as free, autonomous being with bearers of inalienable rights is not inclusive of women. In the light of this context the feminist arguments on the liberal democratic state and the position of women in the democratic set-up needs to be highlighted.

Position of Women in the Democratic Set up

Gender equality is a pre-requisite for effective participation of women in strengthening the institutional structure of democracy. According to Rowbothom Sheila, it has been a persistent thought of political theory that women and democracy do not go together. Women have been outside the rubric of democracy. The issue of women's freedom under democracy hinged on whether woman was subsumed in the term man! According to Rowbothom if man and women's rights are identical in nature then the democratic society needs extensive changes as woman were not regarded as free and independent individuals but as attached to fathers or husbands. [17] Democracy falls within the domain of politics where the definition of politics is characterized as male-dominated, specific to 'public sphere' and therefore not necessarily women friendly.

For these reasons despite the increasing popularity of the concept and practice of democracy, the question regarding why democracy is gendered remain unanswered. In this context Georgina Ashworth laid down three arguments as "First, women's political rights with politics being broadly defined to include everyday concerns are an integral and inseparable part of their human rights; and human rights, in turn, are a fundamental aspect of any democratic framework. Second argument for linking gender and democracy is that in a democracy the points of view of the different groups involved must be taken into account in formulating any decision or carrying forward any strategy. In other words, democracy must be inclusive of the opinions and perceptions of women as well as men. Finally, perhaps the single most important rationale for linking democracy and gender is that women effectively constitute half the world's population, and half of each and every single national population. Women's studies and the amalgamation of practical experiences repeatedly have pointed out that women are not and should not be considered a minority. Indeed, women are as much a "minority" as men are in such a context. To conceptualize issues and develop policies which will affect, directly or indirectly, citizens' lives without taking into account the situations, perspectives and realities of all those who will be affected is no longer credible in today's world." [18]

Mary E. Hawkesworth, Kelly and Bayes in the book Gender, Globalization and Democratization defined full democracy as the one which recognizes women as citizens equally with men and where the institutionalized gender relationships are egalitarian (Hawkesworth, Kelly, Bayes, 2001, p. 1). They argued that: "if established pattern of interaction between men and women in the family, the market place, and other non-governmental institutions in the society deny women physical and economic security, access to education and access to social and political institution and offices, then the democratization process, although it may be constitutionally claim that men and women are equal, can be no more a facade, a thin veneer. So long as women are confined to a "separate sphere", confined to reproduction, housework and child care, so long as women are left uneducated, unable to control their bodies, and recognized as citizens on an equal footing with men, democracy cannot be observed in true in sense." [19]

Mary E. Hawkesworth asserts that democracy as a mode of governance is most widely understood as a Euro-American model of male-dominant democratic elitism. The 'democratic' concepts and institutions (both political and economic) that are exported to other countries carry with them this bias. According to her, the most advanced of the Western liberal democracies have very poor records in areas of gender equity. Women were drastically underrepresented in positions of power in liberal democratic nations, holding only 12-21 percent of the positions in the legislative bodies. In most advanced capitalist economies (e.g. The group of 7 nations-the

US, Canada, Great Britain, Germany, France, Italy and Japan with Russia sitting as a non voting member), women are still confronting a glass ceiling that is remarkably low. At the opposite end of economic spectrum within advanced capitalist nations, women are overrepresented among the poor. In the US for example, women and their children constitute 80 percent of the poor, a higher percentage than exists globally. [20]

Many feminist analyses of politics have been the fact that women have been excluded from the exercise of political power. For centuries women had to fight for the right to vote in Western democracies, as women were regarded as irrational to share in political power with men. Political theorist such as Plato, Aristotle, Hobbes, Locke and Rousseau asserted that there is a natural difference between men and women and men are more superior and rational than women thus men are regarded as more suitable for joining the so called 'Public Sphere' i.e. the 'Politics'.

This divide sees women's gender roles and responsibilities as lying in the family, caring and childrearing, and men's gender roles as being to do with decision-making, formal politics, economics and the workplace. This division of roles and labour is important for understanding citizenship, which traditionally saw men as the holders of citizenship rights on account of their position in the public arena. Men were seen as political agents and women as being under their protection. Women and their concerns were outside the realms of citizenship, and their roles, though contributing to society, were not valued as worthy of membership in terms of decision-making and public activity. [21]

Although these arguments that classify women as naturally unfit for political power have been diminished or modified, feminists today point to women's continuing exclusion from full political citizenship, an exclusion that can be traced to underlying assumptions about women's proper role in society, and to continuing masculine domination of structures of power. [22] Carole Pateman in this regards laid down the most explicit argument for her views regarding feminism and democracy in her book The Sexual Contract (Cambridge, Polity, 1988) and in the essays in the Disorder of Women: Democracy, Feminism and Political Theory (Cambridge, Polity, 1989).

To quote Pateman: “for feminists, democracy has never existed: Women have never been and still are not admitted as full and equal members and citizens in any country known as democracy.” [23] To substantiate her point, Pateman examined the theories laid down by the social contractualist specially Rousseau, John Rawls and also liberal ideas of J.S. Mill who is regarded as a feminist thinker. Pateman tried to explore the contradictory ideas inherent in liberal democracy between ideas about women’s nature and those about individual equality. [24] Rousseau in his educational treatise titled: Emile, asserted that nature has made women inherently different from men, suiting them physically and morally and intellectually to their primary task of reproduction.

Their education and the place of society therefore should reflect this difference and their natural feminine instincts channelled advantageously into civilized domesticity. [25] Rousseau according to the liberal feminist Mary Wollstonecraft was committed to sexual dimorphism i.e. to a belief that “rational man” is the perfect complement for “emotional woman” and vice versa. His ideal male student, Emile, studies the humanities, the social sciences, and the natural sciences while Rousseau’s ideal female student Sophie, dabbles in music, art, fiction and poetry, which would help to refine her homemaking skills so that Emilie’s mental capacities will make him a rational, moral, self-governing, self-sufficient citizen and husband/father and that the development of Sophie’s sensitivities will create in her an understanding, responsive wife and a caring loving mother. [26]

Within this context of the prevalent social belief that women’s natural role in the private sphere and natural subjection to men tends to undermine the basic pillar of liberal democracies i.e., liberty, equality, justice, rule of law etc. Carole Pateman in this regard also questions the notion of consenting individuals while forming the social contract of the contractualist liberal theories. Pateman considers that natural subjection of women to man creates significant problems with women's capacity to consent both in private and the public spheres.

Susane Mollar Okin in her Gender, Justice and Family (1989) opined that democratic equality is favoured by Rawls because it does not directly block the means or mobility with in society. According to Okin, Rawls focuses on the Heads of Family in his model of Justice. The general belief of society that all the contracts are formulated by the head of the family, i.e. the superior male in the family is supported by Rawls's standpoint that the distribution of income and wealth must not always be equal as long as it is to everyone's advantage.

Also equality of wealth distribution among the heads of the family is just as long as the position of authority as the head of the family is accessible to all. [27] Because democratic equality compensates for this ideology, Rawls argues for it to be recognized as the most just of systems. John Rawls's book *A Theory of Justice* also refers to three psychological factors: morality of authority, morality of association and morality of principles. Rawls claims that the society can sustain itself only if its members have a sense of justice and identified the family as a just structure based on morality and love. Okin's question is how Rawls assumes the family is just through these psychological factors? Rawls in this regard does not recognize the possibility that the family is not just due to the hierarchical family structure where sex roles are different and unequal. Rawls opined that the morality of authority is the first stage in moral development.

As family is a moral authority Rawls continues to say that the principles taught by the parents are justified, that they are part of assumed familial duties and that the parents love the child. But he fails to answer how the child is supposed to learn a balanced understanding of justice when it is not prevalent in the child's own home due to its hierarchical set up based on gender discriminations. [28]

The liberal democratic thinker of the Utilitarian fame, J.S. Mill despite being the proponent of liberal feminism, faced criticism from Carole Pateman due to his failure to question the natural division of labour within home. Mill in The Subjection of Women (1869) held view that women are pre-occupied with her own concerns and her family and overestimates her family wants. He believed that if women are given equal education then she would have a better idea of public good and will come out of her restricted family needs. Mill pleaded for universal suffrage so that women could be given the right to vote, which would help women to know that charity begins at home and it must not hen there but needed to be extended to the whole society.

Mill opined that even given the same education, economic opportunities and civil liberties as men women will still choose marriage and motherhood over other competing occupations due to the biological differences that are inherent in women's nature. At the same time he argued that if women remained sequestered in their private roles as a mother, care-taker, wife and confine to the domestic sphere, they will also lack the opportunities to learn what it means to be a democratic citizen. In view of this Pateman opined that Mill's argument for democratic citizenship applies only to men. [29]

Pateman in her essay on "The Patriarchal welfare state" concludes that the women are seen primarily as members of the family, a sphere which is regarded as separate from civil society and the state. In the liberal democratic theories, women are regarded as unequal individual so they lack equal standing as citizens and workers in the democratic polity. She argued that category of citizen is premised on phallocentric notions of paid work and independence. So the welfare state tends to privilege the male bread winner and protect the patriarchal rights where women are perceived as dependents not as equal citizens. [30]

Women are still dramatically underrepresented in formal political institutions and decision-making bodies worldwide. In many countries women are not at all adequately represented in political parties, legislatures or the courts of law. Thus, it can be said that politics continues to be a masculine dominated activity. Even if women are admitted into the higher levels of government, they are entrusted with responsibilities which may be characterized as feminine. Although women were incorporated in large numbers into the workforce and although quotas ensured their presence in political institutions, little effort was made to change cultural attitudes or to challenge the domestic division of labour.

Ultimately, economic and political mechanisms to sustain the public role of women collapsed with the regimes that introduced them and that role in itself was discredited. Further, attention is drawn to the revival of local patriarchalism in the form of conservative, religious and nationalist forces. Politics has been constituted as a man's business to which women are not suited and male participants have been mandated to intervene in the domestic sphere in the form of legislation and constitutional clauses explicitly oriented towards 'enabling' women to stay at home, limiting their capacity for reproductive self-determination and thus their access to the public sphere. [31] Thus democracy has defined itself in fairly restrictive terms; it allows for formal equality but obviously this is not enough. A very little attention or no attention is given to factors that prevent or inhibit women from participation in the democratic process or public sphere on an equal basis, factors such as institutional structures and relationships in the workplace, the family, the community etc. The mere granting of rights doesn't help to alter people's attitudes and perception regarding those they consider inferior, whether these are women or dalits.

Gender discrimination has been a universal phenomenon

in human history from time immemorial. On account of her biological constitution, social taboos and scriptural sanction, the social position of the woman has always been considered as inferior and subordinate to man in society. In every society people as male and as female are expected to make some exclusive role performance. This role internalization is done through the process of gender socialization. The expected role performance of the female places them in a secondary position in the social structure and in the minds of men and women alike. Women are never viewed as persons on their own rights.

Moreover, women don't view themselves as autonomous being due to their cultural socialization. Because of their marginalization in society, women hardly exist as a public phenomenon. Psychological orientations develop in the given social environment. Interest in Politics or Public sphere is created through the socialization process. The socialization process conforming to cultural norms continue to create interest in politics. But female roles are traditionally defined to be home oriented along which the learning develops. Interest is therefore created in the private sphere activities. The political and democratic rights conferred by the democratic system serve as opportunities for the citizens to participate, but if there are significant differences in motivation and societal inputs, the new participatory opportunities under the democratic polity would mean more inequality in participation. [32]

At present even though, the society is developing and women are today more educated than before, and enabled them to go beyond the confines of their mother's world or private sphere into the male's sphere of public affairs, still women couldn't enjoy their democratic rights in the public sphere due to the static social norms. For example, women faces double burden whenever they steps in the public sphere as this change of women's sphere (private sphere) which the society has assigned is not accompanied by shifts to greater social provision for children. Thus, young mothers who had been educated for equality found themselves tied to the home when they had children. Thus to quote Sheila Rowbotham, "Women might not have anyone to talk to, but she could aspire to a fridge, a washing machine etc". The market for domestic goods is flourishing, but there are no equivalent development of social provision to meet women's needs as careers and domestic workers. [33] In this context one can assert that democratic rights do not apply to women and are only used in terms of 'man'. If the rights of man also meant the rights of women, even more extensive changes were needed in society. For women were not regarded as free and independent individuals but as attached to fathers or husband.

The definitions of democracy for women must include domestic inequality, identity, control over sexuality, challenge to cultural representation, community control over State welfare and more equal access to public resources. The feminist political theory claims that women have been consistently marginalized within domestic ideas and institutions. They argue that discrepancies that prevent the participation of women in the political/public sphere and limit their role as political citizens. A major drawback in democratic political thought, according to the feminist, lies in its rigid establishment and gendering of private and public spheres.

Women's lives have been mainly confined to the private sphere and inequality in the private has been largely ignored by democratic theory, and is beyond the preview of notions like political equality, freedom and citizenship. Modern democracy rarely acknowledges that women be active in the public realm or that she exercises her rights as a citizen. The process of democracy is limited to activities in the public sphere of government and women, whose lives came to be restricted largely to the private sphere, have been left out of the liberal-democratic process. Most democratic institutions are of a public kind and don't really affect or even attempt to influence domestic and familial life. When they do, it is in the form of laws, which again are interpreted through a haze of ideas that have to do with masculinity and feminity. [34]

The widespread acceptance of a distinction between public, political life and private, domestic life has been particularly attacked by the feminists. It may be noted here, that since time immemorial, the society has created two different spheres and likewise the society has entrusted different roles to man and women. The private sphere is assigned to women whereas the public sphere to men. The society expects them to act in their assigned roles and rewards them if they work within the limits of the two spheres and punishes them if they don't. The spaces are sharply divided into masculine and feminine; the space of home is identified with women and the outside world is considered as exclusively male sphere and likewise women's identity rests on their roles as wives, mothers, as homemakers, whereas male identity is linked to productive work, public visibility and power. [35]

Women's continued association with the domestic outside the political is seen to naturalize relations of inequality between the genders in both realms and to ensure that most women remain politically invisible is a great challenge towards the functioning of democracy. It may be mentioned here that women in the private sphere too is powerless and feminine subjectivity are retained in this sphere under the patriarchal control of man. It is men who are dominant in the private sphere where domestic violence takes place. In this case too the public control of the private coercion is needed because the family is frequently the site of domestic violence. The private space should be opened up for intervention, which will reduce crime against women.

The feminists tried to uncover the double standards maintained by the so called democratic society in distinguishing the two spheres. Public space is theorized as a sphere where norms like competitive, rational, self-interested and ignores his/her familial, social constitution and emotional ties. These norms refer to a masculinist view of human nature. Thus the dominant spaces of liberalism have no place for traditional feminine traits. Women in order to be competent in the public sphere has to adopt herself to masculine traits which are not her own and thus curtails women's free development and expression of her individuality. [36] In this spectrum it may be cited here that the philosopher Aristotle holds that women are naturally lacking in intelligence and rationality which are regarded as masculinity traits.

Thus being natural fools, women don't deserve to be citizens who participate in public affairs and they must leave these matters to their men who could represent their interest better! The feminist slogan "The personal is political" opened up the barriers and the possibility for understanding the extended public sphere of democratic rights in the domestic and sexual life. Moreover, the feminists questioned the dilemma related to the public and private debate in the modern liberal democratic set up and call for a rejection of artificial separation of these two spheres. The liberal democratic State at present use to intervene in the private lives of its citizens for instances-regulating the divorce laws, inheritance laws, legislation concerning marriage, formulating population control measures etc.

However, when analyzed these laws and the structural adjustment policies formulated by State has further led to the subordinate status of women which is maintained by the power of the State. It may be mentioned that, regarding rape, domestic violence and abortion the State and legal systems of the liberal democratic state falls back on the position of non-intervention and respect for privacy of the individual. Thus dual standards maintained by the law as applied in the private sphere exists legitimizing discriminatory practices against women. Non-intervention of the State in the private matters-family or community is a myth created by the liberal-democratic norms of the State. [37]

Thus women have become increasingly marginalized as political actors within many of the new regimes. Although women are incorporated in large numbers into the workforce and even though quotas ensured their presence in political institutions, little effort was made to change cultural attitudes or to challenge the domestic division of labour. Thus, it can be argued that a democracy would fully worth its name if citizens are able to enjoy their entitled rights which allow them to command democratic participation. Political institutions, development plans, technology, information and knowledge, free media, are inputs and instruments through which a democracy works. But when these institutions, instrumentalists and inputs don't deliver the desired service based on the fundamental norms of democracy i.e.. gender equality, justice, order and freedom and instead become agencies of oppression for women. Thus the recent wave of liberal democratization generally has not served women well.

Feminist historian, Gerda Learner in her book The Creations of Patriarchy (1986) asserted that most of the theoretical work of modern feminism beginning with Simone de Beauvoir and continuing to the present has been a historical and negligent of feminist historical scholarship. Here history referred to the recollected memories and recorded and interpreted past of human kind. Like men, women are always have shared the world and worked equally with men and are central, not marginal to the making of society and to the building of civilization. But though women have made history according to Learner, yet they have been kept from knowing their history and from knowing their history and from interpreting history. Learner opined that in many historical periods considered progressive, men and women did not benefit equally from developments that were lauded as great democratic improvements over the past. [38]

Media and Its Role in a Democratic Set Up

After going through the above discourses on liberal democracy and its feminist criticism, it could be debated that democracy would be fully worth its name if citizens are able to enjoy their rights which allow them to command democratic participation and to treat it as an entitlement. Successful democracy demands a system of constant interaction with all the people, accessibility at all levels, a public ethos which allows conflicting ideas to contend, and which provides for full participation in reaching the consensus on socio-cultural, economic and political goals. Within this context the role of a democratic media becomes the prerequisite of democracy to infuse change and inculcate democratic values in the society.

The world is changing and developing fast and the development in the communication technologies are very deeply impacting the institutions all over the world and at the same time the lives of each and every individual. Media has become a powerful and necessary tool in today's changing world. Media has always played a very important role towards democratization. Looking at history in most the countries, the media has played a very significant role towards transition of democratic system itself. For example: Periodic Election for materialization of a respective government. But the converting democratic practices and democratic procedures into substantive means for fulfilling people's security, the media has played a very significant role.

The media facilitate this process by providing a platform for public debate and as a carrier of public opinion. In a democratic country the free access to knowledge and information is the inalienable right of each citizens and addition to this people's voice irrespective of caste, class, gender and other differences should be equally represented in the media. It is now widely accepted fact that the fate of a democratic political system depends on the efficient, accurate, and complete transmission of social, political, and cultural information in society and for this reason the main role of the media is that it should always act in the public interest.

However, there are conflicting ideas defining the pre-requisites of democratic media. According to the liberalist thinkers, a minimalist state which allows for private media ownership, does not censor its contents are the most important attributes for a democratic media. On the other hand, media democracy advocates argue that corporate ownership and commercial pressures influence media content, sharply limiting the range of news, opinions, and entertainment citizens receive and argues for a more equal distribution of economic, social, cultural, and information capital, for empowering the citizens enabling to actively participate in the democratic process. Moreover with the increasing debate on the role of democratic media, *alternative media* as a counteracting force against the mainstream media basically owned by business corporate came to being. The exponents of alternative media are of the view that the mainstream media is heavily biased, and are class biased which includes the political interests of the owners, government influence or a profit motives in them while disseminating information.

As, a democratic media is a must for a functioning democracy, it is also an established fact that a true democracy can never exist unless there is true participation of women both in governance and developmental programmes. But the social roles assigned to both the sexes all over the globe demonstrate a world full of opportunities for men and restrictions for women! Hence, despite the rapid advancement of 'democratization' and growing 'civil society', women remain underrepresented in parliaments, and absent in decision-making bodies and leadership positions in all the countries in comparison to men. In this regard, the media is expected to represent women's voices and also impart in women new values and progressive action and the information of those issues affecting them as well as to give a complete view of their life situation. Media mediates and shapes people's reality.

It is supposed to reflect the economic, political, social and cultural situation of local, national or global issues. The mass-media have the potential to shape peoples perception and also to alter the perceptions around them in addition to its capacity to mould public opinions and attitudes. In view of this, the task to shape gender realities by changing public opinion and attitude towards the existing gender misconceptions lie more with the, mass-media. With the growing consciousness about the role of media towards gender equality, over the past twenty-five years, analytical critique of the interconnections between women, media institutions and media content has come to occupy an ever more central place on the international agenda. The media at the onset of liberalization during the 90s underwent a dramatic transformation. Under the aegis of the market forces the globalized media opted for a new form of homogenization of people and cultures intensifying the alienation of peoples mostly the indigenous groups, people with disabilities, older women, etc.

Through the homogenization of peoples and cultures, through media, the corporations have marketed their way to more societies and more into women's lives, both in developing and developed countries. The market and media have intensified consumerism through advertisements by creating the myth of beauty among women and became an effective market instrument in creating artificial needs to sell products that guarantee to mould women to perfection. With gradual transformation of media and its power in shaping people's values, attitudes, perceptions and behaviours, it is recognized as a strong socializing agent and platform for women's struggle for eliminating sexism and violence against women. In view of this the 1995 Fourth World Conference on Women in Beijing, China propelled international concern and action on the role of media in perpetuating women's subordination as well its importance in advancing women's rights. The Beijing Platform for Action (BPFA) gave an overview of problems and issues surrounding women and the media and spelled out specific strategies for governments, media organizations, non-government organizations and other civil society actors.

It called for: (a) women's increased participation in and access to media and new information and communication technologies (ICTs); (b) promotion of a balanced and non-stereotyped representation of women in the media. [39] Based on the above recommendations a Global Monitoring Report on reviews of the recommendations of Section J, Beijing Platform for Action on *Alternative Assessment of Women and Media* was prepared by network of NGOs working on Media all over the world. The report revealed that there is a continued negative portrayal and representation of women; women continue to have limited access and participation in decision-making in the media industries and governing authorities and bodies that oversee formulation and implementation of media policies and Women media practitioners continue to face gender-based discrimination including sexual harassment at the work place, proving that the power to shape and influence media still eludes women.

The research study revealed that the traditional polarization of gender roles and identities are still reflected in the media. Studies were also conducted in India monitoring the gender coverage in news. [40] The Media Advocacy Group's Survey conducted in 1994 found that: (a) Gender representation to be biased-men are portrayed in diverse roles, women almost always in traditional feminine roles. (b) Women accounted for 7 percent of the time in the hard news section (political and economic segment of news) and 14 percent in soft news programmes. [41]

Media acts as the cornerstone of democracy, which imparts information on public issues and through which citizens convey their opinions to policy makers. In contemporary times no discussion on the public sphere is complete unless it takes into account the role of media in representing concerns of citizens. Media serves as a powerful institution of the public sphere in today's society. Media plays a dominant role in empowering individuals by providing a platform for public debate where the individuals are reconstituted as a public body in the form of public opinion. The content of media such as entertainment, news, educational programmes, advertising and images of various kinds have tremendous impact in sustaining and weakening if not destroying the fabric of social life. [42] In a democratic society, every citizen has the right to receive information on public issues and convey their opinion. A democratic media is a must for a functioning democracy, it is also an established fact that a true democracy can never exist unless there is true participation of women both in governance and developmental programmes. In this regard, the media needs to play a positive role in representing women's voices and also impart in women new values and progressive action and the information of those issues affecting them as well as give a complete view of their life situation.

Women represent half of the world's population and have acquired political citizenship in most of the societies. Yet their concerns and status have remained marginalized within the social, economic and political structures. Likewise, the media, which forms a dominant part of the public sphere, has left many women's concerns invisible in a democratic polity. Women's issues are often sensationalized, trivialized or distorted by the media. They are not seen as important constituents in decision making positions, in governments. As a result, women often bear the burnt of the chronic problems which beset the country and in addition, carry other burdens related to the gender based division of labour, the general devaluation of women by the society which are rarely presented by the media to carry women problems to centre stage in the nation's affairs. [43]

The mass media texts are very powerful and their messages are more or less irresistible. Media are seen to behave like a hypodermic needle, injecting audiences with their messages. The media images are generally conceived as a system of signs that work to position the female readers for their later roles as wives and mothers by means of the ideology of teenage femininity it cultivates. The culture of femininity is a part of the dominant ideology which has saturated the lives of the young girls, colouring the way they talk to each other. [44] In view of this, feminists from varied philosophical and theoretical positions in analyzing women's problems and solutions in relation to their representation in the media. The representation of women in Media has always been an important battle ground for contemporary feminism. The women's movement is not only engaged in a material struggle about equal rights and opportunities for women, but also in a symbolic conflict about definitions of femininity. [45] Zoonen identified three areas which attracted much of the feminist media scholars. They are stereotypes and socialization, pornography, and ideology.

The theme stereotypes and socialization was dealt by Betty Freidan, Margharet Gallaghar and Tuchman extensively. Tuchman in her book Hearth and Home: Images of Women and Media (1978), tried to focus that at present the media failed to live up to its democratic function. According to her, the society transmits its culture from one generation to another and the society for its survival must be prepared to meet changing condition. But though an impressive social transformation has taken place where over half of all American women joined the labour force, television shows, the media hardly portrays these positive changes. By the very nature of their marginality in society women hardly exists as a public phenomenon with the result that their concern doesn't constitute news and hence are of little value.

Thus media symbolically annihilates women and portrays to the society that women are not important. Thus she opined that the symbolic annihilation of women would endanger social development and girls and mature women would lack positive images and this would hamper them in their development into complete human beings and socially valuable workers. [46]

Another research conducted in this area as identified by Zoonen was by Margheret Gallagher. Gallagher in the projects conducted by her titled Unequal Opportunities: Update (1985), Women and Men in the Media (1992) and Unequal Opportunities: The case of women and the media (1990) found that the under-representation of women in media is common in both western industrialized societies and also the developing countries. Moreover, there were commonality in all these countries that the women who appeared in the media had to be young, pretty and they were portrayed as passive, indecisive, submissive, dependent etc. [47] Likewise in the other feminist research theme in Media Studies, researchers like Thelma McCormack concentrated on the study of Pornography where she opined that pornography objectifies women for men's pleasure and it contributes to the eroticization of power and violence and hence the construction of forms of masculine sexuality which seeks pleasure through power and violence.

She argued that Pornography harms women's opportunities for equal rights, that it creates harassment and private degradation, that it promotes sexual violence and inhibits a just enforcement of the laws, and that it significantly restricts women from the full exercise of their citizenship and participation in public life. [48] Lastly Zoonen identified, the areas of feminist media research comprising of theories of ideology such as Radical ideology, Marxist ideology and Socialist Ideology dealing with the communication and cultural studies.

The liberal feminism is essentially a reformist approach which opined that only by providing equal opportunities, policies and affirmative action programmes, the gender inequality in media could be abolished. It rarely questions the power dimensions in society that maintain male superiority of status and female inferiority. The Radical feminists basically focuses on how women are misrepresented in the media and they investigate the effects of patriarchy on women that is, the system whereby all men directly or indirectly dominate and oppress all women. They are particularly concerned about the media's role in the construction of consciousness and gender identities instead of specific stereotypes. They identified that the male dominance in the media and other social institutions requires women to separate themselves from male-controlled systems and create their own organizations and structures to speak on their behalf with ample representation.

The Socialist feminism, on the other hand does not concentrate exclusively upon gender, but takes the middle way of the radical and liberal feminists and basically analyses the social class, ethnicity, sexual preference, age and disability into the discourse. The socialist feminist theory appears embedded in socioeconomic conditions where media are perceived as ideological apparatuses that represent the essential rightness of capitalism as a social system. It is based within a Marxist framework of reference, namely Gramsci's (1971) theory of hegemony.

For example, the news items might serve as the means by which a dominant class, could condition a population of subordinate classes (women, minorities) to adopt prevailing values and behaviours, by legalizing them by indoctrinating the values with the help of ideological hegemony through media thereby perpetuating an inherently unequal system of power. The media are texts- complex structures of linguistic and visual codes organized to produce specific meanings. They are the bearers of ideology which in the way of seeing appears to us to be universal and natural but which is in fact the product of the specific power structures which contribute our society. Simone de Beauvoirs's account in the Second Sex of the process by which one is not born but rather becomes a women is also cantered on the cultural construction of women as Other can be applicable to the media construct of women.

According to the Psychoanalyst film critic, Laura Mulvey in her book, Visual Pleasure and Narrative Cinema, discusses the way how the Unconscious of patriarchal society has structured the film texts subordinating women's status. According to her, the sign women in film or media is one constructed by and for a patriarchal culture, enabling man to live out his fantasies and obsession by imposing them on the silent image of women. Within this spectrum one may apply Jaques Lacan's theory of image formation during the mirror phase. Laura Mulvey interprets Lacan's theory of psychoanalyst.

According to Jaques Lacan during the mirror phase, when the child see his image in the mirror, the ego formation takes place and the child imagines itself to be a whole and powerful individual by identifying his own mirror image. Likewise when the child views a cinema, he immediately internalizes himself with the figure of the hero. But women in films are projected as objects not subjects so media images are created only for providing pleasure to the male spectator. Female spectator imagines herself with the eroticized bodies of the heroine as projected in the film. This division between active/male and passive/female, argues Mulvey, also structures films narrative. It is the film's hero who advances the story, controlling events, the women and the erotic gaze. Women in contrast, functions as erotic spectacle, interrupting rather than advancing the narrative. [49]

Thus what media portrays goes deep into the subconscious and unconscious mind of people and has wide implications not only on their lives but also on the life of those around them. The media images have lot to do with perceptions. Thus media representation of women has a major role in shaping their self-image and also the concept of women among the policy makers and the audiences. Media while highlighting the biological and domestic role of women, almost neglect the major contributions they make to the development of the nation socially, politically and economically. In other words, media tend to be silent about the productive and economic role of women. [50] The patriarchal nature of socialization of the media personal and the readers/ viewers force them to see women only in subordinate gender roles and construct their images always in relation to men often as their playthings. This definitely indicates the power of the media to throw back women a version of themselves, which then is presented as the norm and gradually they internalize the same.

Betty Freidan in her book, The Feminine Mystique (1963)

argues that by pushing women into the role of happy home makers, society denied them the opportunity to fulfil potential as human beings. Media advertisements manipulated women into believing that they could achieve fulfilment by using the latest models of household appliances, which made household chores easier and faster. Women's magazines romanticized domesticity and presented an image of women as *Gaily Content in a world of bedroom, kitchen, sex, babies and home.* [51]

The media have always been at the centre of feminist critique. Freidan accused the media and a range of allied experts such as doctors, psychiatrists and sociologists of installing insecurity , fear and frustration in ordinary women who couldn't and wouldn't live up to the ideal of happy housewife heroine. According to her, the media and in particular women's magazines during the revival of the American women's movement in the mid-60's contributed to "the Feminine Mystique" the myth that women could find true fulfilment in being a housewife and a mother. [52]

According to Theodor Adorno and Max Horkheimer, the media or the culture industry (Films, radio and magazines) make up a system which is uniform as a whole and in every part. The basis on which these media technology acquires power over society is the power of those whose economic hold over society is greatest. A technological rationale is the rationale of domination itself. The different stories in magazines in different price ranges depend not so much on subject matter as on classifying, organizing, and labelling consumers.

The public is catered for with a hierarchical range of mass-produced products of varying quality thus the consumers appear as statistics on research organization charts, and are divided by income groups into red, green, and blue areas; the technique is that used for any type of propaganda. [53] Thus the mass is divided in various classes in a hierarchical manner. Likewise the projection of the media industry depends upon the market interest of the proprietor class who happens to be the rich class and mostly dominated by man. In that case women issues are given less importance being a class belonging to the private sphere as assigned by the societal values.

Globalization has brought new challenges to the democratic role assigned to the media. The advertisers become the primary customer of the print and visual media through which they reach the customers who happens the readers or viewers of the media. With the economic liberalization in the third world countries including India, the fashion industry has developed. The fashion industry in collaboration with the media creates role models in order to urge women to look this way and that, promote products which, they claim will enhance or even enable one to be beautiful. Thus with the growth of fashion industry women's beauty became one of the most important definition of femininity.

Media projects ideal feminine norms as a thin, elegant, works hard to be beautiful, diets, exercises, is not averse to intelligent conversation, but is not on that account an intellectual women, loves to charity and ultimately longs to settle into a marriage of love. But with this perception, the media aligns traditional feminine attributes to a modern purpose while blending traditional patriarchal values in connection with women with the modern one. Feminists argue that the ideal of beauty has to be viewed as a construction a myth imposed on women. They claim that this myth serves a particular purpose in patriarchal society. According to them the media are dividing women into beautiful and ugly. Those one can't live up to the norm of beautification by using the market products are afflicted with a sense of inadequacy, guilt and jealousy and fails to attain male gaze. The media makes women feels empowered and free by transforming herself into an object. In the process she fails to see that she is really not making a choice but merely working a pro-given and limited role to advantage. [54] All these consequences show the inherent limitations of women's rights narratives and discourses of the media in a liberal democratic society.

Conclusion

The precondition for successful democracy is gender equality so that both men and women could equally participate in governance and developmental process in a country. Even though women in a democratic society is assumed to be enjoying their rights to the fullest extent, in reality women's democratic freedom are curtailed by the rigidity of the prevalent social customs of the society. The position of women in the society is determined on the basis of the social values, and the trends or tendencies prevailing in the society. Thus the relation between women and media in the Indian democratic setup could be determined after analyzing the position of women in the Indian society and culture. The Indian society is highly stratified one and thus the position of women depends upon the class they belonged to.

Media mediates and shapes people's reality and reflects the economic, political, social and cultural situation about local, national or global issues. It plays a great part in shaping society's perception on women. The role of media is crucial in communicating and popularizing women's issues, concerns and actions from a gender perspective. Media plays a very crucial role as a facilitator of developing the society because it informs and create awareness about new ideas, bridge the geographical gap between various regions and communities. Media doesn't operate in vacuum, but is influenced by the cultural set-up of the society. The media issues and representation are seen not only in terms of social institutions and practices, but also in terms of symbolic meanings, the formation of identities and deeply-rooted belief systems.

Culture concerns the conditions and the forms in which meaning and value are structured and articulated within a society. [55] The media/journalists cannot proceed without values prevalent in society. Due to the control of patriarchy in the media, women's concerns have been looked through the eyes of patriarchy. Thus, regarding projection of women in the media, it has been projected through the eyes of patriarchy. In the advent of globalization, media is proliferating. With the opening up of the private media, which is going on, many newspapers and channels are entering in the frame. But at the same time is it really helping towards liberation of women or not is highly debated.

Notes

1. Merkl, Peter H., Political Continuity and Change, Allied Publishers Pvt. Ltd., Indian edition, 1975, p. 113.
2. Locke, J. [1698] 1988. *Two Treatises of Government* Edited P. Laslett. Cambridge: Cambridge University Press, p. 287-288.
3. Roy Anupama, *Gendered Citizenship: historical and conceptual explorations*, Orient Longman, 2005, p. 9.
4. Deol. D, Liberalism and Marxism: An introduction to the study of contemporary politics, Sterling publishers, New Delhi, 2nd edition, 1977, p. 215.
5. Ibid, p. 216.
6. Konstantinov F. V. (ed.), The Fundamentals of Marxist-Leninist Philosophy, Progress Publishers, Moscow, 1982, p. 37.
7. Hayek, F.A., *New Studies in Philosophy, Politics, Economics and the History of Ideas*, Routledge and Keagan Paul, London and Henley, 1982 [1978], p. 130.
8. Vermani R.C., An introduction to Political Theory, Gitanjali Publishers, New Delhi, 1996, p. 187.
9. Bhagawati Dhiren, *Democracy and People*, In Journal of Politics, Department of Political Science, Dibrugarh University, Vol. III, December, 1996, p. 20.
10. Ullah Samina, *Gender and Liberal Democracy: The Deconstruction of Liberal Imperialism in Afghanistan*, In Undercurrent, Vol. III No. 2, 2006. p. 2.
11. Pantham Thomas, *Political theories and social reconstruction*, Sage Publication, New Delhi, 1995, p. 19.
12. Chandhoke Neera, *State and Civil Society: Explorations in Political Theory*, Sage Publication, New Delhi, 1995, p. 34.
13. Ibid. p. 9.
14. Ibid. p. 12.

15. Ibid. p. 161.
16. Ibid pp. 169-170.
17. Rowbotham Sheila, *Feminism and Democracy*, In Held David, Pollitt (ed.), New Forms of Democracy, Sage Publication, New Delhi, 1994, p. 78.
18. Georgina Ashworth, *Introduction: Gender and Democracy Why?* International Institute of Democracy and Electoral Assistance (IDEA), archive.idea.int/women/parl/ch1a.htm.
19. Hawkesworth. E. Mary, *Democratization: Reflections on Gendered Dislocations in the Public Sphere*, in Kelly, Rita Mae, Bayes Jane H, Hawkesworth. E. Mary and Tong, Brigitte (ed.), Gender, Globalisation and Democratisation, Rowman and Littlefield Publishers, INC, 2001, pp. 225-226.
20. Ibid.
21. Report on Gender and Citizenship, Institute on Development Studies, 2004, p. 21 downloaded from: http.www.bridge.ids.ac.
22. Freedman Jane, *Concepts in the Social Sciences: 'Feminism'*, Viva Books, New Delhi, 2002, p. 56.
23. Pateman Carol, *The Disorder of Women: Democracy, Feminism and Political Theory,* Cambridge, Polity, 1989, p. 210.
24. Sullivan Barbara, *Carole Pateman: Participatory Democracy and Feminism*, In, April Carter, Stokes Geoffrey (ed.), Liberal Democracy and its Critics: Perspectives in Contemporary Political Thought, Polity Press Publication, 1998, p. 180-181.
25. Roy Anupama, *Gendered Citizenship: historical and conceptual explorations*, Orient Longman, New Delhi, 2005, p. 80.
26. Tong, Rosemary, Feminist Thought, Routledge, London, 1995, p. 14-15.
27. Hartline Taylor, *Rawls's A Theory of Justice: Addressing the Criticism of Okin and Pateman*, downloaded from: http.www.cupr.org.
28. Okin Mollar Susane, *Gender, Justice and Family*, New York, Basic Books, 1989, pp. 99-100.
29. Sullivan Barbara, *Carole Pateman: Participatory Democracy and Feminism*, In, April Carter, Stokes Geoffrey (ed.), Liberal Democracy and its Critics: Perspectives in Contemporary Political Thought, Polity Press Publication, 1998, p. 187 and also see, Tong, Rosemary, *Feminist Thought*, Routledge, London, 1995, pp. 18-21.
30. Ibid, pp. 182.

31. Eschle Catherine, *Engendering Global Democracy*, 2000, downloaded from www.sussex.ac.uk.
32. Panda Snehlata, *Determinants of Political Participation: Women and Public Activity*, Ajanta Publications, 1990, p. 226.
33. Rowbotham Sheila, *Feminism and Democracy*, In Held David, Pollitt (ed.), New Forms of Democracy, Sage Publication, New Delhi, 1994, p. 85.
34. Geetha V., *Gender*, Stree, Calcutta, 2002, p. 43.
35. Ibid, p. 45.
36. Borgohain Alpana, Borgohain Alpana, *An Analysis of certain Perspectives of Feminist Critique of Liberalism*, Unpublished Ph.d. Thesis, Dibrugarh University, 2003, p. 112.
37. Ibid, pp. 135-136.
38. Lerner Gerder, *The Creation of Patriarchy*, Oxford University Press, New York, 1986, pp. 3-5.
39. Carolina Rodriguez Bello, *Women and Media: Progress and Issues*, October, 2003, appeared in www. whrnet.org/docs/issues-media.html, 2003.
40. *Who makes the news? Global Media Monitoring Project, 2005*, analysis written by Margharet Gallaghar, downloaded from: www.whomakesthe news.org.
41. Centre for Advocacy and Research, Report on: *Representation of Issues in News and Current Affairs Programmes on Television,* 2000 (Unpublished).
42. Ambirajan S., *Globalization, Media and Culture*, In, EPW, June 17, 2000, pp. 21-41.
43. Joseph, Ammu and Sharma Kalpana, EPW, OCT. 26, 1991, WS-75.
44. Fenton Natalie, *Feminism and Popular Culture*, in Gamble Sarah (ed.), The Routledge Companion to Feminism and Post-Feminism, Routledge Publisher, 2001, New York, p. 111.
45. Zoonen Liesbet Van, *Feminist Media Studies*, Thousand Oaks, California, 1994, p. 12.
46. Ibid, p. 16.
47. Ibid. p. 17.
48. Ibid. p. 20.
49. Thornham Sue, *Feminism and Popular Culture*, in Gamble Sarah (ed.), The Routledge Companion to Feminism and Post-Feminism, Routledge Publisher, 2001, New York, p. 97.
50. Prasad Kiran, *Women and Media: Challenging Feminist*

Discourse, The Women Press, New Delhi, 2005, p. 19.

51. Borgohain Alpana, Borgohain Alpana, *An Analysis of certain Perspectives of Feminist Critique of Liberalism*, Unpublished Ph.d. Thesis, Dibrugarh University, 2003, p. 119.
52. Zoonen Liesbet Van, *Feminist Media Studies*, Thousand Oaks, California, 1994, p. 11.
53. Theodor Adorno and Max Horkheimer (1944): *The Culture Industry: Enlightenment as Mass Deception,* Transcribed: by Andy Blunden 1998; cited from http://www.marxists.org.
54. Geetha V., *Gender*, Stree, Calcutta, 2002, p. 22.
55. Zoonen Liesbet Van, *Feminist Media Studies*, Thousand Oaks, California, 1994, p. 6.

9

Political Significance of Fifteenth Lok Sabha Polls (2009)

M.R. Biju

The election to the fifteenth Lok Sabha was a land mark in the politics of India in more than one sense. The Personality of Dr. Man Mohan Singh, Policies of the UPA Government, Rahul Gandhi's contribution to the Congress party particularly in UP, weaknesses of the NDA especially the BJP and confusion in the third and fourth fronts were responsible for the spectacular victory of the Congress and its allies. Belying expectations of a fragmented verdict, the mandate was decisive in favour of the Congress led United Progressive Alliance. The alliance has managed to win 261 seats with the Congress itself winning 206 seats, its best tally since the 1991 elections when the party had won 244 seats.

The UPA came on top in 17 out of 29 states including Delhi. Excepting the Biju Janata Dal (BJD) in Orissa, the performance of the regional and left parties in the Third Front ranged from underwhelming to the disastrous. The National Democratic Alliance won overwhelmingly in Bihar, Karnataka, and Chattisgarh but was defeated in many a major state by the UPA in direct fights. In general terms, the country voted decisively for continuity and stability by giving the Congress led UPA one more term in office. In Contrast to 2004, the UPA with close to 260 of the total 543 seats, not required the support of the Left parties. In terms of seats, it was the best performance by the Congress since 1991. Verdict 2009 also gave little scope for the smaller parties or groupings to engage in back room negotiations to decide the future course of action of the new government.

The triumph of the Congress was actually an aggregation of specific success across different States. The party retained its base in Andhra Pradesh, cut its losses in Madhya Pradesh; recovered lost ground in West Bengal, Kerala, and Rajasthan; and combined well with its allies in Maharashtra and Tamil Nadu. There was no one big surprise anywhere, but the party pulled out one small surprise after another across the regions of India. When it seems to take the long view in Uttar Pradesh and Bihar and spurned alliance offers by regional players, few predicted any immediate gains for the party. But now, one of the significant features of this election is surely the re-emergence of the Congress as a key player in Uttar Pradesh, India's most populous state. The same strategy did not work of course in Bihar, where the alliance of the Janata Dal (United) and the Baharatiya Janata Party rode on the good track record of Chief Minister Nitish Kumar. All the same, the Congress seems to have sown the seeds of its own resurgence by adopting a long-sighted strategy in the two key Hindi speaking States.

The principal opposition party, the Bharatiya Janata Party needed to expand beyond its core support base to get ahead of the Congress. This it was unable to do. In 2004, the BJP fared very well in Rajasthan, Madhya Pradesh, Chattisgarh, Gujarat, and Karnataka, the States where it is locked in a more or less direct fight with the Congress. To merely repeat that success would have been a considerable achievement. But this time, it lost badly in Rajasthan and yielded some ground in Madhya Pradesh. The success in Gujarat, Chattisgarh, and Karnataka could not compensate for the losses sustained in Rajasthan and Madhya Pradesh. To have a realistic chance of forming the government, the BJP not only had to hold its ground in the Hindi belt; it also needed its allies to do well. While the JD (U) obliged in Bihar, the Shiv Sena disappointed in Maharashtra.

The honours were more or less even in Punjab. But more importantly, potential post-allies such as the Telugu Desam Party and the Telangana Rashtra Samiti in Andhra Pradesh and the All India Anna Dravida Munnetra Kazhagam in Tamil Nadu did not do as well as they were expected to. And this came after the demoralizing loss of a long-time ally, the Biju Janata Dal, in Orissa. After reaching a plateau in the Hindi belt, the BJP needed to grow outside its traditional strongholds to really threaten the Congress. In recent years, its only success in this regard has been Karnataka. But in other States in the south, the party is far from being a player of any significance.

Other than the BJP, the big loser in the current election is the Left. In both West Bengal and Kerala, the Left parties suffered severe reverses; if the loss in the southern State can be explained in terms of the customary swing of the pendulum, the failure to win a majority of seats in the eastern State is the first in more than three decades. This has meant that the Left parties will no longer be the influential force they were at the Centre between 2004 and 2008. Although they were not part of the UPA government, the Left parties helped shape a Common Minimum Programme and kept up pressure on the government to comply with it. Factional infighting in Kerala, and a strong oppositional, even if opportunistic, alliance in West Bengal, have succeeded in beating back the Left, which will need to do serious introspection on where it went wrong.

In a tough contest, the UPA surpassed not only the anti-incumbency factor, but also the shrill, communal campaign of the BJP. But the mandate must not be read as an unqualified endorsement of all that the UPA government did in the last five years. In many States, regional issues came into play. The Sri Lankan Tamil issue dominated campaign rhetoric in Tamil Nadu, but the voters rewarded neither those who advocated the cause of the LTTE nor those who blamed the humanitarian crisis in Sri Lanka on alleged complicity and inaction by the Central and State governments. In Bihar, the fight became a virtual referendum on the performance of the Nitish Kumar-government after years of Lalu-Rabri rule. In Maharashtra, the split in the Shiv Sena engineered by Raj Thackeray seems to have played as big a role as the coming together of the

Nationalist Congress Party and the Congress.

The 2009 poll was held at time when the country was facing a series of internal and external challenges: namely the impact of the global economic slowdown, and the tensions and instability in the neighbourhood etc. In this juncture, the UPA must guard against complacency and must use this second innings to improve governance and respond effectively to the big challenges.

Verdict: A Close Watch

Against this backdrop at attempt has been made in this part on the political dynamics, undercurrents and after-effects of the poll.

- **Popular Will Based on Wisdom:** The electorate indisputably noted this time for a stable government at the centre but it was certainly something more than stability. Majority of the electorate felt that only the Congress can provide a stable and secular government. Further, it was widely acknowledged across the country that Sonia Gandhi is the tallest leader and the Congress is the largest party with moderate, middle path views. It was also supplemented with the track record of the Man Mohan Singh Government, particularly its social sector initiatives such as the NREGS and the bank loan waiver.
- **Successful Implementation of NREGS:** In several states like Andhra Pradesh, Rajasthan where the Congress is in power, the State Governments have took bold efforts to implement the National Rural Employment Guarantee Scheme in sharp contrast to the prevailing situation in Left ruled West Bengal (Whose record in Muslim Welfare too is dismal, as seen from Sachar Committee Report on the issue and this helped them to reap rich electoral dividends. The farmer's loan waiver scheme was also a factor that assisted the Congress to win popular support in rural areas.
- **Verdict against the CPM and other Left Parties:** Of course the real surprise for the CPM came from West

Bengal and Kerala. In West Bengal, where the Left Front which is in power for 32 years suffered its worst humiliation since 1977. The Left garnered just 15 out of 42 seats, with the largest partner or 'big brother' the CPM collecting a paltry nine while the other three smaller constituents shared two seats each. At the other end Mamta Banerjee's Trinamul Congress won 19 seats and its ally, the Congress, six. This the net result of the CPM's high handedness, brutality, arrogance of power, pro-corporate sector and anti-farmer attitude exemplified in Nandigram and Singur besides the total alienation of the Left supporters in both the rural and urban areas due to maladministration, corruption and anarchy in every sphere of development.

In Kerala too, the Left suffered severe reverses—though these were expected—due to rampant infighting within the CPM and the LDF. A series of poll-eve decisions of the CPM went wrong and the anger of large sections of the state electorate, including significantly the powerful Catholic Church, turned against the CPM, the UDF won a swathe of 10 southern and Central Kerala constituencies from Thiruvananthapuram to Thrissur (except Attingal) and the rest of turn in the north, except Palakkad, Alathur, and Kasargod. The UDF has triumphed in 100 (out of 140) assembly segments. That should serve as a wake up call for the CPM and the coalition it leads, as they enter their fourth year in Government on 17 May 2009.

The CPM had to pay a heavy price for its questionable association with the People's Democratic Front of Abdul Naser Madani who was the principal accused in the Coimbatore blast case that had targeted L.K. Advani. This alliance cost the CPM both ways the Muslims disliked this association with an overtly communal outfit and voted in masse for the Indian Union Muslim League (IUML) while a Hindu Backlash took place at the other end which benefited the Congress immensely.

In short, nationally the Left has come down from its historic high of 61 seats in 2004 to 24 in 2009. The political context, the party system and the nature of issues wee quite different in West Bengal and Kerala that would be hard to see both these defeats as constituting the same phenomenon. Further, a similar situation happened in Tamil Nadu and Andhra Pradesh. This stagnation may point to a deeper difficulty in the social base of the political support enjoyed by the Left. There is no doubt that the support for Left parties comes more from the poor and very poor classes.

In its strongholds, the Left has drawn disproportionately from marginalised social communities such as Dalits, adivasis and in some cases Muslims. More than half of those who voted for the Left parties belong to the poor or very poor sections. In terms of the social profile of Left voters, about 42 percent are Dalits and Muslims. Despite their claims of representing the proletarian classes, these parties draw 80 percent of their vote from rural areas, significantly more than the 'bourgeois' parties. Notwithstanding their self-image of drawing upon the youth, who are generally prone towards radical political ideologies and practices, the Left parties do not any longer enjoy greater than average support among younger voters. In West Bengal at least, the Left is expanding its base among the rural well to do and the urban middle classes at the expense of- the small and marginal farmer.

- **Congress Gains in U.P:** The Congress gains in U.P have been most striking and for that lavish praises have been showered on Rahul Gandhi for his tenacious campaign as also “go alone” approach. Definitely Rahul did shine in contrast to his cousin Varun, whose hate speech found Muslims scurrying for shelter in the Congress and the BSP since the SP’s marriage of Convenience with Kalyan Singh of the Babri Masjid demotion ‘fame’ left then stunned, to say the least. While Varun’s anti-Muslim tirade did not came to the aid of the BJP either in U.P or else where the Kandhamal violence the Orissa mauled it in the

Parliamentary polls in the State.

- **Non-productive Campaign of the BJP and NDA:** Further the BJP Campaign for the elections was generally non-productive. The party sent mixed signals even on its leadership by projecting Narendra Modi as a potential Prime Minister midway through the elections. This caused great embarrassment even to L.K. Advani. The manner in which Advani condoned Varun Gandhi's communal utterances in Pilibhit also did not go down well with the electorage. The open tussle between party President Rajnath Singh and General Secretary Arun Jaitley over the organizational preparations for the elections in Assam and some of the caustic comments made on Sonia Gandhi and Man Mohan Singh by Modi and other leaders also boomeranged. Over and above the election issues high lightened by the NDA such as internal security and the bringing back of black money from Swiss Banks, failed to generate popular appeal.

The BJP tried to focus on "national security" as its core issue and attempted to make the elections a referendum between personalities pitting its prime ministerial candidate L K Advani against the UPA leadership and Prime Minister Manmohan Singh. The NDA since 2004 had shrunk and the BJP was left only with the Janata Dal-United [JD(U)], the Shiv Sena, the SAD and other minor parties as its allies. The erstwhile NDA allies—the Telugu Desam Party, the All India Anna Dravida Munnetra Kazhagam (AIADMK), and the BJD had all left the NDA at some point or the other citing the communal politics of the BJP.

This had made the NDA'S prospects dimmer even before the elections and expectedly, the NDA managed a tally of only 159 seats, way behind in second place to the UPA. The BJP's overall tally was reduced to 116 (18.8 percent vote share) from 138 (22.2 percent) in 2004. Both the defection of erstwhile partners as well as the reduction in the party's overall vote share was indicative of the decline in resonance of the party's communal Hindutva agenda, which came again to the fore in the run-up to the elections. The BJP managed to win with reduced margins in its strongholds such as Gujarat and Madhya Pradesh, but won handsomely in Chhattisgarh and Karnataka. The performance of the JD (U) was significant as Lalu Prasad's Rashtriya Janata Dal (RJD) and Ram Vilas Paswan's Lok Janshakti Party were trounced in Bihar. It is too early however to suggest that the politics and efficacy of caste alliances in the state has been overcome, as many claim to be the reason for the victory of the JD (U)-BJP alliance, which pitched its state government's "development record" as the agenda for the elections.

- **BJP in Retreat:** The BJP posted its lowest vote share since 1989. The party won just 116 seats, down from 138 seats it had in 2004. Its vote share of 18.8 percent was 3.4 percentage points down in 2004. This is the third successive poll that its support base has shrunk since the high watermark of 1998. The party suffered a negative swing in all most all states, except Karnataka and Himachal Pradesh. Its vote share fell from less than one percentage point in Punjab, Bihar, and Kerala to a whipping 12.4 percentage points in Rajasthan. But the party managed to defend its seats in Karnataka, Gujarat, Chathisgarh and U.P.
- **Resurgence of the Congress:** The 2009 poll handed over an unambiguously positive verdict for the Congress at a time when the party least expected it. The party won 206 seats, crossing the 200 seat threshold for the first time since 1991. A close look at the vote shares and vote changes reveals that initial reactions may have over estimated the Congress gains. Despite boosting its tally by an impressive 61 seats. The Congress did this by increasing its vote share by a mere two percentage points from 2004. Overall, it won 28.6 percent of the vote, almost identical to its vote share in 1999, when the NDA triumphed.

An analysis of the State-wise picture shows that the Swing in favour of the congress was far from uniform. Among the major states it varied from a loss of 7.6 percent points in vote share in Orissa to a gain of 11 percent points in Punjab.

- **The BSP:** This election was to be the Bahujan Samaj Party's big leap forward. The BSP's electoral victory in 2007 in Uttar Pradesh, Mayawati's projection as a Prime Ministerial candidate, and the expectation of her growing clout provided the perfect setting for the party to expand its footprint. The final result was a big setback for Mayawati's ambitions. With just 20 seats in her bag and that too in a Lok Sabha where no one needed these seats, she was left with no option but to join the herd that was over-eager to extend unconditional support to the UFA. However, the BSP has quietly pushed its vote share up by one point, from 5.3 percent to 6.2 percent. This is the third consecutive election in which the BSP's national vote share has grown significantly. If we look at the vote share in U.P., the BSP is still by far the largest party in the State and has fallen only marginally below its vote share in the Assembly elections of 2007.

The party also made significant gains in Haryana and Uttarakhand in terms of vote share. In several other States such as Madhya Pradesh, Delhi, Maharashtra and Jharkhand, the BSP made small but significant accretions to its vote share. Yet, there is no clear upward trend in the party's gains outside U.P. It achieves a breakthrough in one State in an election only to surrender it the next time. In Delhi, for instance, the BSP polled only 5.3 percent of the vote against 14 percent in the 2008 Assembly election. Similarly in Maharashtra, where the BSP hoped to capitalise on the Republican Party of India's eroding Dalit base, it failed to win a single seat, its only consolation coming from four of its candidates securing more than 1 lakh votes. The party is still disproportionately dependent on Uttar Pradesh.

- **Muslim Votes:** At the national level the Congress and its allies bagged less than half the Muslim votes. Muslim support for the Congress and the Left fluctuates, while that of the Samajwadi party has headed consistently downward since 1996. The state level pattern of how Muslim votes voted in 2009, shows that it seems to be consolidating in those states where the community's electoral chances were limited. In include states like, Delhi, Gujarat, Rajasthan, and Madhya Pradesh. In contrast the Muslim vote seems to have split among many parties wherever multiple chances were available states like U.P, Andhra Pradesh, Kerala, Bihar, Tharkhand and Maharashtra. A notable exception to this was Assam, where Badaruddin Ajmal's AUDF garnered 61 percent of Muslim votes. In UP, the Congress, the SP and the BSP together bagged about two-third of Muslim vote. The fragmentation of the Muslim vote may have led to a decline in the number of Muslim MPs—from 36 in 2004 to just 28 in the new house.

Moreover, the Muslim community felt increasingly disenchanted with the parties it supported in the past two decades, including the Lalu Prasad led RJD (Rashtriya Janata Dal) and Mulayam Singh Yadav led S.P. (Samajwadi Party) and Mayawati led BSP (Bahujan Samaj Party).

- **Substantial Rise of Women MPs:** In 2009 Poll saw a substantial rise in the number of women in Parliament as many as 59 against 45 in 2004. The Poll results shows that there was a slight consolidation of the women vote in favour of the Congress, through the list is less than what the party has gained overall.

Year wise details of women members in Lok Sabha are given in brackets.

1952 (22), 1957 (27), 1962 (34), 1967 (31), 1971 (22), 1977 (19), 1980 (28), 1984 (44_, 1989 (28), 1991 (36), 1996 (40)*, 1998 (44),* 1999 (48), 2004 (45)* and in 2009 (59)
(* includes one nominated member).

Concluding Observations

In 2009 Polls, the voters appeared to have delivered a

decisive mandate, came that heralded a new era in Indian politics. The verdict provided greater stability to the national government and reduced the bargaining and black mailing capacity of coalition allies vastly. Moreover, the verdict eliminated the need for a Congress Left coalition and was widely seen as paving the way for greater economic liberalization. The verdict, especially the success of the Congress in U.P catapulted Rahul Gandhi to the centre state of National Politics. The verdict was no doubt a vote for stability, ongoing economic reforms and certainly a vote against, the regional and caste based parties like RJD and BSP. The new and vibrant strength of the Congress will give rise to the impression that national parties were back at the centre-stage of Indian politics.

Further, the 2009 Poll also proved as to how state-level alliances failed and the entire poll process was centred around national political issues. The credibility of the stable government by the third front was doubted by electorate' thus they noted for an alliance which they thought would offer a stable government.

In short, the electorate indisputably noted for a stable government at the Centre. The vote was for a dispensation which was wedded to help the poor and the middle class. The progressive forces of all lives must comprehend the essence of these results and extend constructive support to the ruling dispensation, which has secured the clear mandate to rule for five years beyond all expectations embodied in poll surveys.

To conclude, in 2004 onwards the UPA Government at the centre initiated a politically conscious approach shifted away from mere technocratic strategies of governance. Both the language of politics and direction of policies were pinpointing for the middle class and downtrodden. It has helped the Congress Party in 2009 to launch a platform aimed at the above said groups. The net result was nothing but the resurgence of the Congress party—party of the middle class and the poor. However, both the party and its leadership have to work over time to retain its mass base in the days to came. Their lies the destiny of the UPA.

Table 9.1: State-wise Seats Tally

State	UPA	NDA	TF	FF	Others
Andhra Pradesh	34		8		
Arunachal Pradesh	2				
Assam	8	5			1
Bihar	2	32		4	2
Chttisgarh	1	10			
NCT of Delhi	7				
Goa	1	1			
Gujarat	11	15			
Haryana	9				1
Himachal Pradesh	1	3			
Jammu & Kashmir	5				1
Jharkhand	1	8			5
Karnataka	6	19	3		
Kerala	16		4		
Madhya Pradesh	12	16	1		
Maharashtra	25	20			3
Manipur	2				
Meghalaya	2				
Mizoram	1				
Nagaland					1
Orissa	6		15		
Punjab	8	5			
Rajasthan	20	4			1
Sikkim					1
Tamil Nadu	27		12		
Tripura			2		
Uttar Pradesh	21	15	20	23	1
Uttarkhand	5				
West Bengal	25	1	15		1
Andaman Nicobar		1			
Dadra and NH		1			
Daman and Diu		1			
Chandigarh	1				
Puducherry	1				
lakshadweep	1				
Total	261	157	80	27	18

Source: Election Commission Web Site.

Table 9.2: All India Tally

Turn out			58.42
Party	Contested	Seats Won	Vote (percent)
Congress/allies	526	261	36.22
Congress	440	206	28.56
JKNC	3	3	0.12
MUL	2	2	0.20
KCM	1	1	0.10
NCP	23	9	1.78
DMK	22	18	1.83
Trinamool Cong.	27	19	3.19
JMM	5	2	0.21
RPI	2	0	0.12
IND (Congress)	1	1	0.11
NDA	512	159	24.11
BJP	433	116	18.81
AGP	6	1	0.43
JD (U)	27	20	1.42
INLD	5	0	0.31
Shiv Sena	22	11	1.51
NPF	1	1	0.20
SDF	1	1	0.04
RLD	7	5	0.43
Akali Dal	10	4	0.96
Left	177	24	7.61
CPI	56	4	1.43
CPI(M)	82	16	5.33
FBL	21	2	0.32
RSP	16	2	0.38
KEC	1	0	0.07
IND (Left)	1	0	0.07
BSP	500	21	6.17
Fourth Front	343	27	5.15
SP	193	23	3.43
RJD	44	4	1.27
LJNSP	106	0	0.45
Others	6,021	51	20.74
Total	8,070	543	100.00

Source: Computations by CSDS, Delhi based on Election Commission data.

Table 9.3: Vote Share and Swing

State	Vote Share	Swing from 2004
All India	28.6	2.1
Andhra Pradesh	39,0	-2.6
Assam	34.9	-0.2
Bihar	10.3	5.8
Chattisgarh	37.3	-2.9
Delhi	57.1	2.3
Gujarat	43.5	-0.4
Haryana	41.8	-0.3
Himachal Pradesh	45.6	-6.3
Jharkhand	15.0	·2 9
Jammu & Kashmir	24.7	-0.4
Karnataka	36,8	0.0
Kerala	40.1	8.0
Maharashtra	19.,6	-4.2
Madhya Pradesh	40.1	6.0
Orissa	32.8	-7.6
Punjab	45.2	11.0
Rajasthan	47.2	5.8
Tamil Nadu	15.0	0.6
Uttar Pradesh	18.2	6.2
Uttarakhand	43.3	5

Source: NES 2009. Weighted data, all figures are in percent, swing in percentage points, rest, no opinion.

Table 9.4: BJP's Vote Share

State	Vote Share	Swing from 2004
Andhra Pradesh	3.7	-4.7
Assam	16.2	-6.7
Bihar	14	-0.6
Chattisgarh	45	-2.8
Delhi	35.2	-5.5
Gujarat	46.6	-0.8
Haryana	12.1	-5.1
Himachal Pradesh	49.5	5.3
Jharkhand	27.5	-5.5
Jammu & Kashmir	18.6	-4.4
Karnataka	39.7	4.9
Kerala	6.3	-4.1
Maharashtra	18.2	-4.4
Madhya Pradesh	43.5	-4.6
Orissa	16.9	-2.4
Punjab	10.1	-0.4
Rajasthan	36.6	-12.4
Tamil Nadu	2.3	-2.8
Uttar Pradesh	17.5	-4.7
Uttarakhand	34	-7
West Bengal	6.1	-2

Source: NES 2009. Weighted data, all figures are in percent, swing in percentage points, rest, no opinion.

Table 9.5: Lok Sabha Elections-Data for Main Parties

Party	Seats Contested		Seats Won		Vote Share (percent)	
	2004	2009	2004	2009	2004	2009
INC	417	440	145	206	26.53	28.56
BJP	364	433	138	116	22.16	18.81
JD (U)	73	55	8	210	2.35	1.52
CPI	34	56	10	4	1.41	1.43
CPM	59	82	43	16	5.66	5.33
BSP	435	500	19	21	5.33	6.17
IND	2385	3829	5	9	4.25	5.16
TRMC (AITC)	33	35	2	19	2.07	3.20
NCP	32	68	9	9	1.80	2.04
SHS	56	47	12	11	1,81	1.55
MUL	10	16	1	2	0.20	0.21
JD (S)	43	33	3	3	1.47	0.82
SP	237	193	36	23	4.32	3.43
JKNC/JKN	6	3	2	3	0.13	0.12
SAD	10	10	8	4	0.90	0.96
JMM	9	42	5	2	0.47	0.40
AIADMK/ADMK	33	23	0	9	2.19	1.67
DMK	16	22	16	18	1.81	1.83
TDP	33	31	5	6	3.04	2.51
PMK	6	7	6	0	0.56	0.47
AGP	12	6	2	1	0.53	0.43
LJNSP/LJP	40	106	4	0	0.71	0.45
RJD	42	44	24	4	2.41	1.27
TRS	22	9	5	2	0.63	0.62
BJD	12	18	11	14	1.30	1.59
DMDK	-	40	-	0	-	0.75
MNS	-	11	-	0	-	0.36

IND: Independent

Source: Computations by CSDS based on Election Commission Data.

References

Biju. M.R., Dynamics of Modern Democracy: The Indian Experience (2 Vols.) Kanishka, New Delhi, 2009.

Biju. M.R, Democratic Political Process, Mittal Publications, New Delhi, 2009.

The Hindu, Thiruvananthapuram.

Economic and Political Weekly, Mumbai.

South Asia Politics, New Delhi.

Mainstream, New Delhi.

Frontline, Chennai.

The New Indian Express, Thiruvananthapuram.

Index

Index